# Culture, Society,
# and Menstruation

# A **Health Care for Women International** Publication

**Carole Ann McKenzie,** CNM, PhD
and **Phyllis Noerager Stern,** DNS, RN, FAAN, *Editors*

# Culture, Society, and Menstruation

*Edited by*

## Virginia L. Olesen
*University of California*
*San Francisco, California*

*and*

## Nancy Fugate Woods
*University of Washington*
*Seattle, Washington*

●HEMISPHERE PUBLISHING CORPORATION
A member of the Taylor & Francis Group

New York    Washington    Philadelphia    London

CULTURE, SOCIETY, AND MENSTRUATION

234567890 BRBR 898

This book was set in Press Roman by Hemisphere Publishing Corporation. The
editors were Christine Flint Lowry and Amy J. Whitmer; the production
supervisor was Miriam Gonzalez; and the typesetter was Sandra Stancil.
Braun-Brumfield, Inc. was printer and binder.

**Library of Congress Cataloging in Publication Data**
Main entry under title:

Culture, society, and menstruation

(Health care for women international publication)
Includes bibliographies and index.
1. Menstruation—Social aspects. 2. Premenstrual
syndrome—Social aspects. 3. Menopause—Social aspects.
I. Olesen, Virginia L. II. Woods, Nancy Fugate.
III. Series. [DNLM: 1. Menopause. 2. Menstruation.
3. Premenstrual Syndrome. WP 550 C968]
RG161.C85 1986        305.4        86-3066
ISBN 0-89116-557-6

# CONTENTS

# CONTRIBUTORS

LAURA BLEDSOE, BS
School of Nursing
Oregon Health Sciences University
Portland, Oregon

MARIE ANNETTE BROWN, RN,
  PhD
Family Nurse Practitioner Program
School of Nursing
University of Washington
Seattle, Washington

R. T. CHATTERTON, PhD
Department of Obstetrics and
  Gynecology
Northwestern University Medical
  School
Chicago, Illinois

GAIL J. M. CORBLEY
Graduate Student
Department of Human Relations
University of Oklahoma
Norman, Oklahoma

ALICE J. DAN, PhD
College of Nursing
University of Illinois at Chicago
Chicago, Illinois

F. A. DeLEON–JONES, MD
Department of Research and
  Development
West Side Veterans Administration
  Hospital
Chicago, Illinois

PAULA ENGLANDER–GOLDEN,
  PhD
Department of Human Relations
University of Oklahoma
Norman, Oklahoma

SIOBÁN D. HARLOW
School of Hygiene and Public Health
Johns Hopkins University
Baltimore, Maryland

SHARON A. HEINZ, MSE
Eau Claire Clinic, Ltd.
Eau Claire, Wisconsin

G. A. HUDGENS, PhD
U.S. Army Human Engineering
  Laboratory
Aberdeen Proving Ground, Maryland

PATRICIA A. KAUFERT, PhD
Department of Social and Preventive
  Medicine
University of Manitoba
Winnipeg, Manitoba, Canada

L. A. MONAGLE, MS
College of Nursing
University of Illinois Health Sciences
  Center
Chicago, Illinois

VIRGINIA L. OLESEN, PhD
Department of Social and Behavioral
  Sciences
School of Nursing
University of California
San Francisco, California

ESTHER ROME
Boston Women's Health Book
  Collective
West Somerville, Massachusetts

NANCY ROSENBERGER, PhD
University of New South Wales
Vaucluse, NSW, Australia

FRANK J. SONLEITNER, PhD
Department of Zoology
University of Oklahoma
Norman, Oklahoma

SUSAN MARIE STOLTZMAN,
  MSN, CPNP
CIGNA Healthplan of Texas
Dallas, Texas

DIANA TAYLOR, RN, MSN
Menstrual Disorder Clinic
Oregon Health Sciences University
Portland, Oregon

MARY R. WHITMORE, PhD
Department of Zoology
University of Oklahoma
Norman, Oklahoma

NANCY FUGATE WOODS, RN,
  PhD, FAAN
Department of Parent-Child Nursing
School of Nursing
University of Washington
Seattle, Washington

PHYLLIS ARN ZIMMER, RN,
  MN, FNP
Family Nurse Practitioner Program
School of Nursing
University of Washington
Seattle, Washington

## WOMEN'S SOCIAL POSITION
## AS MENSTRUATING BEINGS

Cultural values concerning menstruation that determine women's position in society affect us all, male and female. A group of men were discussing *Culture, Society, and Menstruation* with a female editor prior to its publication. They welcomed its release, they said, because menstruation tends to be a hidden part of women's lives, and one that women avoid discussing with men. An older man said that he had been educated by women to think of the menstrual period as a vague "trying time" for women, then he spoke of cramps, nausea, emotional outbursts, and the "old idea" that a woman is "unclean" and "off limits" during this time. These men spoke of their frustration with women for keeping important information from them, information that might help men be more understanding and supportive toward women. They said that women seemed more willing to discuss their bowel movements than the specifics of their menstrual experience. One young man pointed out to the editor, several years his senior, that "I would never be having this conversation with my mother." These men resent their exclusion from the sense of meaning menstruation has for women:

> You can live with a woman for years, and go through her periods with her, and yet, your experience is about ten times removed from hers. I feel like saying, "For Christ's sake, tell me about it: Either sound off or buzz off."

That most women have been carefully taught to feel ashamed of being women, in part because they menstruate, is a fact of life we all deal with. We cannot know how it started, why this normal physiological event was singled out for such special attention that it was kept hidden, spoken of only among individuals of the same sex, and then but rarely. One can ponder that the menstrual link with reproduction and the awe with which all humans view pregnancy and birth grants menstruation this unusual power. But as scientists we realize that logic never replaces data, and that none of us was around before individuals learned to record their histories. We must confine ourselves to the here and now. We observe behavior, we ask questions, we read historical records, we attempt to gain understanding from these data, and we advise our audiences about how we think things might be better for us all.

The papers gathered here by Woods and Olesen mean a giant step forward in refocusing the menstrual life of a woman to an integrated and valid part of a total individual: an individual who deserves equal importance in society with her male counterpart. The breadth of the subjects reported by these writers gives us some indication of how the social role of woman as a being that menstruates has an effect on business, on politics, on private life, on her youth, her middle life, and on her health care. The papers are well documented, and most are study reports; nevertheless, one feels the rage at women's unequal place in their social world that inspired these investigators, these writings.

We may not learn how women began to be treated as different, more fragile, more emotionally labile than men, but these authors tell us that they want it stopped! Olesen and Woods have moved us a long way in that direction.

*Phyllis Noerager Stern*

# PREFACE

## SOCIOCULTURAL PERSPECTIVES ON MENSTRUAL CYCLE RESEARCH

This text adds to the substantial research momentum around menstrual cycle issues and highlights significant issues and departures in this burgeoning field. The essays presented here underscore the fact that there is much within the menstrual cycle that can be profitably investigated, analyzed, and reported not only to other scholars, but to policy makers and activist groups. It is significant that all the papers place women's reproductive cycle in a sociocultural, rather than an exclusively biological, context, thus placing these issues in a larger female symbolic system and leading to new perspectives on women and this part of their lives. yet the papers do not fail to heed a woman's biological life, a perspective sometimes troublesome to feminist researchers who fear that acknowledgment of this aspect will continue to define women as biological, rather than socio-bio-cultural actors.

When we were invited to prepare this collection, we drew upon a wide range of researchers and critical analysts: colleagues from the Society for Menstrual Cycle Research, other researchers whose work had become familiar to us, researchers whose new work was just being completed, and researchers whose investigations would round out what was to be presented. Because the nature of the topic and the variety of work being done on it are so extensive, we cannot claim that this volume exhausts the topics or the issues. Rather, we hope that each paper here will excite some reader to replicate, to go beyond, or to develop new frameworks within what is found here. If this volume succeeds, those catalytic impulses should produce many more papers on the subject.

Prominent among the themes in these papers is that definitions of menstruation and menopause and the attendant "problems" come to be the focus of considerable struggle, which has implications for understanding the phenomenon, for doing research upon it, and for action. Rome highlights this in her discussion of premenstrual tension, as does Olesen in her review of the controversies around toxic-shock syndrome. Kaufert's paper focuses the definitional issue even more finely as she argues that the choices among definitions of menopause, the epidemiologist's, the woman's, and the physician's, are not value free. It carries an impact for methodological issues in any research on the topic.

We wish to acknowledge with appreciation the support of the Society for Menstrual Cycle Research in technical preparation and the assistance provided by the Department of Social and Behavioral Sciences, University of California, San Francisco.

Altering definitions in turn are influenced by social change in institutions where women work and by material conditions in societies. Using data from Japan, Dan shows that menstrual leave is losing its legitimacy as new definitions emerge in Japanese institutions. Olesen ties the emergent phenomenon of toxic shock to altering technological and economic conditions in American life.

These analyses resonate with several others that highlight the issue of women and work as variables in research on the menstrual cycle. Brown and Woods examine the interplay between work and menstruation, while Harlow argues in a historical view that scientists have ignored the topic of menstrual dysfunction in the workplace as one requiring scientific scrutiny. These issues are also implicit in Englander-Golden's research on male and female cycles and her findings that social events, such as the social week cycles are more influential than biological cycles in producing mood changes.

Several papers deal with the critical interplay of interpersonal communications around menstrual issues, recognizing that realities are shaped in the give and take of meaningful symbols between women and their male companions, parents, and others. Stoltzman's analysis of adolescents' and their mothers' attitudes toward menstruation points up a provocative difference between these young women and their mothers: Symptom expectancies for adolescents are more negative than the actual symptom experiences of their mothers, a finding that has implications for investigation of the influence of socialization on menstrual attitudes. Brown and Woods note that socialization as a female is not responsible for making women symptomatic, but socialization does influence women's attitudes toward menstruation as does the severity of symptoms and disability, a point made by Woods. Monagle and her colleagues show the existence of multiple menstrual syndromes.

These analyses of interpersonal exchanges around the menstrual cycle are paralleled in Dan's and Harlan's papers, which point to the fact that members of social institutions hold views that help the institutions reinforce ideas of women as ill or as needing special support during the cycle. Dan further argues that this reflects conditions of the workplace as well as contemporary beliefs about women's health. Difficulties with symptoms and physical ailments during the menstrual period may be helped by social support from other women, a point made by Heinz writing about a model clinic program on PMT and by Taylor and Bledsoe reporting research. Heinz further argues that acknowledging the validity of women's complaints is a significant part of therapy offered by the Eau Claire, Wisconsin clinic, but such treatment programs must be regarded with care, as they may also serve to keep women satisfied with their lot in life. Support from other women, as well as active resistance to the medicalization of PMT is urged by Rome, whose paper presenting the work of the Boston Women's Health Collective on this issue constitutes an intriguing companion piece to the Heinz report on the Eau Claire Clinic. Brown and Zimmer analyze women's experiences as they seek help from clinics and others for premenstrual symptoms.

At the other end of the reproductive cycle, menopause is equally the focus of definition and negative definition, as Rosenberger's analysis of Japanese urban and rural women shows.

Readers will find illustrations of a variety of research approaches in these papers, demonstrating that researchers who prefer qualitative or quantitative work will equally be at ease in addressing the many issues posed. Most of the studies start from interviews with women themselves, but several utilize historical or documentary analyses.

If there is a single theme running throughout the text, both implicitly and explicitly, it is the dynamics of the meaning of issues around the menstrual cycle, particularly as they seem to reflect medical perspectives. Indeed, many of the papers make it clear that medicalization of menstruation and menopause is reflected in assumptions of researchers as well as therapists. This theme prompts us to reiterate the critical influence of research such as contained in this issue. Working carefully and heeding the admonitions found in several papers on definitions and variables to be considered, researchers have the potential to yield information and knowledge that can move thinking away from a purely medical view to one that incorporates other perspectives. Stated most dramatically perhaps in the Rome essay on PMT, this theme constitutes a challenge to researchers. As is clear throughout the papers contained herein, consequences of some magnitude for women flow from framing and institutionalizing of such definitions. We hope that this text and its readers can and will build on these papers to make their own research contribution to the shaping of those definitions.

*Virginia L. Olesen*
*Nancy Fugate Woods*

# THE LAW AND WOMEN'S BODIES: THE CASE OF MENSTRUATION LEAVE IN JAPAN

Alice J. Dan, PhD

College of Nursing, University of Illinois at Chicago

The right to take leave during menstruation is an unusual institu-ionalized practice, permitting an examination of the impact of social definitions of menstrual function. This research utilized in-depth in-terviews with 30 knowledgeable Japanese informants to gather data on history, rationale, and use of menstruation leave, as well as opin-ions on the controversy about abolishing it. Materials were systemati-cally content analyzed; findings indicated that social factors were pri-mary determinants for use of menstruation leave. These factors included working conditions, labor union strength, and company at-titudes. Major themes in the controversy over abolishing menstruation leave included the power to define menstrual experience as normal or pathological; the legitimation of menstruation leave as related to ma-ternity; and strategies for improving women's status at work. In sym-bolic interactionist terms, menstruation leave represents the lack of fit between social institutions of work and women's experience.

## INTRODUCTION

Japan is unique among modern industrialized countries in pro-viding women workers with the opportunity to take leave during menstruation. This provision is contained in the Labor Standards Law of 1947, and it permits leave for any woman worker under either of two conditions: 1) if a woman suffers heavily from men-struation, making it hard for her to work, or 2) if the work itself is injurious to her body during menstruation. It does not specify the number of days or whether the leave is to be paid.

I want to thank the National Public Health Institute, Tokyo, Japan (especially the Department of Nursing); Dr. Hajime Saito; the Japanese Ministry of Labor; the College of Nursing at St. Luke's Hospital, Tokyo; Atsuko Ichikawa and Keiko Hosoi who ably inter-preted for me; and my interviewees.

The emergence of this law and its application in practice are of interest for several reasons. First, although we know that social meanings influence women's experiences of their bodies, this process is complex and not well understood. The existence of an institutionalized practice concerning menstruation requires explicit and public definitions for matters that usually remain implicit and private. Thus, the social process becomes more accessible to study, particularly in light of the recent controversy over the proposed abolition of this law.

Further, the perspectives of various social groups about menstruation leave reflect their views of women. Using menstruation leave as a focus can reveal characteristic Japanese cultural interpretations of female biological functions and proper social roles for women. This paper uses a symbolic interactionist framework emphasizing an understanding of the perspectives of participants in their own terms. The following research questions guided my work in Japan.

1. What social views and political forces contributed to the emergence of menstruation leave in Japanese law?
2. How is menstruation leave used and what factors determine its use?
3. What alternative perspectives on menstruation and female biological functions are available to women in Japanese society?
4. What are the connections between the current controversy over menstruation leave and the larger social issues facing women in Japan?

## BACKGROUND

A summary of the various arguments for and against menstruation leave is presented by Renate Herold (1976, 1980). She identifies the following major categories of arguments in favor of menstruation leave.

1. Menstruation causes lowered work efficiency and increased vulnerability to physical problems.
2. Women with pain during menstruation or other difficulties, such as unusually heavy bleeding, should not be required to work during menses.
3. Taking leave during menses prevents problems during later pregnancy and childbirth, including miscarriage and premature labor.
4. Women work under poor conditions and lack sanitary facilities.

Like other Western observers (Cook & Hayashi, 1980), she argues persuasively against menstruation leave. Her critiques of studies purporting to show increased vulnerability or decreased work efficiency during menstruation are devastating. In agreement with a government-appointed medical committee, she shows the flaws in labor union studies linking poor pregnancy outcomes to lack of time off during menstruation. In addition to the lack of medical justification, she argues that menstruation leave is difficult for women to take and benefits only a few women. Those who need time off because of pain or other menstrual difficulties should take sick leave. Finally, she argues that menstruation leave contributes to discrimination against women. It is used by employers as an argument against providing equal positions for female workers, at the same time that its meager benefits pacify women and keep them from fighting for more substantial benefits like higher wages and better working conditions.

These arguments over menstruation leave are bewildering and inconsistent. One of the greatest discrepancies in the available data is that, despite the low percentage of women using menstruation leave, most surveys show very strong feelings against abolishing the leave among large majorities of working women. As Nomura pointed out in a recent paper,

> The issue of seirikyuuka (menstruation leave) is probably the most controversial topic in women's labor in Japan. It is often cited as the reason why employers feel that women cannot perform work equal to men and, therefore, are not deserving of equal pay. Yet the women of Japan were the driving force behind the enactment of seirikyuuka and are the driving force behind the retention of the provision. (1980, p. 45)

Given the apparent logic in favor of abolishing the leave, why do Japanese women insist on its retention? Have they been duped by labor unions into believing nonsense, or is there something else going on?

## Conceptual Framework

In my previous work, I have found it useful to conceptualize a "socially constructed menstrual cycle," separate and distinct from the tangible experience of women, as a way of thinking about such discrepancies (Dan, 1982). These ideas, drawn largely from the work of Berger and Luckmann (1966), are briefly outlined below.

As shown in Figure 1, three levels of reality are seen as quali-

### SOCIAL "OBJECTIVE" REALITY

(retrospective self-reports, cultural history,
ideas of non-menstruating groups)

↑↓

### SUBJECTIVE  REALITY

(on-going self-reports, experience
of menstruating individuals)

↑↓

### BIOLOGICAL SUBSTRATE

(physiological changes)

**Fig. 1. Levels of reality.**

tatively different but constantly interacting with each other. Social reality is the "objective" world shared by others; subjective reality reflects the experience of individuals—what we are immediately aware of; and biological reality consists of all that is happening in our bodies.

One's subjective reality is formed by the socially available categories of experience, by language and by custom; but one also shares with others, through talking, writing, and other forms of expression, one's own particular experience, which then can become a part of the social reality. Berger and Luckmann characterize this ongoing interaction as a dialectical process with 3 moments or aspects (Figure 2).

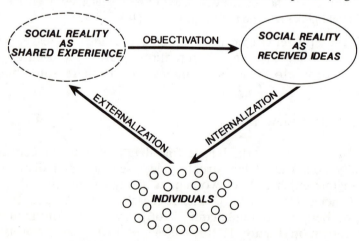

**Fig. 2. Dialectic of social and subjective (individual) reality.**

Externalization, the first moment, is that part of the process in which individuals share their experience and create social reality. As common understandings grow, reciprocal roles and eventually enduring social institutions develop. The third moment is internalization, through which social reality is embodied in individual consciousness. And the second moment, objectivation, results from the need to transmit social reality to new individuals who did not participate in developing the original roles, understandings, or institutions.

At this point in the process (objectivation), the set of activities that constitute an institution become detached from their original motivation in the lives of individuals, and require a legitimating logic. In order to justify social institutions, bodies of knowledge accumulate. It is important to recognize that these bodies of knowledge serve to control behavior and to maintain institutions that are now separated from subjective experience. Objectivation requires resources, often unavailable to women. For this reason, subjective female experience, even shared experience, may not be adequately represented in the dominant social reality (c.f. Spender, 1983).

This insight that the dominant social reality is largely defined by males, and does not include significant aspects of female experience, has been a topic of considerable scholarly analysis among feminists. Adrienne Rich (1976) for example, has examined the discrepancies between the institution of motherhood and the mothering experience. McBride and McBride (1981) suggest that social views of what is normal for women's bodies are often at odds with women's "lived experience," and that women's health depends on getting back in touch with this subjective level of reality. Kate Millet comments on the effects of internalization, "Patriarchal circumstances and beliefs seem to have the effect of poisoning the female's own sense of physical self until it often truly becomes the burden it is said to be" (1970, p. 47). Many others have commented on the lack of symmetry between female experience and institutionalized social reality, including Ann Wilson Schaef (1981) and Catharine MacKinnon (1982), to name only two.

To understand women's menstrual experience, then, we must look at the relationship between women's lived experiences and the larger structure of social reality and its maintenance systems.

## APPROACH

To explore menstruation leave as an institutionalized practice, in-depth interviews and written materials were collected during a six-month stay in Japan, from September 1982 to March 1983.

I contacted women's groups, health scientists and professionals, government officials, and labor union leaders to recruit a sample of knowledgeable informants representing many different points of view. Through the assistance of researchers and faculty in Japan, my requests for interviews were met with utmost cooperation. I was frequently referred to additional individuals with an interest in menstruation leave. In all, 30 formal interviews were conducted, with 25 women and 5 men:

8 physicians
7 writers and journalists
5 nursing leaders
4 staff nurses
4 labor union representatives
2 government officials

In addition, field notes were kept on more informal contacts with many other individuals, including students, housewives, researchers, health professionals, and feminists in various fields.

Most of the work was done in the Tokyo area, and I visited several other cities to meet with informants there as well. My knowledge of the Japanese language was enough for rudimentary conversations, but I was fortunate to have the help of capable interpreters for conducting interviews. About one-third of the interviewees were fluent in English, so that those interviews could be done entirely in English. Another third understood almost no English, so those interviews were simultaneously translated by my interpreters. The rest were conducted in a combination of both languages, with simultaneous translation assistance when needed. Although the initial statement of my interest in menstruation leave was often greeted with laughter, I found little reluctance to discuss the topic at length. The interviews were tape recorded, lasted from one to three hours, and covered the history and rationale for menstruation leave, how it is used, reasons for and against abolishing this leave, attitudes of women and men about taking menstruation leave, attitudes about menstruation itself, health issues, and role changes affecting women in Japan. Written materials such as newspaper and magazine articles, pamphlets for women workers, government reports, and legislation were also gathered and translated for content analysis.

This paper presents an overview of the findings, including traditional ideas about menstruation in Japan, historical and political origins of menstruation leave, current usage of the leave, and major issues for women emerging from my interviews.

## FINDINGS

### Traditional Ideas about Menstruation

There are both positive and negative aspects to traditional views of menstruation in Japan. The custom of celebrating a girl's first menses is described in a small pamphlet on festive Japanese dishes:

> When a daughter has her first menses, the custom is to invite the family friends and celebrate. The guests are not told verbally the reason for the celebration. Instead, a candied apple or pear, with a small branch or leaves of bamboo, pine, or other greens, accompanies the main tray. The guests, when they see the dyed fruit, understand that the daughter has become a woman and celebrate together. (translated by Teruki C. Dan)

This picture, corroborated by my informants, contains both the negative sense of something to be hidden, not spoken of, and the positive celebration generally associated with the ability to have a child.

Other traditional ideas about menstruation are more negative—that menstruation is unclean, that women are dangerous because they menstruate. Most of my informants assured me that these ideas do not influence women today, but one person told me of a recent incident during the construction of a tunnel under the sea between Honshu, the main island of Japan, and Hokkaido, the large island to the north of Honshu. Members of the legislature often visit massive federal construction sites in Japan, as in other countries, and several male Diet members had inspected the progress of this project. A woman Diet member who travelled to the area, however, was refused permission to enter the tunnel, because workmen were afraid that the sea god would be angry. So these traditional ideas do still exert some influence.

### Origins of Menstruation Leave

Menstruation leave first emerged as an issue in the 1920s and 1930s when employed women were mostly young, and working conditions for them were difficult. Since the majority of women workers were under 21 and unmarried, menstruation leave had a broader appeal than maternity leave. The lack of adequate sanitary facilities and materials made management of menstruation especially difficult for factory and transportation workers. Bus conductors and textile workers were among the first groups to request menstruation leave.

Although a general meeting of the national labor federation came out in favor of requiring menstruation leave in 1931, it was not acted on until the last days of World War II. One informant, a woman who had been active in prewar women's labor organizing, reported that before World War II, menstruation leave was a symbol for women's emancipation. It represented their ability to speak openly about their bodies, and to gain social recognition for their role as workers. At the same time, the struggle for menstruation leave dramatized the need for better working conditons for women workers.

Menstruation leave was supported as part of the Labor Standards Law passed in 1947 at the urging of the American Occupation forces. In part, this was characteristic of a general policy of the United States to support labor union and women's issues (Nomura, 1980), to promote more democratic politics in Japan. Americans were also scandalized by working conditions for some groups of women, particularly in factories and mines. Health professional informants pointed out the lack of medical involvement in developing the law regarding menstruation leave. It was an issue of concern mainly for women labor union organizers, and even the name, seirikyuuka, is euphemistic, referring to "physiological leave," rather than to the more specific term for menstruation (gekkei).

Following the passage of the Labor Standards Law in 1947, menstruation leave became a focus of struggle between labor unions and employers. The women's divisions of many labor unions saw menstruation leave as a good instrument for organizing all working women, and they began to press for paid leave and for a broader interpretation of the reasons for taking the leave. They argued that menstruation is a "barometer" for reproductive ability, and that even women without symptoms ought to take leave to protect their future motherhood. Employers considered this an abuse of the law, and in some cases they harrassed women who took the leave. During the last 10 years, several official bodies have undertaken studies of menstruation leave. As part of a response to the United Nations Decade for Women, the government has proposed to eliminate menstruation leave as contributing to discrimination against women workers. However, labor unions and many women's groups do not agree, and the controversy continues.

## Use of Menstruation Leave

Over the last 20 years, use of menstruation leave has steadily declined from a high of over 25 percent to the present 13 percent of

### Table 1. Percentages of All Employed Women Using Menstruation Leave: 1960-1981

| | Percentage | | | | |
|---|---|---|---|---|---|
| Number of employees | 1960 | 1965 | 1971 | 1976 | 1981 |
| 500 or more | 29.4 | 39.4 | 30.9 | 25.5 | 18.5 |
| 100 to 499 | 21.1 | 26.4 | 27.4 | 19.3 | 17.7 |
| 30 to 99 | 10.3 | 14.9 | 12.2 | 10.0 | 8.6 |
| Total | 19.7 | 26.2 | 22.8 | 16.6 | 13.4 |

*Source:* Japanese Ministry of Labor (1982).

all employed women taking it one or more times a year (Table 1). Those who use it apply for the leave six times per year, on the average, and take off about seven days altogether (Herold, 1980).

The decline in usage was attributed by my informants to several factors. First, the average age of women workers has increased in recent years, with more women remaining employed after marriage and even after childbirth, and more women returning to work after their children are all in school. Older women presumably have less need for menstruation leave, especially if its major purpose is seen as protection of future maternity. In addition, my informants cited generational differences in attitudes toward menstruation, such that nowadays young women are ambitious, want to achieve in their jobs, and do not see themselves as incapacitated by menstruation. Another important reason for the decline is the improvement in working conditions. With better rest facilities, less harsh physical demands, and more paid holidays for the work force in general, women feel less need for special menstruation leave. Finally, several informants reported increased pressure from employers not to take the leave. Particularly after the "oil shock" of 1973, economic conditions worsened, and leave of any kind was discouraged by employers.

Differences in patterns of use can also be noted, by size of company (Table 1) and by type of industry (Table 2). Some industries showed little decline in use from 1965 to 1981, or even increased use of the leave over that time, while dramatic decreases were seen in manufacturing, and finance and insurance fields. Labor union strength was thought to be a major factor in these patterns of use, for several reasons. Labor contracts determine whether menstruation leave is paid or unpaid, thus powerfully affecting whether women can afford to take the days off. Some unions have

Table 2. Use of Menstruation Leave by Industry: 1965 and 1981

| Industry | Percentage | |
|---|---|---|
| | 1965 | 1981 |
| Mining | 1.41 | 11.6 |
| Construction | 9.4 | 12.8 |
| Manufacturing | 26.0 | 11.8 |
| Wholesale and retail | 20.6 | 11.1 |
| Finance and insurance | 20.1 | 8.7 |
| Real estate | 18.4 | 18.0 |
| Transportation and communication | 54.1 | 48.2 |
| Electricity, gas, and water supply | 21.3 | 14.5 |
| Service | 15.9 | 13.3 |

Source: Japanese Ministry of Labor (1982).

been able to negotiate for several paid days per month, while others limit the paid leave to one or two days. In addition, unions vary in how much they emphasize the "duty" of women workers to take menstruation leave. Thus, the larger companies and more strongly unionized industries, such as transportation and communication, show larger percentages of female employees taking the leave. However, management attitudes towards menstruation leave are also important, because it is not hard to institute procedures making the leave embarrassing or cumbersome to take. Some of the larger companies, particularly in manufacturing industries, have limited or decreased use of the leave in this way, despite the presence of strong labor unions.

Working women themselves strongly support the necessity of menstruation leave. Even though few use it regularly, there is near unanimity in supporting menstruation leave as a benefit needed by women. Table 3 summarizes surveys conducted by the Japanese National Railway Union, the Japanese Nursing Association, Zen-I-Ro (the general medical union), the Mitsubishi Trust Bank employees' union, and an independent study of over 400 women who volunteered to fill out questionnaires circulated by a group of Japanese feminists [published as a book, Onna-tachi no Rhythms ("Women's Rhythms"), Terasaki et al., 1982].

Regular usage varies greatly among and even within groups. Generally one-quarter to one-half of the women surveyed say they do not need menstruation leave, because their personal experience of menstruation does not cause them any difficulty. Most of these same women still support the necessity of the leave for women who do need it. An interesting category included in all of these surveys is those women who want or need to take the leave, but are unable to. These figures range from almost none to well over half, in various groups. The most frequent reasons given are that they are too busy, or that they do not want to inconvenience coworkers.

## Major Themes

Several themes recurred throughout my interviews. These included issues of defining menstrual experience, legitimating menstruation leave through its relation to maternity, and strategies for advancing women's status.

Who has the power to define what is physiologically normal versus what is pathological in menstrual experience? A 1974 report from a largely medical committee appointed by government officials stated:

> Women who have difficulty working during the menstrual stage should be considered as patients with dysmenorrhea.... Symptoms like dysmenorrhea can be improved or recovered by adequate treatments. Therefore, women who have menstrual pain should quickly undergo appropriate therapy. (Japanese Ministry of Labor, 1974, October, p. 33)

From this perspective, menstruation leave can even be seen as harmful to women, because it may be taken in lieu of obtaining proper treatment for a pathological condition. Comments from other infor-

Table 3. Reports of Use of Menstruation Leave in Independent Surveys

| | Percentage | | |
|---|---|---|---|
| Source | Regularly use | Want to but cannot | Do not need |
| Japanese National Railway Union (1979) | 48.8 | 17.5 | 24.1 |
| Japanese Nurses Association (1979) | 19.3 | 40.0 | 37.5 |
| Zen-Iro (General Medical Union, 1980) | 8.9–32.6 | 18.4–42.3 | 15.3–34.2 |
| Mitsubishi Trust Bank Union (1979) | 4.3 | 68.2 | — |
| Onna-tachi no Rhythms (1982) | 10.3–43.2 | 4.1–14.3 | 35.2–55.3 |

mants, on the other hand, indicated disagreement with this perspective:

> Doctors don't take into account how women feel about themselves and their bodies. . . . Young women can't easily go to a gynecologist. . . . It is unthinkable that women will go to a doctor for menstrual cramps.

Everyone agrees, of course, that menstruation itself is normal, not an illness, but the symptoms—which range from mild to severe and disabling—are they a normal part of being a woman? The crux of this issue is the power to define reality. I believe that some of the strong support for menstruation leave among working women represents resistance to medical control over this defining process.

The second major issue I identified was the legitimization of menstruation leave through its relation to maternity. The labor union rhetoric about protecting mother's body reinforces the implicit meaning of work as harmful to female reproductive function, and of what women do at home as "not work." The dilemma posed for women is that they must choose, as one of my informants stated: "This is a difficult question for women. Do you want to be a hard worker or a protected mother? It's a little funny to have to select only one of the two." Many women, especially in the younger generation, are ambitious and believe they can work as well as men. Although they want to be valued as workers, they feel social pressure to give up motherhood if they want to be committed workers. At the same time, motherhood is seen as the only safe role for women. As one informant said, "Women hold to motherhood to feel safe." And another, "Women don't exist in Japan, only mothers." Perhaps menstruation leave has represented a way for women workers to express their continuing identification with motherhood.

The final issue emerging from my interviews concerned the best political strategy for advancing women's status: Is total equality in the workplace the best way to improve the status of women, or do women need protective laws that recognize the reality of their dual roles? The rhetoric of protection versus equality is used to discuss the question of abolishing menstruation leave. Employers take the position that "If women demand to be treated equally, they should work under the same conditions as men," while women in some feminist groups say, "If women are equal only at work, they will not be equal, because they carry a double burden." These groups resist removing any protective provisions, because they doubt that equality for women will result. They demand equality first, before eliminating protections. This controversy seems to indicate the impossibility of legislating equality for women in employment as if it were an isolated sphere of activity.

## DISCUSSION

Despite the apparent intent of the law, my research suggests that the actual use of menstruation leave depends more on social processes than on physical symptoms. Neither the menstruation leave law as it is written and interpreted, nor the proposal to abolish it, reflects women's experience accurately. I believe that this lack of symmetry between social reality and subjective reality is the basis for the accusations of abuse of the leave. Women appear dishonest to male employers because their use of menstruation leave does not correspond to the "objectively" legitimate reasons for this leave.

How would we go about correcting the distortions in social reality to make it more accurately reflect women's actual experience? It is important to emphasize that social reality does not change because it is proven wrong. It can only be changed through the processes of externalization and objectivation. And objectivation is particularly related to power, because resources are required for the work of maintaining and legitimating social institutions.

Menstruation leave represents an uneasy compromise; it is a symbol of the lack of fit between social institutions of work and women's biologically grounded experience. As a solution to the "problem" of women as workers, menstruation leave seems to be losing its legitimacy as social definitions change.

## REFERENCES

Berger, P. L., & Luckman, T. (1966). *The social construction of reality.* New York: Doubleday.

Cook, A. H., & Hayashi, H. (1980). *Working women in Japan.* Cornell International Industrial and Labor Relations Report No. 10. Ithaca, NY: Cornell University Press.

Dan, A. J. (1982, April). The social construction of the normal menstrual cycle. Paper presented at meeting of Midwest Nursing Research Society, Columbus, OH.

Herold, R. (1976). Japan's menstrual leave—anachronism or ideal? *International Quarterly for Asian Studies, 7*(1–2), 75–93.

Herold, R. (1980). *Die Blume am Arbeitsplatz: Japans Frauen im Beruf.* Tubingen and Basel: Horst Erdmann Verlag.

Japanese Ministry of Labor (1982). *An outline of the status of female labor in 1982.* Tokyo: Foreign Press Center.

Japanese Ministry of Labor (1974, October). Igaku-teki senmon-teki tachiba kara mita joshi no tokushitsu [Sepcial characteristics of women: Considered from the standpoint of medicine and technical specialties] (Report of the 2nd subcommittee of the Labor Standards Law Research Group). Tokyo: Author.

MacKinnon, C. A. (1982). Feminism, marxism, method and the state: An agenda for theory. *Signs, 7*(3), 515–544.

McBride, A. B., & McBride, W. L. (1981). Theoretical underpinnings for women's health. *Women and Health, 6*(1–2), 37–55.

Millet, K. (1970). *Sexual politics.* New York: Doubleday.

Nomura, G. H. (1980, August). The Labor Standards Law of 1947 and its effect on women workers. Paper presented at the International Conference on the Occupation of Japan, Amherst, MA.

Rich, A. (1976). *Of woman born.* New York: Norton.

Shaef, A. W. (1981). *Women's reality.* Minneapolis, MN: Winston Press.

Spender, D. (1983). *Women of ideas and what men have done to them.* London: Routledge and Kegan Paul.

Terasaki, A., Kobayashi, A., et al. (1982). *Onna-tachi no rhythms.* Tokyo: Gendai Shokan.

**Request reprints from Alice J. Dan, University of Illinois College of Nursing, 845 S. Damen, Chicago, IL 60612.**

# MENOPAUSE AS A SYMBOL OF ANOMALY:
# THE CASE OF JAPANESE WOMEN

**Nancy Rosenberger, PhD**

University of New South Wales, Vaucluse, New South Wales, Australia

Doctors tell Japanese women that the reason for the intensity of their menopausal symptoms is isolation and leisure. Still identified with the home, but urged to do hobbies or part-time jobs that do not give her full membership in society, the middle-aged woman is in an anomalous position in the social structure. She uses menopause as a catchall symbol for psychological and physical complaints. Cosmopolitan doctors encourage the idea of psychological causation of menopause by identifying menopausal symptoms with the autonomic nervous system. Chinese medicine offers a traditional physical-psychological approach.

This paper is an analysis of the meanings of menopause in Japan. While menopause has a biological base, it is an experience that differs according to cultural values. Menopause draws its meanings from more basic concepts within the culture, such as the meaning of women's reproductive power, the role of women in the social structure, and the relationship of the physical and the psychological. Such concepts form an image of menopause that is communicated to women through friends, husbands, doctors, and so on. Middle-aged women draw on this image to define and seek treatment for their symptoms. This is not to deny menopause as a valid physical experience. However, the interpretation, timing, and intensity of the symptoms are closely tied to the individual's experience of her own meaning as a menopausal-aged woman in society.

Menopause is a symbol of transition and anomaly, which can give meaning to the physical and psychological changes of the forties and fifties. For the purposes of this study, a symbol of anomaly is defined as a person or object that is in between cultural categories and has characteristics of both categories. A symbol of anomaly can represent the transition of a person from one social classification to another (Douglas, 1970; Van Gennep, 1960). In

15

this analysis, menopause is interpreted as a period of transition from fertility to infertility in which the menopausal woman herself is between categories. The hypothesis is that menopause increases as a meaningful symbol of transition and anomaly as the middle-aged woman's position in the social structure becomes less clearly defined.

The data were collected in the early 1980s by the author via interviews in Japanese with 150 women between the ages of 35 and 60. One-third were interviewed in their homes in a provincial Japanese city and two-thirds in a Tokyo clinic where they came for a yearly checkup. Also interviewed were cosmopolitan doctors and practitioners of Chinese medicine. Their writings were also analyzed. Additionally, a survey on attitudes toward menopause was conducted with 100 men and 20 women in Tokyo. They were drawn from people who came to a mid-sized hospital for an annual general checkup. The remainder of this sample is composed of 189 women in the Northeastern provincial city, drawn mainly from public exercise classes (Tables 1–3).

Conclusions have been reached by analyzing the informants' narratives for underlying assumptions that show the social meaning of menopause. To check the ideas that emerged in the narratives, statistical evidence from the survey questionnaires was used.

Menopause in Northeastern Japan was traditionally called the "Path of blood." It was closely connected with birth and the "impure" blood of birth. A 75-year-old woman in rural Japan told me that her period ended at 42 with a half-year sickness. She said:

> It used to be that we felt like we weren't finished with menstruation until we had a big sickness. That was several years after the birth of my youngest child, and I always thought that my menopause was hard because of having all those children and not resting much after their births.

By 50, this woman was already a grandmother. At 75, she was living with her son's family and still farming. Her transition into infertility was fast and decisive at a time when she was still busy with her home responsibilities. She experienced a gradual transition into an active old age within the household structure.

The "path of blood" was an expression that was used in Chinese medicine, the medical system that women turned to for relief from menopausal symptoms. In postwar Japan, cosmopolitan medicine came to influence the interpretation of menopause. A linguistic switch occurred from the "path of blood" to a scientific-sounding phrase, "damage of the changing years," translated here as menopausal symptoms.

## Table 1. Questionnaire Results from the Tokyo Survey

| Item | Percent agreeing[a] | | | | |
|---|---|---|---|---|---|
| | A | B | C | D | M |
| It is natural that in menopause women suffer physical symptoms | 32 | 12 | 41 | 57 | 35 |
| It is natural that in menopause women suffer irritability and psychological instability | 74 | 73 | 66 | 71 | 60 |
| Most "menopausal problems" occur because of bodily changes rather than because of psychological stress | 79 | 54 | 80 | 57 | 80 |
| Most "menopausal problems" occur because of psychological stress | 29 | 68 | 63 | 71 | 60 |
| "Menopausal problems" are light or heavy according to the attitude of the woman | 89 | 100 | 84 | 86 | 35 |
| With free time and energy for the woman, menopause is the best time of her life | 63 | 72 | 70 | 43 | – |
| Menopausal frustrations are increasing in contemporary life with its frustrations and stress | 53 | 72 | 59 | 86 | – |
| Menopause has more psychological stress than any period in a woman's life | 47 | 60 | 66 | 71 | – |
| More than menopause, the five to ten years before that are the time of most stress | 71 | 64 | 67 | 57 | – |
| After menopause is over, women recover their strength and will do things | 71 | 65 | 76 | 71 | – |
| In menopause women lose their feminine attractiveness | 18 | 12 | 16 | 14 | – |
| In menopause women start to get old | 26 | 13 | 16 | 14 | 30 |
| In menopause women lose the meaning of their lives | 17 | 8 | 13 | 29 | 0 |
| In menopause women's personalities change | 6 | 13 | 14 | 29 | – |
| In menopause the woman's interest in sex goes down | 42 | 45 | 50 | 60 | 50 |
| One of the big reasons for "menopausal problems" is problems with the husband and sex | 16 | 21 | 24 | 17 | 20 |
| After menopause women again develop an interest in sex | 31 | 19 | 27 | 0 | 20 |
| "Menopausal problems" are light if the woman has a good sexual relation with her husband | 61 | 76 | 83 | 80 | 70 |
| "Menopausal problems" are light if the woman is always in the home | 0 | 0 | 10 | 0 | – |
| If a woman is busy with children or elders her "menopausal problems" will be light | 63 | 58 | 72 | 83 | – |
| If a woman works outside of the home, her "menopausal problems" will be light | 82 | 75 | 81 | 83 | 80 |

17

Table 1.  Questionnaire Results from the Tokyo Survey (*Continued*)

| Item | Percent agreeing[a] | | | | |
|---|---|---|---|---|---|
| | A | B | C | D | M |
| A housewife who is involved in outside activities or hobbies get lighter "menopausal problems" than the woman who works outside the home | 61 | 44 | 58 | 80 | — |
| Women in menopause shouldn't be given important work to do | 11 | 8 | 13 | 17 | 35 |
| Menopausal women should put up with their problems and not complain to their families | 16 | 9 | 7 | 33 | 30 |
| Usually there is no need for the menopausal woman to see a doctor | 11 | 36 | 47 | 50 | 70 |
| Menopausal women depend on doctors too much | 33 | 54 | 52 | 60 | — |
| Menopausal women should take hormone therapy to lighten their symptoms | 44 | 32 | 44 | 33 | — |

[a]A = age 25–34 ($N = 19$); B = age 35–44 ($N = 30$); C = age 45–54 ($N = 35$); D = age 55–60 ($N = 7$); M = men ($N = 20$).

Menopause came to be a convenient catchall label for all non-specific complaints of the changing years. The menopausal label is thought to account for feelings such as extreme dislike of housework in the late 30s, frequent anger in the early 40s, stiff shoulders at 46, or bad headaches at 55. The average age for the end of menstruation is 50. However, in a provincial city, the average length of perceived menopausal symptoms was 6.7 years with an average beginning age of perceived menopausal symptoms of 44.5.

In the last 20 years Japan's economic prosperity has provided a longer life span and has moved the center of economic activity out of the home. The typical 35-year-old woman today has two children in school and is culturally infertile, as almost all pregnancies over 35 are aborted. She faces increasingly fewer responsibilities within the home for the next 15 years or more. While her free time increases greatly, she remains on call to the needs of the family structure. If parents-in-law require her care or if children require extra attention during test periods or sickness, the middle-aged woman must be ready to give up her individual activities to fulfill her family responsibilities.

If she stays home alone with no one to care for, the woman is pictured as falling victim to her own individual self-will. She loses a symbol of maturity in Japan—the ability to control the self-will.

This ability is thought to be maintained by active membership in vertically ranked social structures, such as the three-generational family or the company. The argument goes that the woman dwells on her loneliness and worries about her children and husband, who is often absent until late evening. The result may be a myriad of nonspecific complaints. From ages 35 to 60, these complaints

Table 2. Questionnaire Results from the Provincial City Survey

|  | Percent agreeing[a] | | |
|---|---|---|---|
|  | A | B | C |
| Menopause is a time of both emotional and physical changes | 72 | – | – |
| My own "menopausal problems" were made worse by stress at the time | – | – | 30 |
| I have (had) emotional symptoms | – | – | 61 |
| Menopausal problems can be controlled mentally | 83 | – | – |
| Entering menopause leads to a feeling of having aged | – | 37 | 37 |
| Women who are working (outside the home) have an easier time at menopause | 76 | – | – |
| I have talked with someone else about menopause (friend 64%, husband 50%) | – | – | 66 |
| I have consulted a doctor about my "menopausal problems" | – | – | 43 |
| It's a natural event, so I didn't consult a doctor | – | – | 60 |
| How do you feel about having entered menopause? |  |  |  |
| I still feel I should be young | – | 16 | 19 |
| Taken aback, surprised | – | 28 | 50 |
| No longer a woman | – | 4 | 7 |
| Do you want hormone shots for your "menopausal problems?" (% "no") | – | 88 | 58 |
| Did you get hormone shots? | – | – | 20 |
| Did you get tranquilizers for your "menopausal problems?" | – | – | 63 |
| Did you go to an East Asian practitioner for your "menopausal problems?" | – | – | 23 |
| Finger pressure:53 |  |  |  |
| Acupuncture: 31 |  |  |  |
| Moxibustion: 6 |  |  |  |

[a]A = All women (N = 189); B = Women who did not consider themselves to be in menopause yet (N = 106); C = Women who considered themselves to be in or past menopause (N = 83).

Table 3. Tokyo Questionnaire Respondents' Feelings
about Having Entered Menopause

| Item | Percent agreeing[a] |
|------|---------------------|
| I feel I am still young | 47 |
| I feel lonely | 34 |
| I feel refreshed, clean (*Sappari*) | 58 |
| My body is weaker | 32 |
| I will be freer from now on | 32 |
| I feel surprised | 47 |
| I've become like a man | 6 |

[a] $N = 81$.

are labeled as symptoms of menopause or the "sickness of luxury." Menopausal symptoms are thought to occur not because of women's productive activity as in the past, but rather because of her lack of productivity.

Doctors are some of the main exponents of the view that it is the woman in isolation who is given to menopausal symptoms. The blame falls not on society, but on the woman herself. A doctor commented, "Menopause reflects how a woman has lived the first half of her life." The solution advised most often by doctors is to get out and take up a hobby or find a job. Women themselves comment that work and busyness are one solution to menopausal problems, although many add that it also helps to be able to rest when one wants to.

Japanese women past the age of 35 fill their free time by participating in hobbies from tea ceremony to volleyball, or by finding work, usually on a part-time basis. Hobbies are considered useful in helping the woman gain control over her mind and body, but they are classified as "play" in contrast to "work" (which is economically productive). Hobbies are usually done within a ranked structure, but the woman has only part-time classification within that structure. As one informant said, "Most women do hobbies because they have to fill their time. They'd rather be working and earning money."

Unless women have training in a particular profession, however, little is open to them except $2.00-per-hour part-time work. As a part-time worker, the woman is not classified as a full member of the company. Opportunities to go back to school are few, and there are strict age limits on jobs with administrative responsibilities.

Both hobbies and work leave the middle-aged woman out of mainstream membership in Japanese society. Urged to get out of the house, but not allowed full participation in society, the middle-aged woman cannot be classified as "inner," which is the traditional classification of a Japanese woman. Nor can she be classified as "in society," which is the traditional classification for men. In her incomplete identification with any ranked structure the middle-aged woman is in an anomalous position over a long period of time. If, during this time, women complain of physical or psychological symptoms that cannot be linked with disease, these symptoms receive the label menopausal. In short, the transition of menopause has been symbolically extended to cover this whole period of transition from young motherhood to old age. A symbol of social anomaly (the middle-aged woman) is linked with a symbol of biological anomaly (menopause).

This symbolic extension of menopause affects the images of menopause and the middle-aged woman. Menopause becomes ubiquitous; it threatens to recur in various forms throughout middle age. Any symptom is suspect as a menopausal symptom. Symptoms of neurosis are especially liable to be labeled as menopausal because people avoid association with mental illness.

Any symptom labeled menopausal may reflect that the woman is psychologically weak. Women themselves feel that one should be able to psychologically control menopausal symptoms. A doctor tells another doctor, "I can't stand these women in their forties and fifties who go on and on about their symptoms. They're hypochondriacs. I give them some medicine and try to get them out." This point of view has been emphasized by those doctors who explain menopausal symptoms as a temporary disorder of the autonomic nervous system, a phrase that usually refers to mental disorder. Many doctors use this phrase as a euphemism for menopausal symptoms that are psychological in nature or are caused by the psychological instability of the woman. Women themselves prefer to use the phrase "hormonal imbalance" as an explanation for their problems because of its more physical image. Still informants ask themselves, "Do I get these symptoms because I'm too soft on myself?"

Doctors and women both recognize that menopausal symptoms are sometimes the result of social problems. Interpersonal problems with husbands, children, or parents-in-law are usually pointed out by doctors, although women often point to their frustration at not being able to reenter society. One doctor went so far as to say that no symptoms were really menopausal, but rather a result of the social problems of the middle-aged Japanese.

There is confusion about the use of the menopausal label. Doctors admit that sometimes they use the menopausal label for easy communication with the patient. Some doctors use it to assure the patient that she is not gravely ill. Others refrain from using it because they feel it will make the patient worry more about her symptoms.

Because the menopausal label is used so generally, many doctors and women fail to differentiate among problems that are a result of social friction, those that are a result of psychological depression, and those that are a result of hormonal imbalance, or menopause. Doctors rationalize their uncertain diagnoses by saying that they only have three to five minutes with each patient, and that patients resist using counselors. In the most sophisticated hospitals, gonadotropin levels are measured. Ordinarily, if the doctor finds no indication of disease, he must make an assessment of personality, age, menstrual irregularity, and symptoms to make a diagnosis. Some doctors give hormones in shot form once per month if they feel there is a hormonal imbalance. Tranquilizers are given for those who have psychological symptoms or are diagnosed by the doctor as neurotic. It is a system of trial and error.

The symbolic extension of the label of menopause from 35 to 55 also affects the image of the middle-aged woman herself. The 44-year-old woman goes to the doctor about heart palpitations and after an EKG is told, "There's nothing really wrong with you. You're just getting to be that age." Or a doctor teases a 48-year-old woman who has come with menstrual irregularity, "What are you worried about? You want another baby?" A female friend tells a woman, "Don't tell your husband when your menstruation ends. Mine ended early and I made the mistake of telling my husband. Now he's gone off and gotten a girlfriend."

The attitude survey showed that women do not feel that they are old, or that they wish for their reproductive power back, or that they feel sexually unattractive. However, the label of menopause attributes meanings to the woman whether she likes it or not. Menopause is classified as a "woman's sickness," and all the social uncertainty of the long middle-age transition is symbolically linked with the image of a woman in her years of reproductive decline. The problems of the social transition get lost in their interpretation as a biological transition.

Many women have doubts about the label of menopause. They

resent the image of decline and psychological instability. Some women go to doctors of various specialties searching for relief and for a label of physical sickness. Other women avoid the doctor. An informant says, "I just put up with the discomfort. It's embarrassing to go to the gynecologist with all the pregnant women, and Chinese medicine doesn't fit my body."

Many women do go to Chinese practitioners of herbal medicine or acupuncture. They feel they receive a "natural" treatment for a "natural" malady. Menopause is fit into the traditional view of symptom causation, which does not differentiate between the physical and the psychological. The problem is defined in terms of the circulation and quality of the blood and "ki" or life energy. With no implication of psychological or social problems, the woman is promised a readjustment of her whole self through a treatment that purifies and balances blood and *ki*. All symptoms are attended to and no label is given. Some Chinese practitioners liken the balance of *ki* to the balance of the autonomic nervous system. This identifies Chinese medicine with a scientific understanding of the body and guarantees the patient stability without the use of hormones or tranquilizers.

The meaning of menopause is undergoing transition as women and doctors try to be positive about the "second half of life." Highly educated, urban informants, and those with full-time careers consider menopause to be brief and with few symptoms. They react to the implications of aging, loss of womanhood, and psychological instability by denying menopause and labeling nonspecific symptoms as either physical symptoms of aging or neurosis. The woman's denial of association with menopause represents an attempt to change her image in middle age to that of a person who has made a successful transition from young motherhood into a productive middle age with a meaningful role in society.

Younger urban women identify with this concept of middle-age and menopause. They express the intention to keep themselves busy in society, keep their *ki* or self-will strong, and sail through menopause. Because of their high level of education and work experience before marriage, these young women expect to reenter society in middle age. However, company policies are not changing to allow their reentry as full members. Growth in the population over 60 and lack of care facilities may increase women's responsibilities at home. The classification of middle-aged women may become even more anomalous. Menopause may continue to be used as a symbol of this anomaly, but it is hoped that women and doctors will make a more careful differentiation of the causation of symptoms now labeled as menopausal.

# REFERENCES

Douglas, M. (1970). *Purity and danger.* Baltimore, MD: Pelican Books.
Van Gennep, A. (1960). *The rites of passage.* Chicago: University of Chicago Press.

# SEX ROLE ORIENTATION, SEX TYPING, OCCUPATIONAL TRADITIONALISM, AND PERIMENSTRUAL SYMPTOMS

**Marie Annette Brown, RN, PhD, and Nancy Fugate Woods, RN, PhD, FAAN**

School of Nursing, University of Washington, Seattle

Historically the study of sex roles and perimenstrual symptoms has produced conflicting results. Nevertheless, a stereotype has pervaded which depicts lack of femininity or rejection of the female role as a major contributor to various kinds of gynecologic problems, particularly perimenstrual distress. This study sample consisted of a nonclinic, community-based, randomly selected group of 179 women ages 18–35 who were interviewed in their homes. Study instruments included the Moos Menstrual Distress questionnaire, Index of Sex Role Orientation, Bem Sex Role Inventory and U.S. government statistics on percentages of men and women in certain occupations. Findings suggest that sex typing and sex role orientation are unrelated to perimenstrual symptom reports. Women who perform more traditionally feminine occupations report more severe perimenstrual negative affect. Investigators in women's health care are urged to look beyond acceptance or rejection of the female role to understand women's perimenstrual symptomatology. Furthermore, clinician's attributions of perimenstrual symptomatology to sex role rejection can lend them to pejoratively and erroneously label women and may negatively affect women's self-esteem.

## INTRODUCTION

In attempting to explain perimenstrual symptoms, most investigators have invoked either physiological explanations or psycho-

This research was supported by grants from Sigma Theta Tau and BRSG S07 RR05758 awarded by the Biomedical Research Support Grant Program, Division of Research Resources, National Institutes of Health.

We acknowledge the collaboration of Dr. Ada Most and Ms. Gretchen Kramer Dery, both of Duke University in earlier portions of this investigation.

physiologic formulations. The influence of social and cultural forces, however, has not been explored as fully.

The influence of feminine socialization, as reflected in appropriate sex roles for women, would seem to be an important avenue for exploring the effects of cultural norms on women's protection from or vulnerability to illness. Nathanson (1975) suggested that women may report more illness than men becuase it is culturally more acceptable for them to do so. Moreover, she suggested that if illness is a culturally acceptable form of expression for women, then women for whom it is more acceptable should report more illness.

Bem's recent work on gender schema theory suggested that individuals who are sex typed, that is women who rate themselves as masculine or feminine, process information on the basis of sex-linked associations that constitute their gender schema. Those individuals who are androgynous, rating themselves as having feminine and masculine characteristics, process information independent of sex-linked gender schema (Bem, 1981). It is also likely that women who process information about their health through a feminine gender schema are more likely than their counterparts to report symptoms; particularly symptoms related to the menstrual cycle, a distinctly feminine function.

Women's behavior in times of illness also differs from that of men, and Nathanson (1975) suggested that the sick role might be more compatible with women's roles than with men's. Extending this argument, she posited that if illness behavior is a function of compatibility with women's other role obligations, then women with less compatible obligations should assume the sick role less frequently than their counterparts with more compatible obligations. Thus it can be hypothesized that women with more traditional conceptions of femininity and in traditionally feminine roles would report more symptoms than their counterparts with more modern conceptions and roles.

Historically, the study of sex roles, masculine and feminine characteristics, and perimenstrual symptoms has produced conflicting results. In the early part of this century, perimenstrual distress was viewed as part of the complex of weakness and vulnerability in women (Jacobi, 1877). Novak (1931) asserted that more rigorous educational experiences had a detrimental effect on women's menstrual health, and that the "educational wave has left in its train thousands of young girls who are broken in health, neurasthenic and anemic. . . . Many an invalid woman is the end product of the delicate, overworked schoolgirl." (p. 108). Schule (as noted in Kisch, 1910) remarked that the mental equilibrium of even a perfectly healthy woman is not a stable one but is subject to a series of oscillations. . . . The menstrual period has a distinct influence on women's mental disequilibrium." (p. 153)

A common assumption during this period was that women were frail and must be protected (Kisch, 1910). Women were taught to deal with their menstrual functions with shame (Weideger, 1975). They were "put to bed" to deal with their "female problems" (Richards, 1928). In fact, most of women's health problems were thought to be linked with the menstrual cycle, which physicians treated as an illness (Jacobi, 1877). It is not surprising then that women adhering to more traditional notions about femininity were assumed to be at greater risk for perimenstrual difficulties. An extension of these ideas remains today in the subtle cultural prescriptions for curtailment of physical activities during the perimenstrual period (Harris, 1979).

Another perspective arose in the 1930s. Initially, studies of perimenstrual symptoms were pursued from a psychoanalytic framework. Menninger (1939) suggested a very particular form of female neurosis—the "unconscious repudiation of women." He theorized that women who rejected their femininity were at greatest risk of menstrual disturbance. Using the theme of penis envy, he suggested that the major task of the little girl was to renounce her aspirations to be like her brother and to repress her envy. If this task were not accomplished, she resented the more favored and envied males, while secretly striving to emulate them. She would both hate men and deny her own femaleness. The somatic consequences of this "unconscious repudiation of women" would run the gamut of gynecologic concerns, including perimenstrual distress, dysmenorrhea, amenorrhea, and infertility (Menninger, 1939).

Deutsch (1944) also attributed a variety of reproductive type disorders to unresolved issues with femininity. Shainess (1961, p. 25) suggested that recurrent premenstrual symptoms represented a process of recurrent self-devaluation in relation to one's femininity. Moreover, they could be traced to unpleasant, humiliating, or unloving experiences in the mother-daughter relationship. These ideas appear to have influenced subsequent writers who suggested that attitudes and values about femininity influence a woman's psychological response to the physiological changes of the perimenstruum (Thompson, 1950; Shainess, 1961). The ideas also continue to pervade more modern gynecology. Greenhill (1971) asserted that painful menstruation often "reflects the unhealthy attitude toward femininity that is so predominant in our society" in his textbook on office gynecology.

With the rise of the feminist movement, another perspective emerged. There arose a strong counterargument to the pervading idea that women were disabled because of their menses and therefore less reliable and capable (Weideger, 1975; Hyde & Rosenberg, 1976; Delaney, Lupton, & Toth, 1977). Studies emerged that examined the idea that while some women experienced perimenstrual distress, for many women the perimenstrual period had no ill effects (Woods, Most, & Dery, 1982; Wilcoxon, Schrader, & Sherif, 1976; Sherif, 1980). Data from Paige (1971) described more negative attitudes toward menstruation in traditional women than their nontraditional counterparts. Therefore, some suggested that it was the more traditional and feminine woman who had perimenstrual problems, rather than she who rejected the traditional female role.

The most recent studies about sex role orientation and perimenstrual symptoms have continued to produce conflicting results. Berry and McGuire (1972) found that of 100 women who were patients in a state hospital, those indicating a lesser acceptance of the female role reported a significantly higher number of premenstrual and menstrual pain, impaired concentration, and autonomic symptoms, as well as nonmenstrual symptoms, than did their more accepting counterparts. There was no relationship, however, between premenstrual tension and sex role acceptance. The Woods and Launius (1979) study of 71 college students revealed a small positive association between the Bem Masculinity Scale and a group of premenstrual symptoms, such as pain, lethargy, and depression.

In contrast, Gough (1975) found that femininity scores on the California Personality Inventory (which reflects nurturant, supportive, and deferent behavior vs. initiating, decision-making, and action-oriented dispositions), were weakly but positively correlated with menstrual, premenstrual, and intermenstrual symptoms in 116 college students and 85 married women from a family planning study. Also using the CPI, Slade and Jenner (1980) found that for 104 teacher training students (19–22 years of age), scores on the femininity scale were positively and slightly correlated with menstrual cycle phase differences in concentration and negative affect scores on the Moos (1977) Menstrual Distress Questionnaire (MDQ). Paige (1973) noted that among 298 unmarried university women, the traditionally feminine women, those who believed a woman's place is in the home and who had no personal career ambitions, had more menstrual symptoms.

Only one study was found that reported no association between sex role orientation and perimenstrual symptoms. Watts, Dennerstein, and Del Horne (1980) compared 25 women with premenstrual symptoms (who had volunteered for a drug study of mefenamic acid) with a control group. They noted no differences between groups in the rejection of feminine role stereotypes, childbearing, and childrearing.

Of the studies cited, three suggested that women who have more traditionally feminine characteristics or who ascribe to more traditional norms are more likely to have symptoms. Two studies suggested that women who do not accept their lot as women have more premenstrual symptoms. One study found no differences. Each of these studies used groups of students or institutionalized women. In addition, the instruments used to measure femininity in several of the studies assumed that femininity and masculinity are unidimensional constructs (Spence & Helmreich, 1979). In much of this literature, investigators do not differentiate the influence of gender, sex role orientation, and sex typing (masculinity and femininity). To date, no investigators have assessed the effects of women's occupations on perimenstrual symptoms.

This study proposed to assess the relationship between sex role orientation, characteristics of masculinity and femininity, traditionalism of the woman's occupation, and perimenstrual symptoms in a population of women residing in the community at large. Special emphasis was placed on differentiation between the influence of sex role norms, sex typing as feminine or masculine, and enacted role.

## METHODS

### Sample

The sample was selected from a population of women residing in five neighborhoods in a large southeastern city. These neighborhoods varied in racial composition (black and white) as well as socioeconomic status. All households were identified from a census listing for the city. Trained interviewers contacted each household by telephone or in person to determine whether or not one of the residents met the criteria for inclusion in the study. To maximize identifying women who were currently not amenorrheic, women 18 to 35 years of age who were not pregnant at the time of the telephone contact only were included in the sample. Of 650 randomly selected households contacted, 241 potential participants were available, and 179 (74%) agreed to participate.

## Procedure

Interviewers initially contacted the women by telephone, and arranged a mutually convenient time for interviewing the women in their homes. The interviewer obtained informed consent prior to the interview; interviews were completed in about one hour. All instruments were administered as part of the home interview.

## Instruments

### Perimenstrual Symptoms

The Moos (1977) Menstrual Distress Questionnaire (MDQ) was used to measure the dependent variable of perimenstrual symptoms. The MDQ has been used by a large number of investigators over the past decade to document the presence and severity of symptoms associated with the perimenstrual period. The MDQ contains 47 symptoms grouped into eight factors, six of which measure negative perceptions: Pain, Impaired Concentration, Behavior Change, Autonomic Reactions, Water Retention, and Negative Affect. Previous analyses from this study revealed that only 16 of the 47 symptoms on the MDQ differed significantly across cycle phase (Woods, Most, & Dery, 1982). Therefore, the present analyses will use only symptoms with demonstrable cycle phase differences. Thirteen of the symptoms were grouped into three factors: negative affect (irritability, mood swings, depression, tension, crying, anxiety, fatigue), water retention (weight gain, painful/tender breasts, swelling), and pain (headache, cramps, backache). The scales were internally consistent (Cronbach's alpha ranged from 0.64 to 0.88). The MDQ requires that women report their perceptions of each symptom for 1) their most recent flow, 2) the week before their most recent flow, and 3) the remainder of the cycle. They are asked to use a rating scale where responses range from 1 (for "no experience of the symptom") to 6 (for "acute or partially disabling"). The premenstrual and menstrual scores were summed to yield the perimenstrual scores used in the following analyses.

### Sex Role Norm Traditionalism

Sex role norm traditionalism was assessed by means of the 16-item Index of Sex Role Orientation (Dreyer, Woods, & James, 1981). A traditional sex role orientation was defined for those women: 1) whose behavior is dictated primarily by rules and rituals from past generations, only slightly modified by current movement toward equality for men and women; and 2) whose satisfaction comes after that of husband or family. In contrast, feminist women were seen as those who 1) advocate social change, either in theory or practice, which will lead to political, economic and social equality of the sexes; and 2) value their own personal growth and achievement as equal to the needs of family and others. Women respond to statements such as "Women who work should not have children." On a 1 to 7 Likert Scale high scores reflect a traditional sex role orientation. This instrument has been shown to be internally consistent ($\alpha = .9$) and reliable in a test-retest trial over one month ($\rho = .62$). It discriminates well between women who have feminist and traditional sex role norms (95% specificity and sensitivity).

*Sex Typing*
The Bem Sex Role Inventory was used to describe women as masculine, feminine, undifferentiated, and androgynous characteristics. The BSRI consists of 20 masculine personality traits (self-reliant, independent), 20 feminine personality traits (affectionate, gentle) and 20 neutral characteristics (happy, truthful). Respondents indicate on a scale from 1 (never or almost never true) to 7 (always or almost always true) how well each characteristic describes them. Androgynous individuals score high (above the median) on both the masculinity and femininity scales, and undifferentiated individuals score low (below the median) on both scales. Feminine or masculine individuals score high (above the median) on their respective scale and low on the opposite sex scale. The scales are internally consistent (average $\alpha = .83$) and stable over a 4 week retest period ($\rho = .93$) (Bem, 1974, 1977). Consistent with Bem's most recent conceptualization of sex typing, we used the women's ratings in the masculinity and femininity scales to indicate degree of sex typing as masculine or feminine.

*Occupational Traditionalism*
Occupational traditionalism was indicated by the percent of women in each occupation listed in U.S. government statistics for 1980. It was assumed that the more traditional occupations were those most highly populated by women, that is, nontraditional occupations for women would have small proportions of women whereas the traditional occupations would have large proportions of women. Women's occupations were given a traditionalism score that reflected the proportion of women in that occupation. The range was 0–100 (high score = high occupational traditionalism). It was assumed that 99.8 percent of all persons whose primary role is homemaker are women (U.S. Dept. of Labor, 1980).

## RESULTS

The participants ($n = 179$) ranged in age from 18 to 35 years, with a mean age of 27.7 ($\pm 4.6$). Sixty-three percent of the women were living in coupled relationships, with the remainder living alone as never married (29.5%), divorced or separated (8.3%), and widowed (0.5%). Sixty-six (33%) of the women were black and 128 (67%) were white. The income of the sample ranged from less than $2000 to more than $40,000 annually, with a median of about $6700. The women had attained educational levels ranging from completion of the 11th grade to doctoral preparation, with a median of fourteen years of education. They also represented a variety of religious denominations: 66.3 percent were Protestant, 10.4 percent Catholic, 2.1 percent Jewish; and 14.5 percent claimed no religion. Seventy-eight of the women in the sample had one or more children, with the mean number of children being 1.7.

Eighty-one percent of the women were currently employed, and 19 percent were not employed outside the home. Twenty (55%) of the latter described themselves as students, with the remainder being homemakers. The employed women reported working 5 to 60 hours per week, with the mode being 40 hours. The social status of the women's occupations varied widely.

### Perimenstrual Symptoms

The average severity rating on each perimenstrual symptom scale ranged from 2 to 3, consistent with these symptoms being barely noticeable to mild (Table 1). T-tests revealed no significant differences in symptom severity across the premenstruum and menstruum for all symptom clusters.

### Sex Role Orientation, Sex Typing, and Occupational Traditionalism

Half of the women scored in the traditional rage ($>68$) of the ISRO (M = 65.3, SD = 8.7). Approximately 25 percent of the sample scored high on the Bem masculinity and femininity scales. Half of the women were employed in occupations that were traditionally female, that is, in which 80 percent or more of the labor force was comprised of women.

**Table 1.** **Scores on Perimenstrual Symptom Scales (Mean ± SD; $n = 179$)**

| | Symptom | | |
| --- | --- | --- | --- |
| Type | Pain | Water retention | Negative affect |
| Premenstrual | 1.988 ± .941 | 2.333 ± 1.015 | 2.238 ± .873 |
| Menstrual | 2.199 ± .933 | 2.062 ± .925 | 2.070 ± .828 |

## Relationship between Sex Role Orientation, Sex Typing, Occupational Traditionalism, and Perimenstrual Symptoms

As seen in Table 2, the only sex role variable related to symptoms is occupational traditionalism, which is correlated with perimenstrual negative affect. Women in the most traditional occupations report the most severe negative affect symptoms. None of the sex role variables was correlated with pain. Marital status was the only variable correlated with water retention.

In order to examine the influence of sex role orientation, sex typing, and occupational traditionalism on perimenstrual negative

**Table 2.** **Relationship between Sex Role Orientation, Sex Typing, Occupational Traditionalism, and Perimenstrual Symptoms (Pearson's $r$; $n = 145$)**

| | Symptom | | |
| --- | --- | --- | --- |
| Variable | Negative affect | Water retention | Pain |
| Sex Role Orientation (ISRO) | −.053 | .055 | .042 |
| Bem Masculinity Scale | −.118 | .015 | −.053 |
| Bem Femininity Scale | .139 | .064 | .155 |
| Occupational traditionalism | .204[a] | .015 | .017 |
| Age (in years) | −.112 | .034 | −.155 |
| Race (1 = nonwhite) | −.093 | .117 | −.071 |
| Pregnancy history | −.032 | .148 | −.084 |
| Income | −.128 | −.049 | −.138 |
| Marital status (1 = married) | −.055 | .183[a] | .006 |

[a]$p < .05$.

Table 3. Influence of Sex Role Orientation, Sex Typing, and Occupational
Traditionalism on Perimenstrual Negative Affect, Controlling for
Demographic Variables (Hierarchical Multiple Regression; $n = 145$)

| Variable | B | $\beta$ | F | p | Squared part correlation[a] |
|---|---|---|---|---|---|
| $(1)^b$ | | | | | |
| Age (in years) | −.216 | −.092 | .869 | .35 | .012 |
| Race (1 = nonwhite) | −.917 | −.042 | .222 | .63 | .004 |
| Marital status (1 = married) | −.147 | −.070 | .531 | .46 | .000 |  .027 |
| Income | −.384 | −.075 | .664 | .41 | .007 |
| Parity | .103 | .051 | .247 | .62 | .004 |
| (2) | | | | | |
| Sex Role Orientation | −.162 | −.001 | .002 | .98 | .000 |
| Masculinity | −.157 | −.120 | 1.988 | .16 | .017 |  .067 |
| Femininity | .283 | .136 | 2.671 | .10 | .019 |
| Occupational traditionalism | .684 | .186 | 4.754 | .03 | .031 |

[a]Percent of variance uniquely accounted for.
[b]Refers to step in hierarchical regression.
Note. ($R^2 = .097, p < .11$).

affect, we employed hierarchical multiple regression analyses (Table 3). Age, race, marital status, income, and parity were entered on the first step to control for their effects on perimenstrual negative affect. Sex role orientation, masculinity and femininity scores, and occupational traditionalism were entered on the second step.

Age, race, parity, income, and marital status accounted for only 2.7 percent of the variance in negative affect. None of the individual variables made a statistically significant contribution to the model. The sex role variables uniquely accounted for 6.7 percent of the variance in negative affect. Of these variables, however, only one, occupational traditionalism, made a significant contribution to the equation. This suggests that women who work in more traditional occupations experience more severe perimenstrual negative affect.

## DISCUSSION

These findings suggest that sex typing has no significant effect on perimenstrual symptom reports. These results are inconsistent with the earlier work of Gough (1975), Slade and Jenner (1980), and Paige (1973), and with Nathanson's (1975) hypothesis about the effects of culture on the reporting of symptoms.

Likewise, sex role orientation seems unrelated to perimenstrual symptom reports. These findings are in contrast to those of Slade and Jenner (1980), who noted more severe menstrual symptoms in women scoring at the extremes of the Sex Role Attitude Scale: very traditional or very egalitarian. Plots of our data failed to reveal a U-shaped relationship.

It appears that women who perform more traditionally feminine occupations report more severe perimenstrual negative affect than their counterparts in less traditional occupations. This relationship is consistent with Nathanson's (1975) hypothesis linking role compatibility to the sick role. Expectations related to performance in male-dominated occupations are inconsistent with exhibiting illness. Women may find less support for and acceptance of perimenstrual symptoms in more male-oriented work environments, and thus may be less likely to acknowledge these symptoms. Alternatively, women who have the most severe symptoms may not enter the male-dominated sector of the labor force or may leave it because of their symptoms. A longitudinal study of labor force experience and symptoms would be necessary to be certain of the direction of the causal path. The episodic and cyclic nature of perimenstrual symptoms, and the fact that they usually are restricted to a few days each cycle, makes it unlikely that they, alone, would lead women to leave the labor force. Yet another alternative is that personal characteristics that lead women to pursue nontraditional careers also make women less likely to experience negative affect.

One important difference between our investigation and earlier studies involves the use of only those symptoms showing significant exacerbation during the perimenstruum. The associations between perimenstrual symptoms and femininity in other studies may be due, in part, to the more general finding that traditional women report more general psychosomatic symptoms (Woods, 1985). Thus, our study probably underestimates the effects of sex role traditionalism and personal characteristics on general symptoms as reported in other investigations.

The results from this study suggest that the larger construct of sex role orientation was not useful in understanding women's perimenstrual symptomatology. Investigators in women's health care are urged to look beyond acceptance or rejection of the female role to explain women's perimenstrual symptoms. These data sug-

gesting that one's view of self as a woman is unrelated to perimenstrual symptoms need careful attention by clinicians as well. Their
attributions of perimenstrual symptomatology to sex role rejection
can lend them to pejoratively and erroneously label women and may
negatively affect women's self-esteem.

## REFERENCES

Bem, S. (1974). The measurement of psychological androgyny. *Journal of
   Consulting and Clinical Psychology, 2,*153–162.
Bem, S. (1977). On the utility of alternate procedures for assessing psychologi-
   cal androgyny. *Journal of Consulting and Clinical Psychology, 45,* 196–205.
Bem, S. (1981). Gender schema theory: A cognitive account of sex typing.
   *Psychological Review, 88*(4), 354–364.
Berry, C., & McGuire, F. L. (1972). Menstrual distress and acceptance of sex
   role. *American Journal of Obstetrics and Gynecology, 114,* 83–87.
Delaney, J., Lupton, M. J., & Toth, E. (1977). *The curse: A cultural history
   of menstruation.* New York: New American Library.
Deutsch, H. (1944). *The psychology of women.* New York: Grune & Stratton.
Dreyer, N., Woods, N. F., & James, S. (1981). The index of sex role orientation
   (ISRO): A valid scale for sex role orientation in health research. *Sex Roles,
   7,* 173.
Gough, H. G. (1975). Personality factors related to reported severity of men-
   strual distress. *Journal of Abnormal Psychology, 84,* 59–65.
Greenhill, J. P. (1971). *Office gynecology.* Chicago: Year Book Medical Pub-
   lishers.
Harris, D. V. (1979). Physical sex differences: Being male and being female in
   sports involvement. In E. C. Snyder, (Ed.), *The study of women: Enlarging
   perspectives of social reality.* New York: Harper & Row.
Hyde, J. S., & Rosenberg, B. G. (1976). *The psychology of women: Half the
   human experience.* Lexington, MA: D. C. Heath & Co.
Kisch, E. H. (1910). *The sexual life of woman.* New York: Rebman Co.
Jacobi, M. P. (1877). *The question of rest for women during menstruation.*
   New York: Putnam.
Menninger, K. A. (1939). Somatic correlations with the unconscious repudiation
   of femininity in women. *Journal of Nervous and Mental Diseases, 89,* 514–
   527.
Moos, R. H. (1977). *Menstrual distress questionnaire.* Preliminary manual.
   Palo Alto, CA: Dept. of Psychiatry, Stanford University and Veterans
   Association Hospital.
Nathanson, C. (1975). Illness and the feminine role: A theoretical review. *Social
   Science and Medicine, 9,* 57–62.
Novak, E. (1931). *Menstruation and its disorders.* New York: D. Appelton & Co.
Paige, K. E. (1971). Effects of oral contraceptives on affective fluctuations
   associated with the menstrual cycle. *Psychosomatic Medicine, 33,* 515–537.

Paige, K. E. (1973). Women learn to sing the menstrual blues. *Psychology Today, 7,* 41–46.

Richards, E. L. (1928). Some common ground between gynecology and psychopathology. In H. A. Kelly (Ed.), *Gynecology.* New York: D. Appelton & Co.

Shainess, N. (1961). A re-evaluation of some aspects of femininity through a study of menstruation: A preliminary report. *Comparative Psychiatry, 2,* 20–26.

Sherif, C. W. (1980). A social psychological perspective on the menstrual cycle. In J. E. Parsons (Ed.), *The psychobiology of sex differences and sex roles,* Washington, DC: Hemisphere.

Slade, P., & Jenner, F. A. (1980). Attitudes to female roles, aspects of menstruation and complaining of menstrual symptoms. *British Journal of Social and Clinical Psychology, 19,* 109–113.

Spence, J., & Helmreich, R. (1979). *Masculinity and femininity: Their psychological dimensions, correlates and antecedents.* Austin: University of Texas Press.

Thompson, C. (1950). Some effects of the derogatory attitude toward female sexuality. *Psychiatry, 13,* 349–354.

U.S. Department of Labor (1980). *Women in the labor force, 1978-1979.* Washington, DC: Author.

Watts, S., Dennerstein, L., & Del Horne, D. J. (1980). The premenstrual syndrome: A psychological evaluation. *Journal of Affective Disorders, 2,* 257–266.

Weideger, P. (1975). *Menstruation and menopause.* New York: Dell.

Wilcoxon, L., Schrader, S., & Sherif, C. (1976). Daily self reports on activities, life events, moods, and somatic changes during the menstrual cycle. *Psychosomatic Medicine, 38,* 399–417.

Woods, N. F. (1985). Employment and family roles, social context and mental ill health in young adult women. *Nursing Research, 34,* 4–9.

Woods, D. J., & Launius, A. L. (1979). Type of menstrual discomfort and psychological masculinity in college women. *Psychological Reports, 44,* 257–258.

Woods, N. F., Most, A., & Dery, G. (1982). Estimating perimenstrual distress: A comparison of two methods. *Research in Nursing and Health, 5,* 81–91.

# FUNCTION AND DYSFUNCTION: A HISTORICAL CRITIQUE OF THE LITERATURE ON MENSTRUATION AND WORK

**Siobán D. Harlow**

Department of Epidemiology, Johns Hopkins School of Hygiene and Public Health

Historically, menstruation has often been cited as the source of women's inferiority as workers. It has been argued that, given the physical and emotional demands of menstruation, the performance of certain jobs might cause a woman to hurt herself or to disrupt the orderly and efficient production of goods. Despite the influence that this reasoning has had on women's lives, the validity of its conclusions have never been demonstrated by scientific inquiry. This paper argues that, in general, scientists have failed to consider the topic of menstrual dysfunction in the workplace as one requiring scientific scrutiny and that when research has been conducted, beliefs about menstruation have systematically biased the results. These failures have led not only to the perpetuation of myths about women as workers, but they have also thwarted the search for organic causes of menstrual dysfunction. A redefinition of the question concerning work and menstrual dysfunction is proposed.

During the last quarter of the nineteenth century, a theory of bodily energy guided medical thinking about physiologic functioning and mechanisms of disease. This medical theory held that the body subsisted on a fixed amount of energy, and that the female reproductive system possessed special energy requirements placing it in competition with other systems for available energy. A particular conflict was believed to exist between the energy demands of the uterus and those of the central nervous system. Overuse of the brain or sustained muscular effort would deny the uterus its necessary energy

This paper is dedicated to the memory of Dr. Anna M. Baetjer. I would also like to acknowledge Thomas Laqueur for his support and guidance, and Marion Moses for her comments on the manuscript.

and, therefore, cause it to malfunction (Ames, 1875; Barker-Benfield, 1979; Clarke, 1889). In the words of Dr. Edward Clarke, a professor of materia medica at Harvard University and leading proponent of this theory:

> The [reproductive] system is then peculiarly susceptible; and disturbances of the delicate mechanism . . . by constrained positions, muscular effort, brain work, and all forms of mental and physical excitement, germinate a host of ills. Sometimes these causes . . . produce an excessive performance of the catamenial function; and this is equivalent to periodical hemorrhage. Sometimes they produce an insufficient performance of it; and this, by closing an avenue of elimination, poisons the blood, and depraves the organization. The host of ills thus induced are known to the physician as amenorrhea, menorrhagia, dysmenorrhea, hysteria, anemia, chorea, and the like. Some of these fasten themselves to the victim for a lifetime, and some are shaken off. Now and then they lead to an abortion of the function, and consequent sterility. (Clarke, 1889, pp. 47–48)

This theory, prevalent during that period when the biology of menstruation was just beginning to be known, assumes that physical and mental weakness is inherently associated with the normal functioning of women's reproductive organs.

The question of whether or not this assumption was an accurate one, and if it was what the implications were for women workers, has provoked considerable discussion among physicians, legislators, and lay people throughout the last century. Recognition of the tenets of the energy theory is, however, essential to understanding the early literature on the relationship between menstruation and work, and to understanding the subsequent, sometimes inconsistent, developments in the field. This paper will trace the history of scientific inquiry on the relationship between menstruation and work by critically reviewing the occupational health literature on the subject. It will examine the effect that the question of inherent weakness associated with menstrual function has had on the development of research models. Finally, it will propose a new theoretical framework for subsequent investigation.

During the first decade after the Civil War, the growing demand for female labor in the industrial work force, the opening of the first colleges for women, and the concomitant concern that these changes would be hazardous to women's health sparked a rather extensive discussion of women's biological limitations in gynecologic and lay literature (Ames, 1875; Barker-Benfield 1979; Clarke, 1889; Howe, 1874; Putnam-Jacobi, 1877). One of the major participants in this discussion was Dr. Azel Ames, a Special Commissioner of Investigation to the Massachusetts Bureau of Labor Statistics, who conducted the first public inquiry into the relationship between work and menstrual dysfunction in 1874.

Ames' book, *Sex in Industry: A Plea for the Working Girl* (1875), provides a vivid picture of the experience of women who worked in female-dominated trades during the 1870s. For each of six trades—typesetting, telegraphy, counting money, counting rattans, basket-making, and sewing with foot-powered machines—Ames describes the tasks performed by women, detailing each movement of their hands or bodies and each moment when thought or memory was required. He also gathered anecdotal reports from physicians, employers, and supervisors on the nature and extent of the menstrual problems experienced by the women.

Referring to his detailed account and the principles of the bodily energy theory, Ames argued that by simultaneously demanding rapid manipulation, intense concentration, and mental activity the industrial labor process overworked women, and thus taxed their emotional, mental, and physical strength. This taxing of strength, he said, drained necessary energy away from the reproductive organs and was thus the causal factor in the development of "too frequent and profuse return of the menses" and other "disturbed menstrual conditions," conditions that he reported to be common problems for women workers.

His conclusion that a causal association existed between laboring in the trades and the development of menstrual disorders, coupled with his medical belief that menstrual disorders were associated with the breakdown of women's health and the development of insanity, led Ames to recommend that women's employment in industry be limited, a recommendation that was subsequently used as evidence to support the passage of the Massachusetts 1874 maximum hours law for women and children (Barker-Benfield, 1979).

*Sex in Industry* was a pioneering work on occupational hazards for working women, and Ames made many recommendations for improving unsanitary conditions. His descriptions indicate that women were in fact overworked and laboring in unhealthy work-places. Typesetters, for example, sat all day in confined positions in hot composing rooms, subject to lead and antimony poisoning, while trying to set and correct 30,000 ems per week for nine dollars. His analysis of the relationship between menstruation and work, however, rested on a belief in women's frailty, and relied on anecdotal evidence of menstrual dysfunction.

Although not all physicians or lay people agreed with his analysis (Howe, 1874; Putnam-Jacobi, 1877), the question of limitations imposed by inherent weakness, not the effects of unhealthy conditions, defined the focus of discussion during the decade and the framework through which work and menstruation were studied.

Despite the influence of Ames' work and the prominence of the issue in medical and social discourse during the 1870s, the subject of menstruation and work did not continue to receive attention. The medical literature, probably reflecting the minimal attention given to industrial hygiene in the United States during this period, remained virtually silent on this subject for almost 40 years.

In 1921, Dr. Clara Seippel, commenting on the silence in a paper delivered at the Eighth Annual Meeting of the International Association of Industrial Accidents Boards and Commissions (Seippel, 1921), noted the lack of statistics on gynecologic illness in industry. Her paper marked a reawakening of interest on the topic within the medical community. Renewed interest coincided with recognition by the business community that health improved employees' productivity and the consequent emergence of the industrial physician (Brown, 1979).

Three papers were subsequently published by industrial physicians on the prevalence of dysmenorrhea (menstrual cramps) and its effect on productivity in 1922 (Meaker), 1923 (Sturgis), and 1931 (Ewing). Their central concern with working capacity is evidenced by their definition of dysmenorrhea in terms of its relationship to inefficiency as the discomfort or pain with bleeding that makes a woman employee less efficient (Sturgis, 1923).

These studies were methodologically adequate and all concluded that dysmenorrhea did not cause a significant loss of work time or efficiency. Sturgis reported that only 4.4 percent of women working in a department store experienced sufficient discomfort to remain home. Ewing (1931) introduced an exercise program at the home office of the Metropolitan Life Insurance Company and reduced menstrual-related absences over a 7-year period from 360 days to 72 days per 1000 women employees per year.

Sturgis' conclusion, that dysmenorrhea did not seriously interfere with productivity, led her to state further that women should not be charged with inefficiency as a result of menstruation since it was negligible in the majority of women. The 4.4 percent with severe discomfort, she noted, probably suffered from either gross pelvic pathology or a specific endocrine disorder.

These investigators did not assume that incapacity was a necessary companion of menstruation. In their research they specifically measured the extent of limitation and subsequently defined incapacitating conditions as abnormal. Their research, however, still focused on the question of limitation as they were trying to determine whether menstruation made women inefficient workers.

Other investigators have periodically reexamined the question of limitation: Dick (1943), Smith (1944), Baetjer (1946), Svennerud (1959) and Bergsjo, Jenssen, & Vellar (1975). Methodologically adequate studies (Bergsjo et al., 1975; Smith, 1944; Svennerud, 1959) reached conclusions similar to Sturgis, Meaker, and Ewing. In her 1946 literature review Baetjer stated that "from the best recent studies it appears that probably not over 10 percent of women employees suffer sufficiently from dysmenorrhea to cause lost time and that not over about 300 work days per 1000 employees per year are lost from this cause" (p. 199). An excellent and extensive investigation conducted by Svennerud in Sweden in 1959 found that dysmenorrhea accounted for 3.7 percent of absences (1100 days per 1000 women per year) in factory workers and 2.5 percent of absences (300 days per 1000 women per year) in office workers.

Despite the consistency of the literature on this point, however, the results have never been widely known or accepted within either medical or lay literature. As late as 1981, *Novak's Textbook of Gynecology* still contended that dysmenorrhea is the most frequent cause of lost work time, and that each year dysmenorrhea is responsible for 140 million wasted work hours (Jones & Jones, 1981, p. 871). The source of this figure of 140 million hours is not cited. Considering, however, that approximately 43 million women were in the labor force in 1979 (U.S. Department of Labor Statistics, 1980), that number represents only three hours per woman per year. Furthermore, data from the 1977 National Health Interview Survey indicates that the greatest cause of lost work time for acute conditions is, in fact, influenza (National Center for Health Statistics, 1978).

To what can one attribute this seeming failure to disseminate information or dysmenorrhea and absenteeism? Perhaps it results from the disparate nature of the literature, or from the lack of a developed analytic tradition. Certainly, after the publications of Meaker, Sturgis, and Ewing a virtual silence once again descended. The topic of menstruation and work did not resurface in the occupational literature until the outbreak of World War II.

In the 1940s, confronted by a rapidly growing female work force in war-related industries such as General Motors, Western Electric, aerospace, and explosives manufacturing, industrial physicians attempted to develop appropriate medical programs for women in industry (Baetjer, 1946; Barlow, 1944; Burnell, 1944a, 1944b; Dick, 1943; Hesseltine, 1943; Hesseltine, 1944; Kronenberg,

1944; Schauffler, 1944; Smith, 1944; Varney, 1944). Noting the lack of information in the field, Dr. H. Close Hesseltine, chair of the American Medical Association's Committee on the Health of Women in Industry, stated that until factual and sufficient data was obtained, their recommendations would be guided by ideas and opinions (Hesseltine, 1944). The articles published during this period thus reflect the then current medical knowledge and practice.

Menstrual disorders for which no gross pathology could be identified were often attributed to individual maladjustments. Primary dysmenorrhea was said to result from psychological maladjustments (Hesseltine, 1944) or to reflect malingering not actual discomfort (Burnell, 1944a; Varney, 1944). Menorrhagia (heavy or excessive bleeding) and amenorrhea (cessation of menses) were said to stem from tension, worry or excitement, or from an inability to handle responsibility (Hesseltine, 1944).

Physicians were aware that women in different occupations experienced different disorders (Hesseltine, 1944; Varney, 1944), and recognized that certain environmental conditions did influence bleeding patterns (Hesseltine, 1943). They did not, however, incorporate these observations into their evaluation of menstrual dysfunction. Hesseltine, for instance, noted that environmental factors such as climate and altitude might be associated with menstrual dysfunction (Hesseltine, 1943), but he attributed the menorraghia and amenorrhea experienced by flight attendants to their holding positions of responsibility (Hesseltine, 1944).

Hesseltine was not considering level of responsibility as an occupational stressor that, in concert with other stressors, might induce a physiologic response resulting in altered menstrual function. Occupation was not thought to play a role in the generation of menstrual dysfunction (Hesseltine, 1944; Varney, 1944). During this period menstrual disturbances were primarily attributed to personal and behavioral causes, indicating that a premise of inherent weakness continued to underlie the physician's medical reasoning.

In the 1940s, the perimenopause and menopause were discussed for the first time in the occupational literature. The articles indicate that inherent weakness was also thought to attend the cessation of menstruation, and physicians expressed concern about the potential effects of perimenopausal changes on productivity. Hesseltine commented that "the [menopausal] employee may because of her emotional instability become irritable and thus lessen production" (Hesseltine, 1944, p. 696)* These perceptions led to recommendations that placement of menopausal women be restricted. In termi-

---

*Copyright 1944, American Medical Association.

nology reminiscent of that used by Azel Ames, Dr. Max Burnell, the medical director of General Motors, advised, for instance, that

> the menopause, with its associated nervous and vasomotor instability, increased excitability and susceptibility to fatigue, along with the frequent attacks of vertigo, limits the type of work they should be allowed to do. . . . It is the responsibility of the physician . . . to insist that she be placed at tasks requiring less nervous energy and concentration. Sympathetic understanding goes far in lessening lost time during this trying period. (Burnell, 1944a, p. 213)

Some physicians and other professionals did not agree with these interpretations of the source of menstrual difficulties in working women. Jennie Mohr, an economist with the Women's Bureau, argued that "it would be of the utmost value if physicians would undertake studies to determine specific effects on women of certain occupations or working conditions about which we can at present only speculate" (Barlow, 1944, p. 691).* Scattered reports had also appeared in the literature over the previous 20 years indicating possible associations between changes in menstrual flow and exposure to lead (Best, 1932; Mettert, 1934, 1936), benzene (Hamilton, 1931), and tobacco (Mettert, 1934, 1936), and changes in the menstrual flow.

It was not until the 1960s, however, that more definitive studies of the associations between occupation and menstrual dysfunction were undertaken. The earliest studies appeared in the flight physiology literature (Cameron, 1969; Farrell & Allen, 1973; Iglesias, Terris, and Chavarria, 1980; Preston, Bateman, Short, & Wilkinson, 1973). Interpretation of the data from these studies on flight attendants and flight nurses is difficult because of inadequate sample size, reliance on recall of cycling history, and lack of controls or appropriate population data. Although a tendency towards longer flows, increased irregularity, and more pain are reported, one cannot assess whether the magnitude of these changes is meaningful.

Since the appearance of these early publications on flying, the literature has not developed extensively. Reports, predominantly from Eastern Europe, have suggested possible associations between menstrual irregularities and exposure to microwaves (Marha, Musil, & Tuha, 1968; Marha, 1970), chemicals (Chase, Barnett, Welch, Briese, & Krassner, 1973; Shumilina, 1975), and heavy vibrations (Frolova, 1975, Glowacki, 1966, Pramaratarov & Balev, 1969). A recent well-designed study from Canada reported an increase in dysmenorrhea among poultry slaughterhouse workers with exposure

---

*Copyright 1944, American Medical Association.

to cold (Mergler & Vezina, 1982). Thus, although the literature of the past 20 years has addressed the question of whether working conditions influence bleeding patterns, such reports are still isolated phenomena that have yet to reflect the development of an analytic tradition.

Reviewing the history of scientific inquiry during the industrial era on the relationship between menstruation and work thus reveals an essential contradiction. To the extent that a literature exists, it cannot support the notion that menstruation interferes with women's ability to work. Yet the theoretical framework underlying most of the extant research is built upon the premise that menstruation negatively affects women's functional capacity. This viewpoint led to the development of an unidirectional research model which tried to quantify degree of limitation and precluded investigation of work-related causes of menstrual disorders.

The central question raised by this model is, "Is it the normal or abnormal that limits functioning?" The term abnormal implies defect and therefore the possibility of determining etiology. When a defect is perceived of as normative, however, it is defined as an inherent characteristic. Search for a precipitating cause is suspended. The failure to develop an analytic tradition on work-related causes of menstrual dysfunction may thus reflect this historical presumption of inherent weakness. The successful development of an analytic tradition, therefore, would require the definition of a new premise. If menstrual dysfunction in working women is not viewed as an inherent characteristic of the menstrual cycle but as a problem of occupational health, dysfunction would be defined as abnormal and the possibility of determining etiology would be implied.

In a work environment, alterations in menstrual function can, in fact, give cause for concern. Changes in menstrual function may themselves be injurious, for instance through increased blood loss or decreased fertility, or they may function as markers of other health problems. Bleeding abnormalities could also signal chemical poisoning, disruption of the circadian rhythm, disruption of steroid metabolism, or changes in blood chemistry. Menstrual disturbances may also inhibit conception or indicate the occurrrence of early spontaneous abortion.

In constructing a new theoretical framework based on a definition of dysfunction as abnormal, the main objective of research would then be to answer a new question: "Do menstrual cycle patterns, either physiologic or dysfunctional ones, vary between occupations?" The central purpose for conducting menstrual cycle research within the context of the workplace would then be to gain information about whether menstrual cycle patterns vary between groups of people, and if so, how they vary. Insights into the causes of variation might be gained, insights which might help explain the generation of dysfunction.

This focus on the possibility of significant variation between groups, given the lack of population-based data on the epidemiology of menstrual variation or dysfunction, requires that initial studies employ a comparative design. Use of prospective diaries would both eliminate the problems of inaccurate recall and recall bias, and provide information in sufficient detail to better describe patterns in the data.

Consideration ought also to be given to potential mechanisms through which occupation may influence bleeding patterns. Four major pathways can be hypothesized through which such an influence might occur. First, environmental stimuli may act on the hypothalamus, altering cycle regulation or affecting the release of stress-related hormones. These stimuli might include social or psychological stressors, noise, or disruption of the circadian rhythm resulting from shiftwork (Bearwood, Mundell, & Utian, 1975; Sackler, Weltman, Bradshaw, & Jurtshuk, 1959; Singh & Rao, 1970; Zacur, Chapanis, Lake, Ziegler, & Tyson, 1976; Zondek & Tamari, 1967). Second, altered peripheral metabolism of hormones may disrupt feedback mechanisms. Altered metabolism might occur through chemical induction of metabolizing enzymes or as a result of liver changes (Duby, Travis, & Terrill, 1971; Heinrichs, Gellert, Bakke, & Lawrence, 1971; Levin, Welch, & Conney, 1968). Third, changes in blood clotting factors may affect clotting mechanisms (Palmblad et al., 1977). Finally, heavy vibration (Frolova, 1975; Glowacki, 1966; Pramaratarov & Balev, 1969), physical agents such as radiation (Marha et al., 1968; Marha, 1970), or chemical carcinogens may cause direct injury to the reproductive organs.

In summary, this paper has argued that the historical presumption that normal menstruation impairs a woman's capacity to work, and that dysmenorrhea is a major cause of inefficiency and absenteeism, cannot be supported by scientific evidence. It has also argued that this presumption has limited the scientific community in developing an analytic tradition. By defining impairment as abnormal, and suggesting that dysfunction may, in fact, be attributable to occupation, an alternative theoretical framework for investigation was constructed. Using this new theoretical framework, we can build on the fledgling efforts of recent investigators and begin to create a tradition of research on the epidemiology of occupationally related menstrual dysfunction.

# REFERENCES

Ames, A. (1875). *Sex in industry: A plea for the working girl.* Boston: James R. Osgood and Co.

Baetjer, A. M. (1946). *Women in industry: Their health and efficiency.* Philadelphia: W. B. Saunders.

Barker-Benfield, G. J. (1979, December). *Menstruation and class: Public policy for women in college and factory 1860-1920.* Paper presented at the Conference of the American Historical Association, San Francisco, CA.

Barlow, F. A. (1944). Proper placement of women in industry. *Journal of the American Medical Association, 124*(11), 687-691.

Bearwood, C. J., Mundell, C. A., & Utian, W. H. (1975). Gonadotropin excretion in response to audiostimulation in human subjects. *American Journal of Obstetrics and Gynecology, 121*(5), 682-687.

Bergsjo, P., Jenssen, H., & Vellar, O. (1975). Dysmenorrhea in industrial workers. *Acta Obstetrica et Gynecologica Scandinavica, 54,* 255-259.

Best, E. (1932). The employment of women in vitreous enameling (Bulletin No. 101). Washington, DC: Woman's Bureau.

Brown, E. R. (1979). *Rockefeller medicine men: Medicine and capitalism in America.* Berkeley: University of California Press.

Burnell, M. (1944a). Gynecological and obstetrical problems of the industrial physician. *Industrial Medicine, 13*(3), 211-214.

Burnell, M. (1944b). Health maintenance program for women in industry. *Journal of the American Medical Association, 124*(11), 683-687.

Cameron, R. G. (1969). Effects of flying on the menstrual function of air hostesses. *Aerospace Medicine, 40*(9), 1020-1023.

Chase, H. P., Barnett, S. E., Welch, N. M., Briese, F. W., & Krassner, M. L. (1973). Pesticides and U.S. farm labor families. *Rocky Mountain Medical Journal, 70*(11), 27-31.

Clarke, E. H. (1889). *Sex in education, or a fair chance for girls.* Boston: Houghton Mifflin.

Dick, A. C. (1943). Menstrual exercises—absenteeism decrease and work efficiency increase. *Industrial Medicine, 12*(9), 588-589.

Duby, R. T., Travis, H. F., & Terrill, C. E. (1971). Uterotrophic activity of DDT in rats and mink and its influence on reproduction in the rat. *Toxicology and Applied Pharmacology, 18,* 348-355.

Ewing, R. E. (1931). A study of dysmenorrhea at the home office of the Metropolitan Life Insurance Company. *Journal of Industrial Hygiene, 13*(7), 244-251.

Farrell, B., & Allen, M. (1973). Physiologic/psychologic changes reported by USAF female flight nurses during flying duties. *Nursing Research, 22*(1), 31-36.

Frolova, T. P. (1975). Features specific for the effect of vibration on the blood supply to the true pelvis at different periods in the menstrual cycle. *Gigiena Truda Professionalnye Zabolevaniia, 19,* 14-18.

Glowacki, C. (1966). The effects of vibration on the female genitalia. *Ginekologia Polska, 37,* 217-222.

Hamilton, A. (1931). Benzene (benzol) poisoning. *Archives of Pathology, 11*, 434-454.

Heinrichs, W. L., Gellert, R. J., Bakke, L., & Lawrence, N. (1971). Persistent estrous syndrome following DDT administration to neonatal rats. *Clinical Research, 19*, 171.

Hesseltine, H. C. (1943). Women in industry: Preliminary report of the Committee on the Health of Women in Industry in the Section of Obstetrics and Gynecology: Recommendations to the Council on Industrial Health. *Journal of the American Medical Association, 121*(11), 799-802.

Hesseltine, H. C. (1944). Specific problems of women in industry. *Journal of the American Medical Association, 124*(11), 692-697.

Howe, J. W. (Ed.). (1874). *Sex and education: A reply to Dr. E. H. Clarke's Sex in Education*. Boston: Roberts Brothers.

Iglesias, R., Terres, A., & Chavarria, A. (1980). Disorders of the menstrual cycle in airline stewardesses. *Aviation, Space, and Environmental Medicine, 51*(5), 518-520.

Jones, H. W., & Jones, G. S. (1981). *Novak's textbook of gynecology* (10th ed.). Baltimore: Williams and Wilkins.

Kronenberg, M. H. (1944). Working conditions for female employees. *Journal of the American Medical Association, 124*(11), 677-683.

Levin, W., Welch, R. M., & Conney, A. H. (1968). Effect of phenobarbitol and other drugs on the metabolism and uterotrophic action of estradiol-17B and estrone. *Journal of Pharmacology and Experimental Therapeutics, 159*, 362-371.

Marha, K., Musil, J., & Tuha, H. (1968). *Electromagnetic fields and the living environment*. San Francisco: San Francisco Press.

Marha, K. (1970). Maximum admissible values of HF and UHF electromagnetic radiation at work places in Czechoslovakia. In S. F. Cleary (Ed.), *Biological effects and health implications of microwave radiation, symposium proceedings* (DHEW Public Health Service, BRH/DBE 70-2). Washington, DC: U.S. Government Printing Office.

Meaker, S. R. (1922). A preliminary note on dysmenorrhea as an industrial problem. *Journal of Industrial Hygiene, 4*(2), 49-52.

Mergler, D., & Vezina, N. (1982). *Dysmenorrhea among poultry slaughterhouse workers*. Paper presented at the Second International Symposium on Epidemiology in Occupational Medicine, Montreal, Canada.

Mettert, M. T. (1934). *State reporting of occupational disease, including a survey of legislation applying to females* (Bulletin No. 114). Washington, DC: Woman's Bureau.

Mettert, M. T. (1936). *Summary of state reports of occupational disease, with a survey of preventive legislation, 1932-1934* (Bulletin No. 147). Washington, DC: Woman's Bureau.

National Center for Health Statistics (1978). Current estimates from the Health Interview Survey, *Vital and Health Statistics,* [DHEW Pub. No. (PHS) 78-1554] Series 10(126), 18.

Palmblad, J., Blomback, M., Egberg, N., Froberg, J., Karlsson, C. G., & Levi, L.

(1977). Experimentally induced stress in man: Effects on blood coagulation and fibrinolysis. *Journal of Psychosomatic Research, 21,* 87–92.

Pramaratarov, A., & Balev, L. (1969). Menstrual anomalies and the influence of motor vehicle vibrations on the conductors from the city transport. *Akusherstvol I Ginekologia (Sofia), 8,* 31–37.

Preston, F. S., Bateman, S. C., Short, R. V., & Wilkinson, R. T. (1973). Effects of flying and of time changes on menstrual cycle length and on performance in airline stewardesses. *Aerospace Medicine, 44*(4), 438–443.

Putnam-Jacobi, M. (1877). *The question of rest for women during menstruation.* New York: G. P. Putnam.

Sackler, A. M., Weltman, A. S., Bradshaw, M., & Jurtshuk, P. (1959). Endocrine changes due to auditory stress. *Acta Endocrinologica, 31,* 405–418.

Schauffler, G. (1944). Women in heavy war work: Obstetrical and gynecological aspects. *Western Journal of Surgical Obstetrics and Gynecology, 52,* 12–20.

Seippel, C. (1921). Medical aspects of women's ills in industry. *Monthly Labor Review, 13*(5), 1–5.

Shumilina, A. V. (1975). Menstrual and child bearing functions of female workers occupationally exposed to formaldehyde. *Gigiena Truda Professionalnye Zabolevaniia, 12,* 18–21.

Singh, K. B., & Rao, P. S. (1970). Studies on polycystic ovaries of rats under continuous auditory stress. *American Journal of Obstetrics and Gynecology, 108,* 557–564.

Smith, F. L. (1944). Causes of sickness, absenteeism peculiar to women in industry. *Industrial Medicine, 13*(3), 217–219.

Sturgis, M. C. (1923). Observations on dysmenorrhea occurring in women employed in a large department store. *Journal of Industrial Hygiene, 5*(2), 53–56.

Svennerud, S. (1959). Dysmenorrhea and absenteeism: Some gynecologic and medical-social aspects. *Acta Obstetrica and Gynecologica Scandinavica, 38,* Supplement 2.

U.S. Department of Labor Statistics (1980, October). *Perspectives on working women* (Bulletin No. 2080). Washington, DC: Bureau of Labor Statistics.

Varney, W. H. (1944). Medical management of complaints of women in the explosives industry. *Industrial Medicine, 13*(2), 122–124.

Zacur, H. A., Chapanis, N. P., Lake, C. R., Ziegler, M., & Tyson, J. E. (1976). Galactorrhea-amenorrhea: Psychological interaction with neuroendocrine function. *American Journal of Obstetrics and Gynecology, 125*(6), 859–862.

Zondek, B., & Tamari, I. (1967). Effects of auditory stimulation on reproduction. In CIBA Foundation Study Group No. 26 (Ed.), *Effects of external stimuli on reproduction.* Boston: Little, Brown.

Request reprints from Siobán D. Harlow, Johns Hopkins School of Hygiene and Public Health, Box 336, 615 N. Wolfe Street, Baltimore, MD 21205.

# ANALYZING EMERGENT ISSUES IN WOMEN'S HEALTH: THE CASE OF THE TOXIC–SHOCK SYNDROME

Virginia L. Olesen, PhD
Department of Social and Behavioral Sciences, School of Nursing,
University of California, San Francisco

Analyzing emergent issues in women's health, where the issue and its implications are still ambiguous but nevertheless have important consequences for women's health, poses particular problems for feminist researchers. Using the toxic-shock syndrome as an example of such an issue, this paper reviews aspects of such analysis involving method, frameworks, and sources of data.

## INTRODUCTION

One of the clear contributions of the social science sector of the women's movement in the U.S. has been to bring to the attention of women *and* the medical establishment taken-for-granted matters in women's health and to make them problematic in a political and practical way. Such work (Ruzek, 1980; Olesen, 1975) places questions in a theoretical context so as to facilitate policy analysis in more useful and sophisticated ways than would otherwise be possible. Much of this analysis, however, focuses on issues already defined as problems. This paper takes up a different aspect of such analysis, namely the investigation of questions and issues that are still emergent, hence labile, sometimes elusive, and frequently difficult to scrutinize. As a context for this discussion, the paper takes the example of toxic-shock syndrome, using this to generate key analytic points not only about this phenomenon, but the more general matter of analyzing emergent issues in women's health.

This paper is a revised version of one presented at the Society for Applied Anthropology, Edinburgh, Scotland, April 1981. The assistance of Katarin Jurich, Sally Maeth, Jan Hitchcock, Rebecca Johnson, Christine Miller, Kim Christopher, and Pamela Sargent is gratefully acknowledged. The author particularly thanks Jane Zones for sharing her extensive files on regulatory issues around toxic shock.

## MANAGEMENT OF MENSTRUAL FLOW: A HISTORY

To discuss the toxic shock syndrome, which is a disease thought
to derive from toxins produced in the vagina by the bacterium
known as *staphylococcus aureus* when some menstruating women
use tampons, it will be useful to review very briefly the history of
the management of menstrual flow, relying heavily on the Delaney,
Lupton, and Toth history of menstruation (1976).

Crude tampons were apparently used in ancient times when in
certain societies (Egyptian, for instance) women inserted grasses to
absorb the monthly flow. After cloth began to be made, reusable
rags, washed monthly, served this purpose. By the late 1800s a crude
sanitary towel and belt were developed, but when Johnson and
Johnson, the manufacturers of baby powder, in 1896 developed
disposable towels, they could not market them because the moral
climate of the day would not permit advertisement.

At the time of the First World War, nurses found that they could
use gauze. Whether this discovery prompted the paper-producing
firm of Kimberly and Clark, the manufacturers of Kleenex, to
develop and market Kotex in 1921 is not clear. What is certain is
that in 1924, the *Ladies Home Journal,* a mass-circulation magazine
of some stature for middle- and upper-class women, carried the first
ad for this product. Ads in the 1920s stressed that the pads decreased
psychological tension. Subsequently other magazines such as *Good
Housekeeping* also carried the ads, which in the 1930s emphasized
the secretive aspect of menstruation and how to manage it discreetly
with the new pads. In the 1950s, when the emphasis returned to the
avoidance of embarrassment, such terms "secure," "confident,"
and "free" were stressed rather than the straightforward issue of
absorbency. Delaney, Lupton, and Toth argue that this constituted
a return to feminine daintiness and was related to what Friedan later
called "the feminine mystique" (1963).

In 1936, Tampax acquired the patent to a tampon, which
eventually became known by the company name to the point where
tampons generally were referred to as "Tampax." Like Kotex, it
was initially made from wood pulp and rayon, but later was produced from cotton. In 1977, manufacturers altered the composition
of the product and began to use more absorbent materials such as
polyacrylate fibers, carboxymythillic cellulose, and high absorbency
rayon cellulose and polyester foam (Shands, Schmid, Dan, et al.,
1980). This new tampon was designed to expand and hence close
the vaginal outlet (Fuller, Swartz, Wolfson, & Salzman, 1980).
It is this later, highly absorbent tampon that is implicated in the

onset of the disease called toxic-shock syndrome in menstruating women.

## TOXIC–SHOCK SYNDROME

Toxic-shock syndrome is the term applied to the physical state that ensues from toxins produced by a bacterial agent known as *staphylococcus aureus*. That state involves diarrhea, fever, vomiting, sloughing off of skin, and, in extreme cases, sufficient shock to the system that death occurs. It had been known for some time in other cases, for instance, persons who have been inoculated or in youngsters. It has also affected nonmenstruating women (Robertson, 1982).

Toxic-shock syndrome in menstruating women emerged in mid-1979 when between July 15, 1979 and January 5, 1980 seven patients, including one male, were hospitalized in Wisconsin with toxic-shock symptoms. All six female patients were menstruating women. The Wisconsin State Health Department immediately asked all physicians in that state to establish statewide surveillance to note any cases they observed then or earlier. Of the cases physicians reported between September 1975 and June 1980, a research team of physicians interviewed 38 patients, 37 of whom were female. Thirty-five of the women interviewed had had toxic-shock syndrome more than once and, of these, 34 used tampons (Davis, Chesney, Wand, & La Ventura, 1980).

This report returned suspicion to the use of tampons, which had been earlier thought not to be implicated, and confirmed the findings from the Center for Disease Control in Atlanta, which on September 12 had revealed a new study indicating tampon use and in particular the Rely tampon manufactured by Procter and Gamble. The day after the CDC report, CDC representatives, along with Federal Drug Administration officials met with representatives of Procter and Gamble who cast suspicion on the CDC findings, noting that the media publicity had biased the outcome (Donawa, Schmid, & Osterholm, 1984). On the following day the FDA and the CDC issued a news release with the findings. Several days later findings from a study at the University of Utah and one at the University of Minnesota supported the CDC conclusions concerning Rely.

On September 21, Procter and Gamble called in a group of scientific advisors—and doubtlessly some lawyers—who, after a review of the available data decided that Rely should be withdrawn from the market, which it was on September 22. The CDC data showed that out of 242 cases analyzed there, in some 76 instances women had used Rely. Eighty-four had used other brands and 102 were not certain. In the meanwhile, the Food and Drug Administration began issuing advice that the risk of toxic-shock syndrome could be reduced by either using tampons and pads during the period or not using tampons at all. They urged that women using tampons who developed the symptoms should stop using tampons immediately and see a physician promptly (San Francisco Chronicle, November 19, 1980). Simultaneously, Procter and Gamble took a series of ads in national and local newspapers advising that Rely had been withdrawn and offering a refund for the unused tampons.

In the meanwhile, consumer interests began to stir, prompted by women's longstanding and even widespread complaints about vaginal ulcers produced by tampons. The Boston Women's Health Collective in 1979 began to look into the tampon question and was followed in the same year by a new organization, Women's Health International. *New West,* a popular magazine focusing on social criticism, published a lengthy review of the history of problems with tampons in October, just as the toxic-shock story continued to escalate (Friedman, 1980).

Writing in the *New England Journal* in December 1980, the CDC group declared that the appearance of toxic-shock syndrome in menstruating women appeared to be a new phenomenon (Davis et al., 1980). Further evidence emerged in January of 1981 when epidemiologists from Minnesota reported that in their study of 80 toxic-shock patients with tampon users who had not become ill, the chances of getting the disease were directly related to the particular absorbency of the tampon used (San Francisco Chronicle, January 31, 1981). The Minnesota investigators established that the rates for those using tampons were 6 cases per 100,000 as against 1 case per 100,000 for those not using tampons.

When, on January 31, 1981, CDC's Kathryn Shands, the physician in charge of the Center's toxic-shock investigation, reported that the number of new cases had declined from 106 reported to CDC in September to 58 in October, 37 in November, and 42 in December, she attributed the decline to a drop in tampon usage by American women and the removal of Rely from the market (San Francisco Chronicle, January 31, 1981). In September, 1980 CDC's telephone survey showed that during that period tampon usage among those sampled dropped from 70 percent in July to 55 percent in November/December. Investigators at the University of California in San Francisco who studied tampon use among adolescents during the summer of 1980 found a similar decline (Irwin & Millstein, 1982). Tampons, and Rely in particular, seemed to be implicated, though some of the studies also reported the possible bearing of other factors, such as exercise and use of birth control pills, which characterize those who did not contract the disease (San Francisco Chronicle, January 31, 1981).

In the meanwhile, in early 1981 the continuing public confusion and publicity prompted industry representatives and some public interest groups to request the prestigious Institute of Medicine, an arm of the National Academy of Sciences, to review available research information and to indicate future directions. With funding from public and private sources, the Institute formed a 10-person committee of physicians, which then heard presentations, evaluated data, and organized an international and interdisciplinary conference in November 1981 (Institute of Medicine, 1982). (The conference papers were published as Part 2 of the June 1982 issue of the *Annals of Internal Medicine.*)

Consumer groups and feminist groups had early entered the public arena with strongly expressed concerns about tampons and the absorbency issues. This continued expression of worries that had earlier taken the form of seeing tampons as a dangerous source of endometriosis, cervicitis, and vaginitis. In the 1970s, Women's Health International had questioned the content of tampons, bringing this to the FDA and questioning the safety of tampons. Proprietary rights were cited by the FDA as its reason for not asking manufacturers to supply this information. By the time the toxic-shock concerns of 1980–1981 had risen, other feminists groups, including the Coalition for the Medical Rights of Women, were asking questions about absorbency and disseminating information about absorbency to their members. In late 1984, the Boston Women's Health Collective, worried about the labelling issue, sounded a call to women to put pressure on the FDA for labelling.

As one review of the earlier history of TSS makes clear (Donawa et al., 1984), the FDA had been involved in the debates over the research and the growing concern and controversy from mid-June of 1980. By July FDA had appointed a task force to work with CDC to review data and future studies. Among other subsequent activities, the FDA began an educational program to inform tampon users about the risks of TSS. By October the FDA proposed a regulation requiring a warning about TSS on all tampon packages and finally obtained this in June of 1982.

Still unresolved, though, was a critical issue of the relationship of tampon absorbency to the risk of TSS. The critical principle of manufacturers' proprietary rights had prevented requiring labelling of absorbent content. This issue had been the focus of a special task force of industry and consumer representatives constituted by the American Society of Testing and Materials. The work of the task force had stopped after disagreement between the consumer representatives, including several feminist organizations (Boston Women's Health Collective, Women's Health International, and the Coalition for the Medical Rights of Women), and the manufacturers over hiring an independent, consumer-chosen statistician to review data related to absorbency provided by the manufacturers.

By mid-1985 it did appear, however, that labelling of absorbency would occur after publication of an FDA recommendation in the Federal Register. Even as this occurred, two manufacturers, Tambrands (the former Tampax company) and Playtex, withdrew super absorbent tampons from the market. This action had been prompted by the anticipation of research findings to be published by a Harvard team. Working on the puzzle of why tampons encouraged growth of bacteria that produced the deadly toxins, these researchers had discovered that materials in high absorbency tampon extract magnesium atoms from the vagina and bind them permanently into the fiber (Mills et al., 1985). In the low magnesium environment produced in the vagina, the bacteria (*staphyloccus aureus*) produce the fatal toxins.

Noting that their experiments had not been conducted in the presence of blood, the Harvard researchers cautiously concluded their paper by noting that menstrual fluid and blood vary in the amount of magnesium made available to the fibers, so future work would need to include this variable. They further commented that the conditions which produce the toxic shock syndrome toxins have not been studied in vivo and the role of the toxin in the pathogenesis of the toxic-shock syndrome is not clearly established (Mills et al., 1985, p. 1161).

## TOXIC–SHOCK: AN EMERGENT ISSUE WITH RESEARCH IMPLICATIONS

Within the seven years of the discovery of toxic-shock in 1978 through the FDA deliberations on labelling content of tampons in 1985, toxic-shock syndrome moved from being a little-understood condition in menstruating women and some others to a health issue of national concern prompting attention from industry, consumer groups, and prestigious governmental regulatory and scientific bodies. However, in spite of the increasing public awareness and scientific concern and the gradual sharpening of understanding, ambiguity has characterized much of the history of the illness and continues to do so.

The syndrome was itself for a time ambiguous—some researchers believed it to be a form of Karpasi's syndrome, while others, in spite of the CDC claims that it was a new entity, defined it as *staphylococcal toxemia* rather than toxic-shock *syndrome* (Toft & Crossley, 1980).

Reporting incidence of the syndrome was difficult because of problems in determining the actual number of cases, which in turn is related to the difficulties of diagnosis in the early stages, since no laboratory marker exists and some symptoms are associated with other illnesses (Institute of Medicine, 1982, p. 22). Compounding this issue was the impact of extensive media coverage, a point which industry representatives used in their argument that CDC's 1980 research could not be used as a basis to withdraw products from the public, since the findings were biased by the publicity (Donawa et al., 1984). The media coverage in 1980 and throughout 1981 generated rapid public awareness and understanding (Reingold et al., 1982, p. 878; Helgerson, 1981), but this did not go uncriticized. Some argued that while the extensive information did create awareness, leading women to report cases of the syndrome and to alter their use of tampons, and thus possibly helping to reduce morbidity and mortality, such publicity was nevertheless hasty and predicated on certain scientific data (Todd, 1981).

While the 1985 Harvard team's findings concerning the magnesium binding properties of super-absorbent fibers further focuses the search for the etiology and consequent management of the illness, much remains unknown. Clearly, toxic-shock syndrome will continue to be an emergent issue in women's health, particularly since some deaths still occur and since it has become a critical reference point in women's decisions to use tampons: "I think about toxic shock every time I reach for a box of tampons. . . . I think a minute and usually buy the pads, too. I use them both. I won't give up tampons, but I do use them less" (*The San Francisco Chronicle*, March 21, 1985).

Like similar issues where ambiguity and controversy has surrounded the evolution of the issue, estrogen replacement, for example (Kaufert & McKinlay, 1985), as a sociocultural issue, the toxic-shock phenomenon poses critical questions in the definition and construction of the issue qua issue and the nature of the parties generating contending definitions. This suggests that even medical or epidemiological knowledge of the problem is socially constructed, an observation delineated in detail elsewhere in studies of medical education (Atkinson, 1981). Certainly in the case of toxic-shock syndrome, different definitions, predicated on the production of research data and the presumed confounding influences of the mass media of communication were and remain in play. Criticisms of feminist organizations who particularly focused on the safety issues further expanded these definitions.

What these different definitions implicity share, but, with the exception of feminist criticisms, do not explicate is that toxic-shock syndrome can not be viewed simply as a biological issue. It is not iatrogenic: It is, rather, cultural or sociogenic. Its origins lie in the sociocultural situation in which women find themselves. Culturally mandated management of the "dirtying" and "polluting" aspects of menstrual flow via products technologically possible in an era of synthetic fibers, is involved (Douglas, 1966). As a socio-genic issue, toxic-shock syndrome must be analyzed not only as an emergent health problem for women which demands safe management, but it should be examined through understanding of the cultural factors that are at play in the definitions of the various parties to the ongoing controversy. (In this connection the prestigious panel convened by the Institute of Medicine on the toxic-shock syndrome included no socially or culturally oriented researcher who works in the area of menstrual cycle research.).

The definitions qua definitions, representing different constructions of the contending parties, are amenable to analysis through the perspectives of symbolic interaction, as Estes and Edmonds have argued in setting out the implications of this theory for policy analysis (1979). This theory is particularly useful in scrutiny of *emergent* issues. When coupled with considerations of the structural issues that impinge on the definers and help shape their definitions, it becomes a powerful analytic approach to these types of issues in women's health. Even taking into account the difficulties of acquiring certain critical data from the industry or researchers working in it (Sun, 1984), one could, for instance, trace the divergent conceptualizations of tampons as a source of risk for menstruating women held by governmental bodies, scientists, activist feminist health groups, and women consumers.

However, analysis of toxic shock necessitates not only symbolic and structural work on the sociocultural properties of the phenomenon, but it requires attention to material circumstances.

The management of pollution, which menstruation symbolizes, along with the emotional consequences of shame and embarrassment, are not only symbolic issues. They are linked to the material or economic base of contemporary American society. Even though the menstruating woman in many, but not all societies, is regarded as a potentially polluting figure and may be restricted from certain activities during her cycle, one is hard pressed to think of other than advanced societies where the very artifacts with which menstrual flow is managed are imbedded in the economics of the society. These are two links between the toxic-shock issue and the material base of modern societies.

Regarding technology, the profitable manufacture of pads was probably not possible in an era before paper processing reached the point it had in the 1920s. Further, the development of printing processes, which would allow mass circulation of women's magazines with advertisements for these products, was another critical technological factor. Once such ads were possible, these communication systems permitted wide diffusion of cultural themes, which continue to underscore the dirtying and dangerous qualities of women's cycle, while promising secure and unembarrassing management with first pads, then tampons, and then superabsorbent tampons.

It is ironic that the ads for tampons, suggesting as they did that it was all right, indeed highly acceptable, for women to insert these devices into themselves, may have facilitated the first step to the much later women's exploration of the interiors of their own bodies via self-administered cervical examinations. Once the ads for tampons had appeared, access to intimate parts of women's bodies became women's prerogative. Removed were the older worries that the offending tampon would breach the hymen, a cultural task reserved, of course, for the male.

One can, however, carry the material analysis further. The past 20 years have seen increasing numbers of women coming to work as full- or part-time productive workers. In 1981 in the United States, 93.5 percent of all white women in the labor force were at work and 85.9 percent of all nonwhite women in the labor force were at work. [The labor force is all persons over 16 not in institutions (Bureau of the Census, 1982).] Most of these working women (85 percent of the white women and 88 percent of the nonwhite women) were of ages where menstrual flow must be managed, and in public work settings rather than in the privacy of home. Development of the superabsorbent tampon with the new materials of the late 1970s is thus related to women's shift to public labor. Sales of vaginal sprays also increased in the 1970s. It is likely that both sprays and tampons were developed to allow women to manage the "cultural impurities" of femaleness in a secure way while in public.

Thus, a symbolic, structural, or material analysis alone cannot comprehend the toxic shock phenomenon as an emergent issue in women's health. All three are interlocking perspectives on such an issue and merit integration into whatever research or policy analysis occurs.

## SUMMARY AND CONCLUSIONS

This paper has discussed the emergence of a new illness designated as toxic-shock syndrome among menstruating women as a case that points to symbolic, structural, and material analysis of emergent issues. The question, of course, remains whether it is useful to analyze situations yet aborning. This paper took the view that it *is* critical to analyze emergent phenomena in women's health. This rescues issues from completely medical views on the one hand or completely rhetorical views on the other, hence such an analysis begins to provide alternative sets of definitions (Olesen, 1975). Taking such a view, however, does not overlook the difficulties that may inhere in attempting to do an analysis, particularly of the type commended here. Those difficulties themselves, are, of course, topics for further analysis.

To locate the conclusions more firmly in a policy context, it is a truism that policymakers of all types, whether in the paper industry that produces tampons, the CDC, the FDA, feminist health organizations, other consumer groups, require information (Olesen & Lewin, 1985). Providing alternative perspectives derived from research yields that type of knowledge. This assumes, of course, that one's research on such an emergent issue, eventually reaches those policy arenas where alternative perspectives can be entertained. As numerous writers about policy have made clear, this flow of information is not without difficulties (Lipman-Blumen & Bernard, 1979). Yet, as Ruzek has shown (1980), some alternative perspectives about women's health issues do move to various policy levels.

The issues treated here constitute prior questions relating to symbolic, structural, and material aspects of this phenomenon, which should be addressed even as the issue of toxic shock moves through yet another stage of controversy and new definitions. In this particular instance, the emergent issue has had and may continue to have fateful consequences for some women. For that reason alone it demands our attention.

# REFERENCES

Atkinson, P. (1981). *The clinical experience.* London: Gower.

Bureau of the Census (1982). *Statistical abstract of the United States.* Washington, DC: U.S. Government Printing Office.

Davis, J. P., Chesney, J., Wand, P., & La Ventura, M. (1980). Toxic shock syndrome. *New England Journal of Medicine, 303,* 1429–1435.

Delaney, J., Lupton, M. J., & Toth, E. (1976). *The curse, a cultural history of menstruation.* New York: E. P. Dutton and Co.

Donawa, M. E., Schmid, G. R., & Osterholm, M. T. (1984). Toxic-shock syndrome: Chronology of state and federal epidemiologic studies and regulatory decision-making. *Public Health Reports, 9*(4), 342–350.

Douglas, M. (1966). *Purity and danger.* London: Routledge and Kegan Paul.

Estes, C. L., & Edmonds, B. C. (1979). Symbolic interaction and policy analysis. *Symbolic Interaction, 4*(1), 75–86.

Friedan, B. (1963). *The feminine mystique.* New York: W. W. Norton.

Friedman, N. (1980). The truth about tampons. *New West,* October 20.

Fuller, A. F., Swartz, M. N., Wolfson, J. S., & Salzman, R. (1980). Toxic-shock syndrome. *New England Journal of Medicine, 303,* 881.

Helgerson, S. D. (1981). Toxic-shock syndrome: Tampons, toxins and time: The evolution of understanding an illness. *Women and Health, 6,* 93–104.

Institute of Medicine. (1982). *Toxic-shock syndrome: Assessment of current information and future research needs.* Washington, DC: National Academy Press.

Irwin, C. E., Jr., & Millstein, S. G. (1982). Emerging patterns of tampon use in the adolescent female: The impact of toxic shock syndrome. *American Journal of Public Health, 72,* 164–467.

Kaufert, P. A., & McKinlay, S. M. (1985). Estrogen-replacement therapy: The production of medical knowledge and the emergence of policy. In Lewin, E., & Olesen, V. L., (Eds.), *Women, health and healing.* London: Tavistock Publications.

Lipman-Blumen, J., & Bernard, J. (1979). *Sex roles and social policy.* Beverly Hills: Sage Publications.

Mills, J. T., Parsonnet, J., Tsai, Y-C., Kendrick, M., Hickman, R. K., & Kass, E. H. (1985). Control of production of toxic-shock syndrome toxin-1 (TSST-1) by magnesium iron. *Journal of Infectious Diseases, 151*(6), 1158–1161.

Olesen, V. L. (1975). Rage is not enough. In Olesen, V., (ed.), *Women and their health: Research implications for a new era.* [Health Resources Administration, DHEW Publication No. (HRA) 77-3138]. Springfield, VA: National Technical Information Service.

Olesen, V. L., & Lewin, E. (1985). Women, health and healing: A theoretical introduction. In Lewin, E., & Olesen, V. L. (Eds.), *Women, health and healing.* London: Tavistock Publications, pp. 1–19.

Reingold, A. L., Hargrett, N. T., Shands, K. H., Dan, B. B., Schmid, G. P.,

Strickland, B. Y., & Broom, C. V., Toxic-shock syndrome surveillance in the United States, 1980–1981. *Annals of Internal Medicine, 96,* 875–882.

Robertson, N. (1982). Toxic-shock. *The New York Times Magazine.* September 19, 30–117.

Ruzek, S. B. (1980). Medical responses to women's health activities: Conflict, accommodation and cooptation. *Research in the Sociology of Health Care, 1,* 335–354.

Shands, K. N., Schmid, G. P., Dan, B. B., et al. (1980). Toxic-shock syndrome in menstruating women: Association with tampons use and staphylococcus aureus and clinical features in 52 cases. *New England Journal of Medicine, 303,* 1436–1442.

Sun, M. (1984). Lawyers flush out toxic shock data. *Science, 224,* 132–134.

Todd, J. (1978). Toxic shock syndrome associated with Phage group I staphylocci. *The Lancet,* ii, 1116–1117.

Todd, J. (1981). Toxic-shock syndrome—scientific uncertainty and the public media. *Pediatrics, 67*(6), 921–923.

Toft, R. W., & Crossley, K. B. (1980). Clinical experience with toxic-shock syndrome. *New England Journal of Medicine, 303,* 1417.

# MENSTRUATION AND MENSTRUAL CHANGE: WOMEN IN MIDLIFE

**Patricia A. Kaufert, PhD**
Department of Social and Preventive Medicine, University of Manitoba,
Winnipeg, Manitoba, Canada

Research on the menstrual cycle has paid scant attention to the experience of menstrual change among women during the years immediately prior to menopause. Using data taken from a cross-sectional survey of Manitoba women in the 40–59 age group, this paper discusses the impact of changes in menstrual pattern on women's propensity to seek medical care and on their perception of their menopausal status. The difference between "subjective" and "objective" definitions of menopausal status is discussed in terms of the implications for the assignment of women to one category or another and in terms of conflict between methodological priorities and the new norms of feminist research.

## INTRODUCTION

Comparatively little information is available on the end phase of a woman's menstrual life, that is, after she has passed 40 years of age and is moving toward being, but is not yet, menopausal. This stage has been largely ignored by researchers interested in the menstrual cycle who tend to find their subjects among women in the early 20s. Menopause research looks at older women, but usually treats those still menstruating as a relatively undifferentiated group, using them as a standard of comparison against which the researcher assesses the changes occasioned by final menses. These later phases of a woman's menstrual career have caught the focused attention of neither menstrual cycle or menopause researchers,

This research was supported by National Health Research and Development Project 6607-1240-42 as well as by a National Health Research Scholar Award No. 6607-1213-48 to the author.

hence there has been little exploration of this period in a woman's menstrual history.

This paper will discuss what a group of women, who are 40 through 54 years of age and still menstruating, report about their current pattern of menstruation, including changes in regularity or other symptoms of hormonal transition. The propensity of women to seek medical care in response to changes in menstrual pattern will be examined, together with the impact of such changes on their perception of their menstrual status. These data will be used in an exploration of two issues in research on women's health. First, the conflict between methodological and conceptual priorities, as opposed to the new norms of feminist research, which are involved when choosing between objective and subjective definition of menopausal (or menstrual) status. Second, the ambiguities inherent with any critique of medicalization in which a balance must be struck between a potential "real" need for health care and the risks of medicalizing a normal process.

## BACKGROUND

This paper is based on a study of the health of women in middle age that is being carried out in Manitoba, Canada. The overall project has three stages. Stage 1 is a cross-sectional mail survey that is now complete and in process of analysis. Stage 2 will be completed in October 1985 and is a longitudinal study extending over a three-year period in which those taking part are a subset of those who completed Stage 1. Stage 3 is a series of semi-structured in-depth interviews with 75 women: a subset of the subset. The data to be presented here are taken from the cross-sectional survey.

## METHODS

The target population were women between 40 and 59, living in Manitoba. Using a stratified random sample of the general population of women in this age group, questionnaires were mailed to those women whose names appeared in either the Henderson's Directories for the urban areas or the Voter's Registration Lists for the rural areas. Following the methods for the mail survey recommended by Dillman (1978), the data collection stage provided 2500 questionnaires completed and available for analysis. After adjustment for errors (such as death or incorrect age identification, or movement

Table 1. Menstrual Characteristics by Percentage of Age Group

| Characteristic | 40-44 ($N = 688$) | 45-49 ($N = 605$) | 50-54 ($N = 590$) | 55-59 ($N = 610$) |
|---|---|---|---|---|
| Menstruated within previous 3 months | 88 | 65 | 29 | 2 |
| Menstruated within last 12 months, but not last 3 months | 1 | 7 | 10 | 1 |
| Has not menstruated within the last 12 months | 1 | 10 | 40 | 71 |
| Had a hysterectomy | 10 | 18 | 21 | 26 |

$\chi^2 = 1352.25$; 9df; $p < 0.0000$.
Missing values $= 7$.

out of the Province) the overall response rate to the cross-sectional survey was 68 percent.

The questionnaire collected extensive data on the health and health behavior of women in midlife, including chronic health problems, symptom profiles, medication use, and patterns of physician contact. Other sections in the study provided information on employment patterns in this age group, family structure, and on women's attitudes toward the roles available to them in midlife as wives, mothers, daughters, housewives, and labor force participants. Some data are particular to women's health, such as their history of gynecological surgery, their menstrual and menopausal status and experience. It is with the variables relating to their current menstrual history that I will be dealing in this discussion.

The study population can be divided into four groups according to their menstrual status (see Table 1). First, women who menstruated within the last 3 months; second, women who menstruated within the last 12, but not within the last 3 months; third, women who have not menstruated for 12 or more months. The fourth group is formed by women who have had hysterectomies or whose menstruation ceased after radio- or chemotherapy. These women form a separate group because their hormonal characteristics cannot be ascertained from menstrual pattern data. This paper is concerned solely with groups one and two; that is with 1254 women who have menstruated within the last 12 months. Their sociodemographic characteristics are set out in Table 2.

Table 2. Sociodemocraphic Characteristics Women 40–54 Who Are
Still Menstruating

| Characteristic | % | N |
|---|---|---|
| Age | | |
|   40–44 | 48 | 607 |
|   45–49 | 34 | 424 |
|   50–54 | 18 | 223 |
| Marital status | | |
|   Married | 87 | 1086 |
|   Widowed | 4 | 45 |
|   Divorced/separated | 6 | 80 |
|   Single | 3 | 43 |
| Parental status | | |
|   No children | 5 | 66 |
|   Children under 18 | 23 | 288 |
|   Children under and over 18 | 45 | 557 |
|   Children over 18 | 27 | 341 |
| Education | | |
|   Less than secondary | 33 | 415 |
|   Secondary | 33 | 410 |
|   Some postsecondary | 27 | 336 |
|   One or more university degrees | 7 | 81 |
| Current employment | | |
|   Currently employed | 61 | 769 |
|   Not currently employed | 39 | 485 |

## RESULTS

### Menstrual Change

Changes in menstrual pattern, known as precursors to menopause, were to be predicted in this population of women given their age and the probable imminence of menopause for many. At question, however, was the proportion of such women within the group, the relationship between menstrual change and age and between one type of menstrual change (such as regularity) and another (such as very heavy menstruation).

The questionnaire asked that a comparison be made between the menstrual cycle today and what it was like one year ago in terms of both regularity and flow. A significant association was found between these two forms of change in a woman's menstrual experience. When controlling for age (as in Table 3), a change in regularity is more likely to be associated with a report of heavier menstruation in the 40–44 age group, whereas in the two older age groups, it is more often linked with a lighter menses. The relationship between the timing of a woman's final menses and these different permutations on menstrual change are being observed in the longitudinal study.

This paper concerns less whether these changes predict to menopause than their impact on behavior and attitude, whether in terms of a woman's definition of her menopausal status or her propensity to seek medical care. For this reason, women are divided into three groups according to their experience of menstrual change; first, those reporting no change in menstrual pattern; second, those who have menstruated within the last 3 months, but who report a change in regularity and/or flow that has occurred within the previous year. The third group is women who have not menstruated within the previous 3 months, but have done so within the previous 12. According to the definitions of menopause adopted by the International Menopause Society (Van Keep, 1979), this last group of women are "perimenopausal." For convenience, the second are labeled "transitional," (implying transitional before menopause) as by including changes in menstrual flow, the group is no longer an exact match to the society's definition of the premenopause: Table 4 sets out the three categories by age group.

## Menstrual Change and Medicalization

"Medicalization" is a blanket term that tends to be used pejoratively, particularly in research on women and health, to denote

Table 3.  Menstrual Flow by Regularity by Percentage of Age Group

|  | 40–44 | | 45–49 | | 50–54 | |
|---|---|---|---|---|---|---|
|  | Regularity unchanged ($N = 535$) | Less regular ($N = 72$) | Regularity unchanged ($N = 291$) | Less regular ($N = 123$) | Regularity unchanged ($N = 112$) | Less regular ($N = 95$) |
| Lighter | 13 | 25 | 18 | 48 | 28 | 62 |
| Same | 73 | 25 | 71 | 29 | 57 | 13 |
| Heavier | 14 | 50 | 11 | 23 | 15 | 25 |
|  | $\chi^2 = 72.4$ | 2df | $\chi^2 = 63.376$ | 2df | $\chi^2 = 44.38$ | 2df |

$p < 0.0000$.
Missing values $= 37$.

Table 4. Menstrual Pattern by Percentage of Age Group

| Pattern | 40-45 ($N = 607$) | 45-49 ($N = 424$) | 50-54 ($N = 223$) |
|---|---|---|---|
| No change in menstruation | 64 | 47 | 26 |
| Transitional[a] | 35 | 43 | 49 |
| Perimenopausal | 1 | 10 | 25 |

[a]Transitional = change in regularity and/or flow during the preceding 12 months.
$\chi^2 = 103.76$; 4df; $p < 0.0000$.
Missing values = 7.

medical intrusion into a natural process. It is used here simply to refer to the extent to which women see the menopause and the attendant changes in their menstrual pattern as events requiring medical management. In this paper, two indicators of medicalization will be examined: first, whether women said they had discussed their menopausal status with a physician; second, whether they had reported any menstrual problems to a physician during the preceding year. Among women without any change in menstrual pattern only 38 percent had discussed their menopausal status with a physician. By comparison, 60 percent in the transitional and 71 percent in the perimenopausal group had done so. In the sense that their menopausal state has been defined to them by a physician, these data suggest a relatively high degree of medicalization.

On the other hand, different pictures emerge using the second indicator of medicalization. Only a few women have discussed any menstrual problem with a   physician. Even among those currently experiencing menstrual change, only 38 percent of the women in the transitional category and 36 percent of the perimenopausal women had done so. In the sense that women have not treated their changing menstrual experience as problems for which they seek medical care, these other data suggest a relatively low level of medicalization.

The disparity between the two items may be explained on methodological grounds. First, in the question on complaining of menstrual problems to a physician, women were asked to recall over a 12-month period, whereas the question on menopausal status had no such time limitation. Second, women are being asked to recall different things. They may recollect that a physician said they were menopausal, but forget that they themselves had discussed menstrual symptoms. (The same questions are to be repeated in the longitudinal study, but with a 6-month recall limit to both questions.) An alternative explanation is that some women do not equate having discussed their menopausal status with having reported a menstrual problem. Accustomed from childbirth to the examination of the normal processes of their bodies by a physician, women may well differentiate the content of a medical encounter and separate out a discussion of menstrual change from a complaint about menstrual problems, an issue to which we will return in the later discussion.

The question on whether menstrual problems were discussed included a section on the nature of these problems. Answers were coded using the International Classification of Disease: 8th Adaptation (ICDA). The number and type of problem are shown in Table 5. Although the occasional psychological (depression), psychosomatic (headaches) or somatic (lower back pain) symptom are reported as a menstrual problem, the majority are changes in menstrual pattern which may not, but probably do, predict the onset of menopause.

As another measure of whether menstrual disturbances had occasioned medical consultation, a comparison was made between women who reported experiencing one or other of three different medical problems and whether they had discussed menstrual problems with a physician. The three problems were severe pain at menstruation, spotting between menses, and very heavy menstruation or flooding. The response rate on these three was low and the results can only be interpreted with great caution. Accepting this proviso, these three problems appear as relatively weak triggers of medical care seeking activity; approximately 28 percent of those reporting heavy menstruation and only 16 percent of those reporting either pain or intermenstrual bleeding had discussed a menstrual problem with a physician.

On balance, these data would suggest not only a relatively low level of medicalization of the menopause, but that women may not interpret their changes in menstrual pattern as other than natural and safe. On the other hand, the majority in both the transitional and perimenopausal categories say they have discussed their menopausal status with a physician. The next section looks at the relationship between menstrual change and the definition of menopausal status.

## Menstrual Change and the Definition of Menopausal Status

Most epidemiologists agree on a definition of menopause as a woman's final menses and treat as postmenopausal anyone who has

Table 5. "Menstrual Problems" Discussed with a
Physician during the Previous 12 Months

| ICD8 | Problem | N |
|------|---------|---|
| 6260 | Amenorrhoea | 4 |
| 6261 | Scanty menstruation | 3 |
| 6262 | Excessive menstruation | 140 |
| 6263 | Painful menstruation | 48 |
| 6264 | Frequent menstruation | 19 |
| 6265 | Irregular menstruation | 76 |
| 6266 | Intermenstrual bleeding | 40 |
| 6267 | Postmenopausal bleeding | 17 |
| 6269 | Menstrual disorder (NOS) | 37 |
| 6270 | Menopausal symptoms (NOS) | 32 |
| 7823 | Flushing | 5 |
| 7881 | Night sweats | 1 |
| 7889 | Chills | 4 |
| 7900 | "Nerves" | 4 |
| 7901 | Fatigue | 4 |
| 7902 | Depression | 4 |
| 7910 | Headache | 4 |
| 7287 | Lower back pain | 2 |
| 7289 | Backache (NOS) | 3 |
| 7805 | Dizziness | 2 |
| 7841 | Nausea (NOS) | 2 |
| 7850 | Abdominal swelling | 2 |
| 7867 | Vaginal pain | 1 |
| 7871 | Cramps | 1 |
| 2800 | Anaemia | 1 |
| 3460 | Migraine | 1 |
| 4600 | Cold | 1 |
| 6294 | Unspecified infection of genital tract | 1 |

not menstruated for one year. Essentially an operational device, it requires no more from the subject than a statement on her menstrual pattern during the previous 12 months. It is the researcher who assigns her to a pre-, post, or perimenopausal category; the question of whether this assignment coincides with the definition the woman herself might make of her menopausal status is not treated as relevant. This paper will explore the relationship between the "subjective" (as made by the individual woman) and the more "objective" (as made by the researcher) definitions of menopausal status.

As transitional and perimenopause have not become the terms of common parlance, women were asked whether they saw themselves as being at the beginning (corresponding to "transitional"), middle, or end (the equivalent to "perimenopause"), or without sign of menopause. They were also asked what they had been told by a physician about their menopausal status. Their self-definition is then compared with the three types of menstrual pattern (no change, transitional, and perimenopausal). Women reporting changes in their pattern of menstruation are significantly more likely to see themselves as at the beginning or in the middle of menopause (Table 6). On the other hand, the match is not exact and it is the women who deviate who raise the more interesting questions.

One way of looking at the difference between the two forms of definition is to take the data in Table 6, assume that the definition by menstrual characteristics is the more objective, and apply the standard epidemiological tests for sensitivity and specificity (Mausner & Bahn, 1974, p. 245). In epidemiology, these tests are employed to determine the number of "false" positives or "false" negatives which are produced by a particular testing procedure. In this situation, they are used to determine which women "incorrectly" define themselves as menopausal (although reporting an unchanged menstrual pattern), and those women who "incorrectly" define themselves as without a sign of menopause (although reporting irregularity or a change in menstrual characteristics). A similar comparison can be made between what a woman says her physician defined as her menopausal status and the definition based on her menstrual change experience.

In this analysis, women at the beginning or at the middle of menopause are treated as one "menopausal" group and the transitional and perimenopausal categories are collapsed together. (Women who said they were "through" with menopause are omitted). The sensitivity (i.e., the number of women who correctly define themselves as menopausal) is 74 percent and the specificity is 71 percent (see

Table 6. Self-Defined Menopausal Status by Menstrual Pattern in Percentages

| Status | No change in menstruation ($N = 621$) | Transitional ($N = 501$) | Perimenopausal ($N = 95$) |
|---|---|---|---|
| Through with menopause | — | 1 | 14 |
| In middle of menopause | 6 | 18 | 49 |
| Beginning menopause | 23 | 52 | 33 |
| No sign of menopause | 71 | 29 | 4 |

## Table 7. Menopausal State

| Definition | Menopausal (i.e., change in menstruation) | Not menopausal (i.e., no change in menstruation) |
|---|---|---|
| By self[a] | | |
| Menopausal | 421 | 178 |
| Not menopausal | 148 | 428 |
| By physician[b] | | |
| Menopausal | 278 | 110 |
| Not menopausal | 76 | 123 |

[a]Sensitivity = 74%; specificity = 71%; false negatives = (148/421 + 148); false positives = (178/428 + 178).

[b]Sensitivity = 79%; specificity = 53%; false negatives = (76/278 + 76); false positives = (110/110 + 123).

Table 7). When women's self-definition is replaced by the definitions of status made by physicians, the sensitivity is higher (78%) but the specificity is lower. Close to one-half of the women reporting no change in menstrual pattern had been told by their physicians that they were either beginning or in the middle of menopause. These results indicate that menopausal status will be assigned very differently, depending on whether a woman's self-definition is being used, or her report of what her physician told her or a definition constructed by a researcher and based on menstrual report.

## DISCUSSION

In a previous paper, feminist and medical definitions of menopause were compared (Kaufert, 1982). According to Reitz (1977) a woman "knows" when she is menopausal. This knowledge is the product of a woman's awareness of changes as they take place within her own body; therefore, by this definition, the ability to classify a woman as menopausal becomes the exclusive property of the individual and is based on self-knowledge. Derived solely from what is personally experienced, this definition is totally subjective.

In the medical model of menopause, only a physician can separate out the truly menopausal symptom from the pathological. To decide whether or not a woman is menopausal, the physician requires information on symptom experience supplied by the patient, plus a clinical examination and laboratory test results; these data are assessed according to criteria established by medical science.

While this medical definition is more "objective," like self-definition, it is individualistic in orientation, for its application depends on a one-to-one clinical interaction with the patient.

The epidemiologist researcher uses a third method to decide whether or not a woman is menopausal. Neither direct contact with individual women or clinical data is required. The definition is based solely on a series of statements made by women on the approximate timing of their more recent menses. Epidemiologists are relying on subjective data in the sense that they are using what the woman reports from her own experience, but their questions are framed to retrieve a relatively narrow, relatively precise set of information. By contrast, the physicians draw on a wider range of a woman's experience (changes in menstrual flow and regularity, physiological and psychological symptomology), but like the epidemiologist, it is the physician rather than the woman who interprets the meaning of what she experiences.

The data discussed in this paper showed that a woman's own definition of her menopausal status and the definition she says she was given by a physician often, but not necessarily, coincide with a definition based on her menstrual pattern. The comparison demonstrated the methodologically relevant point that studies using different approaches to the definition of menopausal status (for example, self-definition, physician report, or the method of the epidemiologist) will assign some, but not all, women to the same category. Any comaprison between such studies can assume some overlap, but not enough to satisfy the purist methodologist that comparison is justified.

Other questions relevant to this discussion of the three methods of defining menopausal status are concerned less with methodological than with theoretical and conceptual issues. One movement in feminist thought would "invite a return to purely "female" subjectivity, leaving rationality and objectivity in the male domain, dismissed as products of purely male consciousness" (Keller, 1982, p. 593).

By this reasoning, both the physician's and the epidemiologist's definition should be discarded. Falsely pretending to objectivity, they are the product of male-dominated medical science and of what men see as relevant in the menopause. For the epidemiologist, it is the end of menses; for the physician, it is this, plus hormone related blood and tissue changes and assorted morbid symptomology. Both definitions discount the complex of sensations and responses, some positive and some negative, such as those which women discussed with Reitz (1977).

Whatever the ideological appeal of this feminist argument, it contains points critical to a discussion of either menstrual cycle or menopause research. Research studies usually start from the hypothesis that women do or do not experience this or that symptom or mood change at this or that point in their cycle or during the menopausal transition. Data is collected and the prediction tested. The results are debated according to whether the correct definition was used, whether or not the subjects were "blind" and whether the statistics were appropriate.

While this is the correct, scientifically legitimate method of doing research, nevertheless it excludes the full range of experience by focusing only on what the hypothesis predefined as relevant (cf. Brighton Women and Science Group, 1980, p. 14). For example, even with the limited framework of this paper, it has been shown that when women are asked about their own perception of their menopausal status, their self-definition is not the same as that of the outsider epidemiologist. (The next step is to use the in-depth interviews to explore with women what "cues" they use to identify their experiences as menopausal). In the reworking of the philosophy of science by feminist thinkers, the price of opting for scientific objectivity is to surrender the power of judgment and understanding that comes to us as women. By this account, both menstrual cycle and menopause researchers are in danger of treating not only other women's experiences as irrelevant, but also the experiences of their own bodies if they be women. Given the context of this conference, the pertinence of the feminist argument is that women's self-definition, whether of their menopausal status or their menstrual experience, should not be dismissed as a form of "false consciousness."

On the other hand, the price of installing subjectivity as a research principle is that the results of research may not be accepted within the scientific community. Yet within the present environment of menstrual and menopausal research, political and economic realities make it essential that scientific (male) theories describing the impact of menstruation and menopause on women's lives should be tested. The current publicity given to the menopause and to premenstrual tension (PMT) can be interpreted as a new development in "biological politics" (Sayers, 1982). Given the current conservative climate, the description of women as unstable by virtue of their hormones may be used to curtail the gains women have made in the economic and political market place. Women researchers have an obligation to challenge these theories; however, if their results are to be accepted as legitimate, cumulative, and comparable between studies, then the rules of scientific method must be obeyed. In the context of menopause research, the definition of menopausal status adopted by the epidemiologist must be used as it is both relatively objective and relatively stable across population groups.

Finally, I will discuss the medical approach to the definition of menopausal status. One of its elements is that the woman must be seen by a physician. Yet changes in menstruation are the natural side-effect of a natural event, the onset of menopause; to see a physician is to "medicalize" menopause, just as menstruation and childbirth have been medicalized, a fact deplored in feminist writing (e.g., Raymond, 1982). At one level, the case for nonmedical interference in the menopause appears stronger than the case against medical intrusion into childbirth. Even those most strongly committed to the "natural processes . . . of spontaneous birth" (as described by Rossi, 1977) recognize that, for some women in some childbirth situations, medical management is essential (Kasper, 1981, p. 182). By contrast, the menopause is not life-threatening, it is without complications, and the recent history of its medical management is that estrogen therapy has been iatrogenic in its consequences for many women. The arguments would seem to be against medical involvement.

The problem is that the signs and symptoms associated with menopause are ambiguous in meaning; for example, changes in menstruation may be related to approaching menopause, but they may be indicative of any one of an assortment of pathologies affecting the reproductive system, including cancer. Diagnosis of these conditions is not open to self-examination, but is dependent on contact with some form of medical care. Even those guides to health which are staunchly feminist in orientation [such as *Our Bodies, Ourselves* (1971) or the series on health published by the Virago Press] recommend seeing a physician as a response to menstrual changes, such as heavy or irregular menstruation. While the menopause itself may be apt to self-management, these other conditions are not.

The dilemma for the researcher is illustrated by the data presented earlier on the women's use of medical care as a response to menstrual problems, such as pain, spotting between menses, and heavy menstruation or flooding. These three were included in the study because they are symptoms with dual meaning. Therefore, the relatively low level of medical consultation in response to the three symptoms is a cause for concern. While one would discourage the definition of menopause as a morbid event requiring medical management, there is an equal responsibility to encourage women to take seriously their experience of menstrual change. To accept that only a physician can define menopause is to agree to its medicalization, if only to this minimal extent. On the other hand, to reject medicalization is to ignore that the physician's ability to distinguish between the pathological and the nonpathological may be critical for some women. The difficulty is that there is no easy rule by which to predict which cases do, or do not, belong to the "safe" majority who do not require medical care.

## CONCLUSION

In menopause research (as in research on the menstrual cycle) questions of status definition are usually treated as methodologically problematic, but ideologically neutral. The object of the preceding discussion was to demonstrate that the choice between three approaches to menopausal definition (the epidemiologist's, the physician's, and the woman's own report) is not value free. As researchers, we must become aware of the implications that underlie our use of one rather than another.

## REFERENCES

Boston Women's Health Book Collective. (1976). *Our bodies, ourselves.* New York: Simon and Shuster.
Brighton Women and Science Group. (1980). *Alice through the microscope.* London: Virago Press.
Dillman, D. (1978). *Mail and telephone surveys.* New York: Wiley.
Kasper, A. (1981). Independent practice as a nurse midwife in Bethesda, Maryland—An interview with Jan Epstein, CNM. *Women and Health, 6*(3-4), 175-187.
Kaufert, P. A. (1982). Myth and menopause. *Sociology of Health and Illness, 4,*141-166.
Keller, E. (1982). Feminism and science. *Signs, 7,* 589-602.
Mausner, J., & Bahn, A. (1974). *Epidemiology.* Philadelphia: W. B. Saunders.
Raymond, J. C. (1982). Medicine as patriarchal religion. *The Journal of Medicine and Philosophy, 7,* 197-216.
Reitz, R. (1977). *Menopause: A positive approach.* Radnor: Chilton.
Rossi, A. (1979). A biosocial perspective on parenting. *Daedalus, 106,* 1-32.
Sayers, J. (1982). *Biological politics: Feminist and anti-feminist perspectives.* London: Tavistock Publications.
Van Keep, P. (1979). Editorial note. *Maturitas, 1,* 227.

# SOCIAL AND MENSTRUAL CYCLES:
# METHODOLOGICAL AND SUBSTANTIVE FINDINGS

Paula Englander–Golden, PhD, Frank J. Sonleitner, PhD,
Mary R. Whitmore, PhD, and Gail J. M. Corbley
University of Oklahoma

By using daily unaware, daily aware, and retrospective self-reports, this study allowed the investigation of 1) self-reports of moods and behaviors across the menstrual cycle under different conditions of awareness and type of recall, 2) social cycles for men and women, and 3) correlations between neuroticism and self-reports of moods and behaviors. Results indicate that 1) retrospective self-reports cannot be used as evidence of PMS, 2) a social cycle exists for both sexes, and 3) discrete symptomatology in discrete phases of the menstrual cycle cannot be dismissed as neuroticism.

## INTRODUCTION

Assessment of the magnitude and prevalence of menstrual cycle effects is of great importance to women both for economic and health reasons. The U.S. Department of Labor (1977, p. 55) reported that "women are considerably more likely than men to be absent from work because of illness" and popular belief is that the illness is menstruation (O'Leary, 1974). Recently, Englander-Golden and Barton showed that child care, rather than personal illness, mediates sex differences in absence from work (Englander-Golden & Barton, 1983). Yet dissipating the myth of pervasive adverse effects due to menstruation is perhaps more difficult today in light of the proliferation of PMS clinics.

Since the late 1960s considerable research has been done on the menstrual cycle from the vantage point of disciplines such as the behavioral, social, and natural sciences as well as psychiatry, medicine, and humanities. Years later there is little consensus regarding results. For instance, which moods and behaviors, if any, fluctuate as a function of the menstrual cycle; what is the prevalence of possible cyclical phenomena; do they occur in normal women or only in neurotic or psychotic women; in women with particular beliefs, psychological makeup; and finally, what are the causal factors for the observed phenomena? (Herbert, 1982; Ruble, 1977; Koeske & Koeske, 1975; Parlee, 1974; Parlee, 1973).

At least some of the contradictory results arise because some of the self-reports of moods and behaviors are elicited by means of retrospective questionnaires while others are elicited by questionnaires administered daily or on specific days of the menstrual cycle. The use of retrospective questionnaires has been criticized by Parlee (1973, 1974) because by necessity they make women aware of the saliency of the menstrual cycle. Therefore, such reports can be affected by cultural expectations about menstruation. Self-reports obtained daily or on specific days of the cycle could also be contaminated with stereotypic responses if subjects were suspicious or aware that the menstrual cycle was being studied. Researchers have usually not assessed the extent to which such awareness or suspicion affects daily self-reports (Dennerstein & Burrows, 1979; Golub, 1976; May, 1976).

It has been shown that daily self-reports of moods and behaviors obtained from women who did not suspect the true purpose of the study differed significantly from retrospective self-reports even when both types of reports were obtained from the same group of women concerning the same menstrual cycle (Englander-Golden, Whitmore, & Dienstbier, 1978). In general, the retrospective reports yielded more pronounced cycle effects. Peaks in negative moods and events were remembered in the paramenstruum while peaks in positive moods were remembered at midcycle; these were not necessarily the positions where the maxima and minima were reported on the daily "unaware" questionnaires. Stereotypic beliefs about the menstrual cycle affected both intensity and position of the peaks.

The present study was designed to allow a comparison between daily "unaware," daily "aware" and retrospective self-reports. This design permits the investigation of an important question not previously addressed; is it the difference in awareness or in type of recall which produces the observed results? It was hypothesized that daily "unaware" self-reports would show the least variability across the menstrual cycle since they are the least likely to be contaminated by stereotypic beliefs, whereas retrospective self-reports would show maximum variability. Furthermore, it was decided to use the daily "unaware" self-reports to investigate variability in moods and behaviors as a function of a social cycle (day-of-week) for men and women and to compare its variability to the women's menstrual cycle. Such a social cycle has been studied by Rossi and Rossi who had men and women fill out daily mood questionnaires (1977). However, since no cover story was provided and women were asked to indicate onset of menstruation during the rating period, it is impossible to assess the state of "awareness" of their subjects. Finally it was decided to see how neuroticism would be correlated with the daily "unaware" self-reports of moods and behaviors in the different phases of the menstrual cycle.

## METHOD

### Subjects

Subjects were undergraduate advanced zoology students in two consecutive years who volunteered to participate in research for additional credit. Daily "unaware" and retrospective self-reports were collected during the first semestter. Subjects were dropped if they did not have at least one complete cycle or stopped participation before the end of the 11 weeks of the study. Thirty-seven women who were not taking oral contraceptives and 16 women who were taking oral contraceptives satisfied the conditions for inclusion. Twenty-three males participated in the collection of daily "unaware" self-reports.

Daily "aware" self-reports were collected during the second semester. Forty-nine women who were not taking oral contraceptives and 15 women who were taking oral contraceptivess satisfied the conditions for inclusion. Eighteen men also participated during the semester. Their data was not used since students were told that this was a study of the menstrual cycle.

### Procedure

#### Daily "Unaware" Condition and Retrospective Condition

The cover story explained that this was a study in psychobiological rhythms that may be common to both males and females. Students were asked to fill out a 70-item daily questionnaire each evening, in terms of "how you felt this day" (see below).

They were told that since illness and some medications can affect moods and behaviors, they would have to indicate every day whether they had been sick and what medication they had taken, be it over-the-counter or prescription such as aspirin, cold medicines, thyroid, insulin, oral contraceptives, antibiotics, and antihistamines. Women were also asked to indicate onset and end of menstruation so that possible effects because of menstrual cycle could be "factored out." Although no students asked how such "factoring out" would be done, the researcher was prepared to say that "there is a computer program that can handle this."

At the end of 11 weeks, when all the daily "unaware" data had been collected, students were reminded that in order to analyze the data for biological rhythms common to both women and men, one had to "factor out" possible effects from menstruation. Female students were therefore asked to fill out the same questionnaire that they had been filling out daily in terms of how they felt during specific phases of their last menstrual cycle. Seven phases were identified: early menstrual, first two days of most recent flow; late menstrual, days 3 and 4 of most recent flow; late premenstrual, days 1 and 2 before onset of most recent flow; early premenstrual, days 3 and 4 before onset of most recent flow; luteal, days 5 through 12 before onset of most recent flow; ovulatory, days 13 through 17 before onset of most recent flow; follicular, days between the 18th day counting back from most recent flow all the way to and including the fifth day after onset of the previous menstrual cycle. A map was provided for the students for easy identification of these phases. Although the identification of these phases follows physio-logical events, the specific choice of days is somewhat arbitrary because of individual variability.

It is important to note that the same definition of menstrual cycle phases was used to pool the appropriate days for the daily "unaware" data. For the social cycle analysis, the daily "unaware" data (collected for 11 weeks) were pooled over each day of the week.

### Daily "Aware" Condition

Students were told that this was a study of the menstrual cycle. Again they were asked to fill out the questionnaire every evening, indicate any sickness, any medication taken, and onset and end of menstruation. All instructions were given in the same manner as in the Daily "Unaware" Condition with the exception that no cover story was used. The men in the class requested that they also be allowed to fill out the daily questionnaire and asked the researcher to see if there were any cycles in men. The researcher agreed to this request. Again, the daily questionnaires were given out for 11 weeks.

### Moods and Behaviors Questionnaire

The questionnaire consisted of 70 items rated from "not at all" to "very" on a 6-point scale. Included were 36 items from Moos'

Menstrual Distress Questionnaire (MDQ) (1968). The items from the MDQ that were excluded were Chest Pain, Ringing in the ears, Heart-pounding, Numbness or tingling, Blind spots or fuzzy vision (all from the MDQ Control factor); Dizziness or faintness (from the MDQ Autonomic factor); Insomnia, and Accidents (both from the MDQ Concentration factor) and Restlessness, Mood swings (both from MDQ Negative Affect factor). These items were excluded because Englander-Golden et al., when doing a factor analysis on self-reports obtained with the MDQ in a daily "unaware" condition, discovered that they could not be located in any factor (1978).

Although 70 items were rated, subsequent factor analysis (see Results section) identified the following factors: 1) Pain: muscle stiffness, headache, cramps, backache, and general aches and pains; 2) Fatigue: fatigue, worn out, weary, sleepy, and tired; 3) Water retention: weight gain, skin disorders, painful breasts, and swelling; 4) Autonomic reaction: cold sweats, hot flashes, flushing, and clamminess; 5) Prostaglandin: nausea, vomiting, and diarrhea or loose bowel; 6) Tension: tension, nervous, and on edge; 7) Depression: crying, depression, unhappy, gloomy, worthless, blue discouraged, and helpless; 8) Anxiety-irritability: lonely, anxious, easily upset, irritable, and grouchy; 9) Vigor: excited, with bursts of energy/activity, active, full of pep, lively, and vigorous; 10) Well-being: affectionate, feelings of well-being, friendly, good-natured, cooperative, and understanding; 11) Sexual arousal: sexy, passionate, and lustful; 12) Behavioral change: lowered school or work performance, stay at home, and avoid social activities; 13) Concentration: forgetfulness, confusion, lowered judgment, difficult concentration, decreased efficiency and lowered motor coordination; 14) Anger: annoyed, angry, and ready to fight.

The factor comprised of nausea, vomiting, diarrhea or loose bowel was given the name "prostaglandin" because it has been reported that a prostaglandin associated with the onset of menstruation produces such effects (Halbert, Demers, & Jones, 1956).

### Maudsley Personality Inventory (MPI)

Neuroticism was measured on the MPI (Eysenck, 1959) which was administered after retrospective self-reports had been collected from the women who also had given self-reports in the daily "unaware" condition during the semester.

### Debriefing

When all data was gathered subjects in the "unaware" condition were asked to fill out a questionnaire that asked about their perceptions of the study. Not a single subject was suspicious that the menstrual cycle was a focus of this study. Subjects were told that data would be analyzed for a variety of possible cycles.

## RESULTS

All analyses were done having first separated women who were not taking oral contraceptives from those who were.

The daily "unaware" data was used to create the 14 factors. The procedure of Nicewander et al. (1969) was used by first creating rational clusters and then determining whether they indeed represented factors. The clusters were obtained from factor analysis of previously reported self-reports of moods and behaviors across the menstrual cycle which were obtained using daily "unaware" data (Englander-Golden, Whitmore, & Dienstbier, 1978). The 14 factors with their specific items (as detailed in the Method section) were replicated for both the nonpill and pill women in the daily "unaware" condition.

Table 1 shows mean responses on 14 factors of 37 nonpill women in the daily "unaware" and retrospective conditions as well as the mean responses of 49 nonpill women in the daily "aware" condition across the seven phases of the menstrual cycle and results of analysis of variance. The scores for the phases were obtained by averaging over the appropriate days, as defined in the Method section, for the 11 weeks of the study.

As can be seen, in the retrospective condition all factors have significant variability as a function of menstrual cycle phase with $p < .01$. Highest levels of pain, fatigue, water retention, autonomic reaction, prostaglandin, tension, depression, anxiety/irritability, behavioral change, and anger were remembered as occurring during the first two days of flow. During the same two days vigor, sexual arousal, and well-being were remembered as being at their lowest. The peak in vigor, sexual arousal, and well-being were remembered as occurring in the ovulatory or follicular phase. Greatest disruption in concentration was remembered for the two days prior to onset of menstruation. Table 1 shows that in the daily "unaware" condition only four factors (pain, water retention, autonomic reaction, and prostaglandin) reached a significant variability as a function of menstrual cycle phase, with each factor reaching a maximum during the first two days of flow ($p < .01$ for the first three and $p < .05$ for the fourth factor). Finally, in the daily "aware" condition 10 out of the 14 factors reached significant cyclical variability. As in the retrospective condition "bad events

**Table 1. Mean Responses of 37 Nonpill Women in the Daily Unaware (DU) and Retrospective (R) Conditions and of 49 Nonpill Women in the Daily Aware (DA) Condition across the Menstrual Cycle and F-Values**

| Factors | | Ovulatory | Luteal | Early premenstrual | Late premenstrual | Early menstrual | Late menstrual | Follicular | F-values |
|---|---|---|---|---|---|---|---|---|---|
| Pain | (DU) | 1.75 | 1.71 | 1.86 | 1.91 | 2.42 | 1.90 | 1.68 | 12.54** |
| | (R) | 1.69 | 1.50 | 1.89 | 2.34 | 3.05 | 1.88 | 1.51 | 30.63** |
| | (DA) | 1.77 | 1.86 | 1.99 | 2.07 | 2.59 | 2.01 | 1.85 | 15.07** |
| Fatigue | (DU) | 2.78 | 2.70 | 2.54 | 2.57 | 2.72 | 2.47 | 2.55 | 1.23 |
| | (R) | 1.94 | 1.73 | 2.14 | 2.34 | 2.64 | 2.02 | 1.66 | 13.78** |
| | (DA) | 2.64 | 2.77 | 2.91 | 2.73 | 2.78 | 2.47 | 2.62 | 2.50* |
| Water retention | (DU) | 1.62 | 1.81 | 1.96 | 2.11 | 2.33 | 1.77 | 1.46 | 24.41** |
| | (R) | 1.82 | 1.73 | 2.32 | 2.84 | 2.91 | 1.98 | 1.60 | 22.71** |
| | (DA) | 1.67 | 1.86 | 2.03 | 2.22 | 2.38 | 1.90 | 1.63 | 21.82** |
| Autonomic reaction | (DU) | 1.23 | 1.27 | 1.32 | 1.34 | 1.53 | 1.36 | 1.23 | 4.28** |
| | (R) | 1.41 | 1.40 | 1.39 | 1.57 | 1.69 | 1.38 | 1.27 | 4.83** |
| | (DA) | 1.26 | 1.23 | 1.31 | 1.34 | 1.42 | 1.27 | 1.28 | 2.62** |
| Prostaglandin | (DU) | 1.33 | 1.38 | 1.33 | 1.28 | 1.51 | 1.25 | 1.25 | 2.80* |
| | (R) | 1.27 | 1.30 | 1.37 | 1.44 | 1.64 | 1.38 | 1.21 | 4.88** |
| | (DA) | 1.27 | 1.21 | 1.30 | 1.25 | 1.54 | 1.33 | 1.23 | 5.92** |
| Tension | (DU) | 2.53 | 2.46 | 2.44 | 2.49 | 2.39 | 2.41 | 2.33 | 0.53 |
| | (R) | 1.92 | 1.85 | 2.19 | 2.35 | 2.62 | 1.98 | 1.67 | 7.46** |
| | (DA) | 2.10 | 2.27 | 2.53 | 2.15 | 2.15 | 2.10 | 2.30 | 3.81** |
| Depression | (DU) | 1.93 | 1.92 | 1.84 | 1.94 | 1.96 | 1.91 | 1.82 | 0.59 |
| | (R) | 1.55 | 1.52 | 1.74 | 2.05 | 2.23 | 1.58 | 1.41 | 16.62** |
| | (DA) | 1.73 | 1.82 | 1.94 | 1.94 | 1.97 | 1.89 | 1.89 | 1.51 |
| Anxiety-irritability | (DU) | 2.17 | 2.14 | 2.10 | 2.21 | 2.29 | 2.18 | 2.02 | 1.40 |
| | (R) | 1.75 | 1.67 | 2.11 | 2.56 | 2.82 | 2.07 | 1.50 | 19.70** |
| | (DA) | 1.89 | 2.01 | 2.16 | 2.13 | 2.11 | 2.12 | 2.12 | 2.01 |

**Table 1. Mean Responses of 37 Nonpill Women in the Daily Unaware (DU) and Retrospective (R) Conditions and of 49 Nonpill Women in the Daily Aware (DA) Condition across the Menstrual Cycle and F-Values** (*Continued*)

| Factors | | Ovulatory | Luteal | Early premenstrual | Late premenstrual | Early menstrual | Late menstrual | Follicular | F-values |
|---|---|---|---|---|---|---|---|---|---|
| Vigor | (DU) | | 2.96 | 2.98 | 2.97 | 2.69 | 2.97 | 2.77 | 1.32 |
| | (R) | 3.33 | 3.18 | 2.75 | 2.56 | 2.12 | 2.64 | 3.20 | 16.64** |
| | (DA) | 3.14 | 3.08 | 3.03 | 2.93 | 2.74 | 3.02 | 3.13 | 3.10 |
| Well-being | (DU) | 3.68 | 3.67 | 3.71 | 3.72 | 3.46 | 3.72 | 3.49 | 1.17 |
| | (R) | 3.89 | 3.82 | 3.44 | 3.09 | 2.88 | 3.41 | 3.91 | 12.50** |
| | (DA) | 3.93 | 3.85 | 3.75 | 3.78 | 3.60 | 3.78 | 3.85 | 2.28* |
| Sexual arousal | (DU) | 2.17 | 2.10 | 2.07 | 2.22 | 2.07 | 2.04 | 1.94 | 0.98 |
| | (R) | 2.27 | 2.12 | 1.83 | 1.81 | 1.55 | 2.05 | 2.26 | 5.72** |
| | (DA) | 2.39 | 2.22 | 2.16 | 2.12 | 1.91 | 2.09 | 2.14 | 3.09** |
| Behavioral change | (DU) | 2.34 | 2.27 | 2.26 | 2.19 | 2.41 | 2.17 | 2.17 | 1.42 |
| | (R) | 1.66 | 1.68 | 1.90 | 2.17 | 2.91 | 2.04 | 1.66 | 16.01** |
| | (DA) | 2.20 | 2.13 | 2.22 | 2.32 | 2.46 | 2.30 | 2.24 | 2.33* |
| Concentration | (DU) | 1.86 | 1.84 | 1.81 | 1.89 | 1.90 | 1.81 | 1.76 | 0.88 |
| | (R) | 1.61 | 1.50 | 1.77 | 2.00 | 1.88 | 1.55 | 1.47 | 5.73** |
| | (DA) | 1.83 | 1.88 | 1.99 | 1.94 | 1.98 | 1.89 | 1.92 | 1.05 |
| Anger | (DU) | 1.93 | 1.90 | 1.82 | 1.89 | 1.87 | 1.75 | 1.69 | 1.78 |
| | (R) | 1.45 | 1.53 | 1.54 | 1.73 | 1.95 | 1.41 | 1.46 | 6.28** |
| | (DA) | 1.70 | 1.80 | 1.96 | 1.80 | 1.79 | 1.85 | 1.81 | 1.48 |

*$p < .05$.
**$p < .01$.
*Note.* F tests for the DU and R conditions have 6 and 216 degrees of freedom; those for the DA condition have 6 and 288.

were reported in the paramenstruum where "good" events were reported at a minimum.

Table 2 shows equivalent data for pill women. As can be seen, the retrospective condition yielded the largest number of cyclical variations with 10 out of 14 factors reaching significance ($p < .01$ or $p < .05$). Peaks in pain, fatigue, water retention, prostaglandin, tension, depression, anxiety/irritability, and disruption in concentration were remembered for the first two days of flow. During these two days well-being and sexual arousal were remembered at their minimum. Peaks for the latter two factors were remembered in the ovulatory phase. Table 2 shows that in the daily "unaware" condition 6 out of 14 factors reached significant cyclical variability ($p < .01$ or $p < .05$). Pain, water retention, tension, depression, and anxiety/irritability reached a peak in the early or late menstrual phase. Sexual arousal reached a peak in the follicular phase. Surprisingly, only 2 of the 14 factors reached significance in the daily "aware" condition ($p < .01$). Both pain and water retention were reported at their peak in the early menstrual phase.

Tables 3, 4, and 5 show social cycles for each group of women and for men. Table 3 shows that for women not taking oral contraceptives, there were 9 significantly varying factors (tension, depression, anxiety/irritability, vigor, well-being, sexual arousal, behavioral change, concentration, and anger). Table 4 shows that for women taking oral contraceptives there were 5 significantly varying factors (tension, anxiety/irritability, vigor, well-being, and concentration). Table 5 shows that for men there were 4 significantly varying factors (prostaglandin, vigor, sexual arousal, and behavioral change). The prostaglandin factor was not expected to be meaningful to men. When results showed that this factor varied significantly across the male social cycle a group of men were interviewed. They readily identified the meaningful component of this factor as being diarrhea/loose bowel caused by drinking beer. Indeed this factor has a peak intensity on Saturday.

Finally, Pearson correlation coefficients between neuroticism and daily "unaware" self-reports were calculated separately for each menstrual cycle phase. For women who were not taking oral contraceptives there was no significant correlation between neuroticism and self-reports in the phase where the peak of a *significantly varying* factor occurred. Thus, as can be seen in Table 6, for the pain factor in the early menstrual phase $r = -.149$, ns; for the water retention factor in the early menstrual phase $r = -.004$, ns; for the prostaglandin factor in the early menstrual phase $r = -.094$, ns; and for

Table 2. Mean Responses of 16 Pill Women in the Daily Unaware (DU) and Retrospective (R) Conditions and of 15 Pill Women in the Daily Aware (DA) Condition across the Menstrual Cycle and F Values

| Factors | | Ovulatory | Luteal | Early premenstrual | Late premenstrual | Early menstrual | Late menstrual | Follicular | F-values |
|---|---|---|---|---|---|---|---|---|---|
| Pain | (DU) | 1.74 | 1.65 | 1.66 | 1.89 | 2.52 | 1.96 | 1.79 | 11.44** |
| | (R) | 1.44 | 1.37 | 1.60 | 2.14 | 2.64 | 1.60 | 1.46 | 9.05*** |
| | (DA) | 1.67 | 1.68 | 1.83 | 1.80 | 2.66 | 2.12 | 1.88 | 9.84** |
| Fatigue | (DU) | 2.86 | 2.55 | 2.28 | 2.51 | 2.69 | 2.60 | 2.80 | 2.08 |
| | (R) | 1.67 | 1.56 | 1.91 | 1.75 | 2.36 | 1.92 | 1.76 | 3.09* |
| | (DA) | 2.47 | 2.56 | 2.80 | 2.44 | 2.66 | 2.73 | 2.48 | 0.82 |
| Water retention | (DU) | 1.63 | 1.71 | 1.78 | 1.83 | 2.16 | 1.62 | 1.54 | 5.88** |
| | (R) | 1.56 | 1.55 | 1.83 | 2.12 | 2.70 | 1.56 | 1.45 | 5.35*** |
| | (DA) | 1.55 | 1.65 | 1.80 | 2.01 | 2.13 | 1.68 | 1.56 | 7.78** |
| Autonomic reaction | (DU) | 1.19 | 1.17 | 1.17 | 1.16 | 1.35 | 1.24 | 1.21 | 1.57 |
| | (R) | 1.14 | 1.03 | 1.19 | 1.17 | 1.34 | 0.97 | 1.16 | 1.84 |
| | (DA) | 1.10 | 1.15 | 1.24 | 1.15 | 1.22 | 1.14 | 1.21 | 1.26 |
| Prostaglandin | (DU) | 1.28 | 1.20 | 1.22 | 1.22 | 1.34 | 1.37 | 1.30 | 1.21 |
| | (R) | 1.06 | 1.04 | 1.21 | 1.12 | 1.58 | 0.98 | 1.12 | 2.80* |
| | (DA) | 1.10 | 1.17 | 1.13 | 1.15 | 1.26 | 1.29 | 1.15 | 1.24 |
| Tension | (DU) | 2.54 | 2.39 | 2.08 | 2.00 | 2.29 | 2.55 | 2.39 | 4.57** |
| | (R) | 1.40 | 1.31 | 1.69 | 1.98 | 2.25 | 1.46 | 1.58 | 4.11** |
| | (DA) | 2.52 | 2.40 | 2.65 | 2.28 | 2.60 | 2.87 | 2.77 | 1.66 |
| Depression | (DU) | 2.04 | 1.85 | 1.79 | 1.73 | 1.88 | 2.25 | 1.82 | 3.22** |
| | (R) | 1.45 | 1.36 | 1.88 | 1.98 | 2.17 | 1.43 | 1.32 | 3.24*** |
| | (DA) | 1.87 | 1.82 | 1.86 | 1.55 | 1.94 | 1.93 | 1.93 | 1.15 |

| | | | | | | | | | |
|---|---|---|---|---|---|---|---|---|---|
| Anxiety-irritability | (DU) | 2.23 | 2.09 | 1.93 | 1.92 | 2.19 | 2.37 | 1.96 | 3.06** |
| | (R) | 1.47 | 1.46 | 1.95 | 2.17 | 2.50 | 1.52 | 1.54 | 4.48*** |
| | (DA) | 2.05 | 2.06 | 2.26 | 1.91 | 2.28 | 2.17 | 2.25 | 1.62 |
| Vigor | (DU) | 2.70 | 2.81 | 2.84 | 2.66 | 2.77 | 2.58 | 2.72 | 0.40 |
| | (R) | 2.77 | 2.41 | 2.57 | 2.24 | 2.02 | 2.32 | 1.35 | 2.11 |
| | (DA) | 2.94 | 3.10 | 3.16 | 3.04 | 2.73 | 2.94 | 3.00 | 1.53 |
| Well-being | (DU) | 3.83 | 3.89 | 3.91 | 3.85 | 3.87 | 3.81 | 4.08 | 0.74 |
| | (R) | 3.96 | 3.62 | 3.37 | 3.01 | 2.75 | 3.25 | 3.77 | 4.11** |
| | (DA) | 4.07 | 4.07 | 3.93 | 4.17 | 3.84 | 3.93 | 3.97 | 1.07 |
| Sexual arousal | (DU) | 2.31 | 2.25 | 2.42 | 2.27 | 1.90 | 2.07 | 2.51 | 2.69* |
| | (R) | 2.81 | 2.10 | 2.29 | 2.01 | 1.81 | 2.10 | 2.48 | 2.58* |
| | (DA) | 2.44 | 2.60 | 2.73 | 2.82 | 2.59 | 2.49 | 2.62 | 0.96 |
| Behavioral change | (DU) | 2.53 | 2.26 | 2.27 | 2.52 | 2.28 | 2.50 | 2.28 | 0.98 |
| | (R) | 1.69 | 1.71 | 2.12 | 2.31 | 2.33 | 1.58 | 1.67 | 1.99 |
| | (DA) | 2.30 | 2.16 | 2.53 | 2.21 | 2.46 | 2.38 | 2.22 | 1.21 |
| Concentration | (DU) | 2.01 | 1.86 | 1.79 | 1.74 | 1.84 | 1.99 | 1.90 | 1.69 |
| | (R) | 1.35 | 1.25 | 1.53 | 1.57 | 1.72 | 1.10 | 1.42 | 2.78* |
| | (DA) | 1.85 | 1.76 | 1.87 | 1.80 | 1.89 | 1.84 | 1.87 | 0.27 |
| Anger | (DU) | 1.84 | 1.89 | 1.77 | 1.69 | 1.80 | 2.03 | 1.73 | 1.06 |
| | (R) | 1.25 | 1.19 | 1.62 | 1.85 | 1.77 | 1.20 | 1.33 | 1.97 |
| | (DA) | 1.51 | 1.59 | 1.67 | 1.61 | 1.63 | 1.63 | 1.60 | 0.21 |

*$p < .05$.
**$p < .01$.
Note. F tests for the DU and R conditions have 6 and 90 degrees of freedom; those for the DA condition have 6 and 84.

Table 3. Mean Responses of 37 Nonpill Women in the Daily "Unaware" Condition across Seven Days of the Week and F-values

| Factors | Sun | Mon | Tue | Wed | Thu | Fri | Sat | F-values |
|---------|-----|-----|-----|-----|-----|-----|-----|----------|
| Pain | 1.78 | 1.82 | 1.83 | 1.89 | 1.85 | 1.81 | 1.85 | 1.07 |
| Fatigue | 2.62 | 2.55 | 2.62 | 2.84 | 2.61 | 2.59 | 2.61 | 2.10 |
| Water retention | 1.75 | 1.79 | 1.75 | 1.78 | 1.79 | 1.75 | 1.81 | .87 |
| Autonomic reaction | 1.32 | 1.32 | 1.35 | 1.32 | 1.29 | 1.33 | 1.32 | .57 |
| Prostaglandin | 1.38 | 1.34 | 1.33 | 1.34 | 1.31 | 1.30 | 1.34 | .91 |
| Tension | 2.24 | 2.39 | 2.39 | 2.68 | 2.55 | 2.47 | 2.29 | 8.95** |
| Depression | 1.96 | 1.86 | 1.90 | 2.03 | 1.89 | 1.83 | 1.80 | 3.84 |
| Anxiety-irritability | 2.13 | 2.07 | 2.10 | 2.25 | 2.17 | 2.11 | 2.10 | 2.55* |
| Vigor | 2.82 | 2.84 | 2.85 | 2.87 | 2.97 | 3.21 | 3.34 | 14.69** |
| Well-being | 3.69 | 3.64 | 3.71 | 3.62 | 3.69 | 3.87 | 3.82 | 3.95** |
| Sexual arousal | 2.08 | 2.04 | 2.03 | 2.03 | 2.07 | 2.30 | 2.29 | 4.38** |
| Behavioral change | 2.39 | 2.22 | 2.30 | 2.33 | 2.30 | 2.09 | 2.20 | 3.41** |
| Concentration | 1.79 | 1.81 | 1.89 | 1.97 | 1.88 | 1.85 | 1.77 | 4.66** |
| Anger | 1.84 | 1.72 | 1.84 | 1.93 | 1.89 | 1.81 | 1.79 | 2.64* |

*p < .05.
**p < .01.
Note. F tests have 6 and 216 degrees of freedom.

88

Table 4. Mean Responses of 16 Pill Women in the Daily "Unaware" Condition across Seven Days of the Week and F-Values

| Factors | Sun | Mon | Tue | Wed | Thu | Fri | Sat | F-values |
|---|---|---|---|---|---|---|---|---|
| Pain | 1.73 | 1.76 | 1.77 | 1.88 | 1.86 | 1.77 | 1.78 | 1.08 |
| Fatigue | 2.43 | 2.51 | 2.58 | 2.74 | 2.55 | 2.54 | 2.52 | 1.16 |
| Water retention | 1.67 | 1.69 | 1.72 | 2.69 | 1.67 | 1.63 | 1.62 | .69 |
| Autonomic reaction | 1.16 | 1.19 | 1.19 | 1.17 | 1.20 | 1.18 | 1.23 | .55 |
| Prostaglandin | 1.24 | 1.29 | 1.23 | 1.32 | 1.27 | 1.20 | 1.28 | 1.06 |
| Tension | 2.04 | 2.34 | 2.46 | 2.50 | 2.62 | 2.15 | 2.11 | 5.84** |
| Depression | 1.77 | 1.92 | 1.92 | 1.88 | 2.05 | 1.68 | 1.81 | 1.98 |
| Anxiety-irritability | 1.93 | 2.02 | 2.07 | 2.19 | 2.25 | 1.96 | 1.94 | 2.56* |
| Vigor | 2.72 | 2.61 | 2.59 | 2.65 | 2.66 | 3.04 | 3.12 | 4.17** |
| Well-being | 4.00 | 3.86 | 3.83 | 3.91 | 3.82 | 4.05 | 4.13 | 2.41* |
| Sexual arousal | 2.28 | 2.21 | 2.15 | 2.22 | 2.32 | 2.47 | 2.54 | 2.13 |
| Behavioral change | 2.45 | 2.30 | 2.47 | 2.29 | 2.48 | 2.17 | 2.22 | 1.85 |
| Concentration | 1.83 | 1.87 | 1.91 | 1.98 | 1.96 | 1.71 | 1.75 | 3.30** |
| Anger | 1.65 | 1.81 | 1.79 | 1.73 | 2.01 | 1.69 | 1.80 | 2.12 |

*p < .05.
**p < .01.
Note. F tests have 6 and 90 degrees of freedom.

89

**Table 5.** Mean Responses of 23 Men in the Daily "Unaware" Condition across Seven Days of the Week and F-values

| Factors | Sun | Mon | Tue | Wed | Thu | Fri | Sat | F-values |
|---|---|---|---|---|---|---|---|---|
| Pain | 1.61 | 1.65 | 1.64 | 1.61 | 1.60 | 1.56 | 1.61 | .80 |
| Fatigue | 2.13 | 2.09 | 2.09 | 2.09 | 2.13 | 2.04 | 2.14 | .45 |
| Water retention | 1.24 | 1.22 | 1.21 | 1.20 | 1.20 | 1.18 | 1.23 | 1.37 |
| Autonomic reaction | 1.17 | 1.17 | 1.16 | 1.14 | 1.15 | 1.18 | 1.19 | .96 |
| Prostaglandin | 1.22 | 1.18 | 1.20 | 1.21 | 1.13 | 1.13 | 1.21 | 2.88* |
| Tension | 1.75 | 1.87 | 1.84 | 1.86 | 1.80 | 1.83 | 1.79 | .73 |
| Depression | 1.55 | 1.58 | 1.63 | 1.57 | 1.57 | 1.56 | 1.56 | .54 |
| Anxiety-irritability | 1.74 | 1.72 | 1.78 | 1.71 | 1.72 | 1.74 | 1.80 | .74 |
| Vigor | 2.63 | 2.64 | 2.66 | 2.71 | 2.71 | 2.82 | 2.85 | 3.36** |
| Well-being | 3.37 | 3.33 | 3.33 | 3.46 | 3.43 | 3.43 | 3.44 | 1.32 |
| Sexual arousal | 2.52 | 2.38 | 2.30 | 2.50 | 2.48 | 2.57 | 2.67 | 3.24** |
| Behavioral change | 2.39 | 2.21 | 2.14 | 2.20 | 2.07 | 2.05 | 2.08 | 2.97** |
| Concentration | 1.76 | 1.72 | 1.81 | 1.82 | 1.77 | 1.73 | 1.74 | 1.39 |
| Anger | 1.55 | 1.64 | 1.66 | 1.60 | 1.61 | 1.64 | 1.65 | .65 |

*$p < .05$.
**$p < .01$.
*Note.* F tests have 6 and 132 degrees of freedom.

the autonomic reaction factor in the early menstrual phase r = −.122, ns.

Table 7 shows equivalent results for women who were taking oral contraceptives. The only exceptions occurred for the factor of tension, where in the late menstrual phase r = .532, $p < .05$; and for the factor of depression, where in the late menstrual phase r = .557, $p < .05$. In both cases higher neuroticism was correlated with higher reports in tension and depression.

## DISCUSSION

The strongest evidence that self-reports of moods and behaviors across the menstrual cycle are least biased by cultural expectations when elicited in the daily "unaware" condition comes from data obtained from women who were not taking oral contraceptives. First, the four factors which showed significant cyclicity across their menstrual cycle in the daily "unaware" condition (pain, water retention, autonomic reaction, and prostaglandin) did not vary across their social cycle. Yet the data for the social cycle came from the same time frame as the data for the menstrual cycle. Second, when these women were asked to remember their moods and behaviors for the last menstrual cycle, the very cycle they just finished reporting in the daily "unaware" condition, they remembered "bad" moods and behaviors for the paramenstruum and "good" moods and behaviors at other times of the menstrual cycle. In the retrospective condition every factor showed significant cyclicity, with remembered moods not necessarily congruent with how they were reported in the daily "unaware" condition. Daily "aware" self-reports, obtained from a different group of women not taking oral contraceptives, showed 10 significantly cycling factors across the menstrual cycle. This result suggests that daily "aware" self-reports are also contaminated by cultural beliefs and expectations, although not as strongly as retrospective reports.

Results from women taking oral contraceptives are not that clear. Since retrospective self-reports yielded most cyclicity (10 factors) while daily "aware" yielded least (2 factors) it is impossible to make a simple statement that these women believed that the pill removes symptomatology. Such a belief should also minimize retrospective reports of symptomatology.

A look at the social cycle of both groups of women shows that such a cycle is at least as important, in terms of cyclical variability, as the menstrual cycle. Indeed, for women not taking oral contraceptives, the moods which have been traditionally linked to PMS

Table 6. Neuroticism Scores Correlated with Factor Means over Cycle Phases for Nonpill Unaware Females ($N = 37$)

| Factors | Phase | | | | | | |
|---|---|---|---|---|---|---|---|
| | Early menstrual | Late menstrual | Follicular | Ovulatory | Luteal | Early premenstrual | Late premenstrual |
| Pain | -.026 | .009 | .136 | .332* | .249 | .435** | .438** |
| Fatigue | .214 | .066 | .256 | .289 | .291 | .362* | .286 |
| Water retention | -.006 | .267 | .230 | .261 | .216 | .182 | .132 |
| Autonomic reaction | .198 | .231 | .244 | .311 | .495 | .388* | .367* |
| Prostaglandin | .131 | .364* | .281 | .446** | .272 | .590** | .342* |
| Tension | .453** | .379* | .423** | .362* | .416* | .477** | .518** |
| Depression | .323 | .393* | .472** | .536** | .489** | .436** | .605** |
| Anxiety-irritability | .256 | .255 | .295 | .422** | .277 | .436** | .491** |
| Vigor | -.050 | -.098 | -.316 | -.246 | -.121 | -.268 | -.189 |
| Well-being | -.101 | -.121 | -.232 | -.209 | -.183 | -.353* | -.219 |
| Sexual arousal | .125 | -.007 | -.121 | -.058 | -.019 | -.353* | -.119 |
| Behavioral change | .195 | .235 | .200 | .121 | .231 | .391* | .409* |
| Concentration | .376* | .329* | .310 | .412* | .447** | .482** | .522** |
| Anger | .211 | .244 | .245 | .271 | .344* | .365* | .353* |

*$p < .05$ (r must be equal or greater than .325 for 35 degrees of freedom).
**$p < .01$ (r must be equal or greater than .418 for 35 degrees of freedom).

Table 7. Neuroticism Scores Correlated with Factor Means over Cycle Phases for Pill Unaware Females (*N* = 16)

| Factors | Phase | | | | | | |
|---|---|---|---|---|---|---|---|
| | Early menstrual | Late menstrual | Follicular | Ovulatory | Luteal | Early premenstrual | Late premenstrual |
| Pain | .390 | .310 | .329 | .188 | .487 | .276 | .462 |
| Fatigue | .649** | .748** | .686** | .417 | .660** | .551* | .457 |
| Water retention | .252 | .385 | .510* | .387 | .491 | .568* | .328 |
| Autonomic reaction | .651** | .414 | .667** | .008 | .470 | .013 | .427 |
| Prostaglandin | .472 | .478 | .392 | .329 | .288 | .394 | .235 |
| Tension | .577* | .532* | .425 | .594* | .495 | .521* | .222 |
| Depression | .593* | .557* | .384 | .487 | .339 | .201 | .194 |
| Anxiety-irritability | .633** | .340 | .652** | .459 | .550* | .474 | .268 |
| Vigor | .182 | -.052 | -.003 | -.075 | .110 | -.167 | -.240 |
| Well-being | .104 | .124 | .133 | .025 | .000 | -.011 | -.023 |
| Sexual arousal | .331 | .382 | .426 | .199 | .319 | .208 | .386 |
| Behavioral change | .507* | .274 | .365 | .506* | .291 | .425 | .310 |
| Concentration | .389 | .416 | .595* | .612* | .531* | .328 | .525* |
| Anger | .481 | .535* | .656** | .323 | .502* | .335 | .225 |

*$p < .05$ (r must be equal or greater than .497 for 14 degrees of freedom).
**$p < .01$ (r must be equal or greater than .623 for 14 degrees of freedom).

(tension, depression, anxiety-irritability), vary more across the social cycle than across the menstrual cycle when self-reports are obtained in the "unaware" condition. Cyclicity across the menstrual cycle is marked by physiological events. Even where such cyclicity occurs, the mean difference between peaks and troughs in self-reports is less than one step on a six-point response scale.

The fact that men had four significantly varying factors across the social cycle (i.e., the same number as women not taking oral contraceptives had across the menstrual cycle) indicates that our concepts of what represents "detrimental" cyclicity may be deeply affected by value judgment. Who can say that a woman's cyclicity in pain as a function of the menstrual cycle is any more detrimental to her performance than a man's cyclicity in vigor? In fact, the previously mentioned results on sex differences in absence from work (Englander-Golden & Barton, 1983) indicate that it is not.

While the above results weaken broad assumptions about pervasiveness of PMS, the lack of correlations between neuroticism and daily "unaware" self-reports, in the phase in which the reports are at their maximum, indicate that women who complain of physical symptoms during menstruation cannot be simply dismissed as neurotic (Coppen, 1963). Thus, if a woman is complaining of cramps during menstruation it is not psychologically the same as when she complains of cramps in the follicular phase. The significant correlations in the premenstruum are not surprising. The neuroticism scale contains many questions that are almost identical to the moods women report as heightened during that time.

It is important to note that the definition of the menstrual cycle phase is somewhat arbitrary. Thus, some differences in menstrual cyclicity across different studies could be due to a different definition of specific phases. Indeed, one such example can be given. In a previously published study Englander-Golden et al. reported significant menstrual cyclicity on the sexual arousal factor for women not taking oral contraceptives (1980). In the present study this factor did not reach significant cyclicity. Yet when this data was analyzed in a manner similar to the previous analysis (considering only one day for the ovulatory phase), significant variability was obtained (Wallis & Englander-Golden, 1985).

In conclusion, the results presented in this study indicate that 1) retrospective self-reports cannot be used as evidence of pervasive existence of PMS, 2) a social cycle exists for both sexes and conceptualizing debilitating effects only due to the menstrual cycle may indeed reflect a cultural bias against women, 3) symptomatology in specific phases of the menstrual cycle cannot simply be dismissed as the report of a neurotic. Thus, this study lends credibility to the arguments against pervasive symptomatology while at the same time acknowledging the existence of discrete changes across the menstrual cycle.

## REFERENCES

Coppen, A., & Kessel, N. (1963). Menstruation and personality. *British Journal of Psychiatry, 109,* 711–721.

Dennerstein, L., & Burrows, G. D. (1979). Affect and the menstrual cycle. *Journal of Affective Disorders, 1,* 77–92.

Englander-Golden, P., & Barton, G. (1983). Sex differences in absence from work: A reinterpretation. *Psychology of Women Quarterly, 8*(2), 185–188.

Englander-Golden, P., Chang, H. S., Whitmore, M. R., & Dienstiber, R. A. (1980). Sexuality and the menstrual cycle. *Journal of Human Stress, 6*(1), 42–48.

Englander-Golden, P., Whitmore, M. R., & Dienstbier, R. A. (1978). Menstrual cycle as a focus of study and self-reports of modds and behaviors. *Motivation and Emotion, 2*(1), 75–86.

Eysenck, H. (1959). *Manual of the Maudsley Personality Inventory.* London: University of London Press.

Golub, S. (1976). The magnitude of premenstrual anxiety and depression. *Psychosomatic Research, 20*(2), 125–130.

Halbert, D. R., Demers, L. M., & Jones, D. E. D. (1956). Dysmenorrhea and prostaglandins. *Obstetrical and Gynecological Survey, 31*(1), 77–81.

Herbert, W. (1982). Premenstrual changes. *Science News, 12,* 380–381.

Koeske, R. K., & Koeske, G. F. (1975). An attributional approach to moods and the menstrual cycle. *Journal of Personality and Social Psychology, 31,* 473–478.

May, R. R. (1976). Mood shifts and the menstrual cycle. *Journal of Psychosomatic Research, 20*(2), 125–130.

Moos, R. H. (1968). The development of a menstrual distress questionnaire. *Psychosomatic Medicine, 30,* 853–867.

Nicewander, W. A., Urry, V. W., & Starry, A. R. (1969). Composite components analysis: A method for factoring large numbers of items. *Proceedings,* 77th Annual Convention, American Psychological Association, 111–112.

O'Leary, V. E. (1974). Some attitudinal barriers to occupational aspirations in women. *Psychological Bullentin, 81*(1), 809–826.

Parlee, M. B. (1974). Sterotypic beliefs about menstruation: A methodological note on the Moos Menstrual Distress Questionnaire and some new data. *Psychosomatic Medicine, 30,* 229–240.

Parlee, M. B. (1973). The premenstrual syndrome. *Psychological Bulletin, 80,* 454–456.

Rossi, A. S., & Rossi, P. E. (1977). Body time and social time: Mood patterns by menstrual cycle phase and day of the week. *Social Science Research, 6,* 273–308.

Ruble, D. N. (1977). Premenstrual symptoms: A reinterpretation. *Science, 291.*

U.S. Department of Labor, Bureau of Labor Statistics Bulletin. (1977). *U.S. Working Women: A Data Book.*

Wallis, J., & Englander-Golden, P. (1985). Female primate sexuality across the menstrual cycle. Unpublished paper presented at the Sixth Conference of the Society for Menstrual Cycle Research Galveston.

**Request reprints from Paula Englander-Golden, Department of Human Relations, University of Oklahoma, Norman, OK 73019.**

# MENSTRUAL ATTITUDES, BELIEFS, AND SYMPTOM EXPERIENCES OF ADOLESCENT FEMALES, THEIR PEERS, AND THEIR MOTHERS

Susan Marie Stoltzman, MSN, CPNP

CIGNA Healthplan of Texas, Inc., Dallas, Texas

Menstrual attitudes, beliefs, self-care practices, communication patterns, and symptom experiences were explored among 4 groups of women. Thirty adolescent volunteers and 19 of their close girlfriends comprised 2 groups. Forty-six biological mothers of these adolescents and friends comprised the other 2 groups. All participants completed self-report questionnaires and a demographic data form. Post hoc analysis revealed significant differences ($p \leq .05$) between the scores of mothers and their daughters, and no differences between scores of adolescents. The adolescents were more likely to view menstruation as debilitating, bothersome, and unsanitary, and less likely to view it as a positive event than their mothers. Adolescents reported significantly more acute pain, water retention, and arousal symptoms than did their mothers.

## LITERATURE

To date, empirical investigation of the sociocultural perspectives of the adolescent menstrual experience is limited. Researchers who have studied samples of adolescents report three general categories of data: attitudes toward menstruation, menstrual symptom expectations and experiences, and sources of menstrual information.

General evaluative attitudes toward menstruation among adolescents have been studied by Brooks-Gunn and Ruble (1980a, 1980b), Clark and Ruble (1978), Whisnant and Zegans (1975), Haft (1973), and Kovar, (cited in Haft, 1973). Clark and Ruble surveyed pre- and postmenarcheal girls and boys in 7th and 8th grades, finding that all three groups had a relatively well-defined set of expectations and attitudes. Most subjects believed that menstruation was "accompanied by physical discomforts, increased emotionality, and a dis-

ruption of activities and social interactions" (p. 231). In view of
the striking similarity and high degree of awareness in all three
groups, Clark and Ruble postulated that these expectations and
attitudes were a reflection of negative sociocultural stereotypes
which are consistent and assessable at a fairly young age. In a
study of 151 adolescents, Kovar reported that girls viewed menstruation as a reminder of restrictions; in contrast, both Whisnant
and Zegans (1975) and Brooks-Gunn and Ruble (1980a, b) found
that the large majority of girls believed that one should "act normal"
during the menstrual period. The adolescents in Haft's 1973 study
graded menstruation generally unfavorably. She found no differences between pre- and postmenarcheal subjects. While Brooks-
Gunn and Ruble reported more negative feelings about menstruation in junior high than in elementary school girls, they too, found
no differences between pre- and postmenarcheal subjects. In addition, these authors note that while adolescents seemed to view
menstruation as more debilitating than college women, they tended
to deny the effects of menstruation more than college men and
women.

Adolescent menstrual symptom expectations and experiences
were examined among a cross-section of girls (5th through 8th
grades) by Brooks-Gunn and Ruble (1980a). These investigators
found that girls, regardless of menstrual status, believed that others
experienced more menstrual symptoms than they themselves experienced or expect to experience. The findings suggested that age,
but not menstrual status, affects girls' reports of menstrual symptomology: the 7th and 8th graders perceived more cycle differences
than the 5th and 6th graders. Since elementary schoolgirls appear
to have somewhat less negative attitudes and less cycle-related
symptoms than junior-high schoolgirls, the investigators suggested
that beliefs about menstruation may develop with age. Golub and
Harrington (1981) also note that age may influence the incidence
and/or perception of menstrual symptoms. While their sample of
158 female adolescents (ages 15–16 years) showed no significant
difference in moods during premenstrual, menstrual, or intermenstrual cycle phases, these adolescents consistently reported more
distress during the menstrual phase of their cycles.

Many of the studies described thus far asked participants about
sources of menstrual-related information. Four major sources were
repeatedly identified: family (parents and siblings); friends (peers
and adults); health care and educational systems (nurses, doctors,
health classes, and teachers); and media (television, books, booklets, and magazines). Brooks-Gunn and Ruble note that in systematic

studies of sources, most girls report learning something about menstruation from their mother, or that their mothers are the primary sources of information. Family members other than mothers seem to contribute little information. The second major informational source is female, not male, friends. Over three-quarters of the girls in Brooks-Gunn and Ruble study (1980a) learned something about menstruation from female friends. Health education classes comprised the third primary source of information; the bulk of information provided by media sources is in the form of booklets prepared by the sanitary products industry. Magazines and television are additional sources of information.

In summary, it seems that several factors: general cultural stereotypes, expectations for self, specific information received from others, and developmental stage, may influence the adolescent's menstrual experience. Direct physical experience of symptoms is also likely to contribute to an adolescent's perception of menstruation, although attitudes, beliefs, and expectations may influence self-perceptions and reports of physiologic states.

## FRAMEWORK

Few studies specifically explore the role that mothers and other sources of information about menstruation may play in the acquisition of menstrual related beliefs among adolescent females. Considering that adolescents identify two primary sources: mothers and female peers, it seems likely that these two sources may strongly influence adolescents' attitudes toward and beliefs about menstruation.

Whisnant and Zegans (1975) found that regardless of the quality of the past relationship, most of the girls in their study turned to their mothers for information at menarche. Most of the girls in the Koff, Rierdon, and Jacobson study (1981) were prepared for menstruation and most listed their source of information as mother. All but one postmenarcheal girl cited mother as the first person told about the onset of menstruation. Brooks-Gunn and Matthews (1979), found that reports of menstrual distress among both pre- and postmenarcheal subjects were related to maternal reports of menstrual distress. If girls believed their mothers experienced menstrual symptoms, they, too, anticipated or reported being negatively affected by menstruation. Experiences of a girl's mother, sister, or female relatives with menses was found to create expectations of similar experiences among the girls in Martin's (1978) study. Delaney, Lupton, and Toth (1976) contend that the chief influence of menstrual disorders in a girl's mother. Dalton (1964) states that despite the wide range of premenstrual symptoms, there is a tendency for these to be similar among female family members.

This central role of mothers in the menarcheal and possibly in the postmenarcheal menstrual experience of a girl may be explained by socialization and identification theories. It has been suggested that a girl's identification with her mother may be particularly intense at menarche, when she can biologically fulfill the role of mother; thus, maternal beliefs, communicated by both word and action, may be a powerful variable in the socialization of beliefs about menstruation as well as in the development of a girl's sexuality (Deutsh, 1944, Friday, 1977, Hammer, 1975, Weideger, 1976).

Menke (1979) constructed a model to describe the relationship between mother/daughter menstrual cycle beliefs and experiences. She describes a reciprocal mechanism, whereby a woman's actual cycle experiences and behaviors influence her beliefs, while her beliefs influence her menstrual cycle experiences and behaviors. Menke suggested that the menstrual beliefs and practices of a mother have a particularly significant effect of the development of her daughter's beliefs and practices, due to the identification of the daughter with her mother. Although she acknowledged some degree of mutual influence, she emphasized that since the mother is a role model, maternal beliefs would be a dominant influence, significantly affecting the daughter's beliefs.

Using Menke's model as a theoretical framework, Schick (1980) and Cain (1980) examined mother and daughter responses to the Menstrual Attitude Questionnaire (Brooks-Gunn & Ruble, 1980b) and the Modified Moos Menstrual Distress Questionnaire (Menke, 1979; Moos, 1977). Schick sampled 15 adolescent females, ages 12–16, and their mothers. She found no significant differences between mother and daughter attitudes about menstruation. In addition, she found no significant differences between the scores of mothers and their daughters on the Modified Moos Menstrual Distress Questionnaire. Cain studied mothers and daughters from different cultural backgrounds. She, too, reported that mothers and daughters hold similar beliefs about menstruation, and have similar symptom experiences with their menstrual cycle. Both Cain and Schick reported statistically significant support for Menke's model.

Thus, theoretical speculation and research data suggest that the acquisition of menstrual attitudes and beliefs may be partially explained by the identification of daughters with their mothers. While empirical validation of these postulates is limited, research findings suggest that a mother's attitudes and beliefs may significantly affect the menstrual experiences of her daughter.

Information concerning the importance and role of peers in terms of the adolescent menstrual experience is scarce. Both Koff et al. (1981) and Whisnant and Zegans (1975) found that whether or not to tell one's best friend about her menarche posed a dilemma for both pre- and postmenarcheal girls. In general, more pre- than post-menarcheal girls expected to tell about menarche; for post-menarcheal girls, menstruation was a private experience held secret from friends. In view of the close peer relationships that develop during adolescence, particularly among adolescent females (Sommer, 1978), and the large number of adolescents who identified close female friends as major sources of information about menstruation, it seems possible that peers may also have a significant influence on the adolescent menstrual experience.

The purpose of the study reported here was to examine the attitudes toward and beliefs about menstruation and symptoms experienced during menstruation of adolescent females 15–16 years old. Data was analyzed to determine whether the attitudes, beliefs and menstrual cycle symptoms experienced by these adolescents were more similar to those of family (mother), or those of peers (close girlfriends). Self-care practices during menstruation and communication practices regarding menstruation were also explored.

## HYPOTHESES

1. There will be no significant differences between adolescents and their mothers on measures of menstrual attitudes, beliefs, self-care practices, communication patterns, and symptom experiences.

2. There will be no significant differences between adolescents and their close girlfriends on measures of menstrual attitudes, beliefs, self-care practices, communication patterns, and symptom experiences.

3. There will be significantly less difference between adolescents and their mothers than between adolescents and their close girlfriends on measures of menstrual attitudes, beliefs, self-care practices, communication patterns, and symptom experiences.

## METHODOLOGY

### Procedure

Arrangements were made by the investigator with the school administration of a medium-sized suburban public high school to have access to the physical education classes for the purposes of volunteer recruitment. Criteria for subject selection were that each adolescent be between 15 and 16 years old, have experienced menarche, and experience menstrual cycles.

On the day of recruitment, the investigator breifly explained the study and selection criteria to female adolescents enrolled in the junior-senior physical education program at the high school. The adolescents were informed that their voluntary participation in the study involved a) completing two questionnaires and a participant data form, and returning them in a self-addressed, stamped envelope to the investigator; b) inviting her own mother and a close female friend of the same grade to participate in the study; c) distributing two questionnaires, a participant data form, and a letter of information to her own mother; and d) distributing four questionnaires, two participant data forms, and two letters of information to her chosen close girlfriend. The investigator then asked for volunteers. The first 40 adolescent volunteers who met the selection criteria were chosen to participate in the study.

Four questionnaire packets were distributed to each of the 40 volunteers by the investigator at the time of recruitment. Each packet contained a letter of information/consent, the Stoltzman Menstrual Questionnaire, the Modified Moos Menstrual Distress Questionnaire, a participant data form, and a self-addressed, stamped envelope. The investigator instructed each adolescent participant to distribute one questionnaire packet to her own mother and the other two questionnaire packets to her selected close girlfriends. Adolescent volunteers were requested to ask their close girlfriends to distribute a questionnaire packet to their mothers. All volunteers were instructed to complete their questionnaires independently (i.e., without conferring or comparing answers with other study participants). Participants returned their questionnaires to the investigator in the self-addressed, stamped envelopes provided. Consent was implied by the return of questionnaires and participant data forms to the investigator.

## Data Collection Tools

The Stoltzman Menstrual Questionnaire (SMQ) is a three-part instrument constructed for this study. It is designed to assess: a) attitudes toward and beliefs about menstruation, b) self-care activity and hygiene practices, and c) communication patterns surrounding the topic of menstruation. Information used to construct questionnaire items was obtained through a review of menstruation literature and a critique of existing tools that measured menstrual attitudes and beliefs. The questionnaire consists of 32 statements pertaining to menstrual attitudes and beliefs, 16 statements related to self-care practices, and 32 statements concerning menstrual communication patterns. The responses to these statements are set on a 5-point Likert scale that ranges from "strongly agree" to "strongly disagree." A mean overall score and several mean subscale scores were computed for each study participant who completed the questionnaire. Six health professionals, an educational psychologist, and a professor of women's studies critiqued this tool to establish face validity. The reliability coefficient (alpha) for the total scale in this study was .78. The coefficients for the attitudes/beliefs, self-care practices, and communication pattern subscales were .75, .79, and .79 respectively.

The Modified Moos Menstrual Distress Questionnaire (MDQ) is a 55-item instrument designed to assess affective and physical symptoms experienced during the menstrual cycle. The original Moos MDQ (1968, 1977) consisted of the 46 symptoms which through analysis has been categorized into the following subscales: pain, disturbance of concentration, behavioral decrements, autonomic nervous system imbalance, water retention, negative affect, arousal, and perpetuations of control. In 1979, Menke added an additional group of 8 symptoms to the test, labeled Positive Affect, thus bringing the total number of questionnaire items to 55, and the total number of symptom subscales to 9. Participants responded to each of these 55 items on a 6-point Likert scale that ranges from "no experience" of the symptom to an "acute or partially disabling" experience of the symptom during menstruation. One overall mean score and nine subscale mean scores were computed for each participant, indicating the intensity to which the symptoms were experienced during their most recent menstruation.

The participant data form was used to request demographic data from study subjects. Questions were formulated to include items identified in menstruation literature as potential influential variables regarding menstrual attitudes, beliefs, and symptom experiences.

## Analysis

Data analysis was accomplished using the Statistical Package for the Social Sciences (SPSS) computer program. Paired $t$-tests were used to compare the SMQ scores and Modified Moos MDQ scores of a) mother-daughter pairs and b) adolescent-close girlfriend pairs. Relationships between mother-daughter pairs and adolescent-close girlfriend pairs were determined by using an analysis of variance and Bonferonni's post hoc multiple comparison analysis. Demographic data were summarized with descriptive statistics.

## RESULTS

### Sample Description

The final study population consisted of 95 Caucasian females. Forty-nine of the subjects were adolescents divided into two groups: 30 adolescents initially recruited for the study and 19 close girlfriends of these adolescents. The average adolescent from both groups was 16 years old, had experienced menarche at age $12\frac{1}{2}$, and was in the 10th grade. The remaining 46 participants were the biological mothers of the adolescent subjects. Twenty-four were mothers of the adolescents initially recruited for the study and 22 were mothers of the close girlfriends. In general, mothers from both groups were 42–45 years old, started menses between the ages of 12 and 13, and averaged $13\frac{1}{2}$ years of education.

Demographic data were collected on all study participants. Most of the adolescents and their close girlfriends had lived with their mothers since birth. Family income ranged from below $15,000 to over $40,000 annually. While no one income group really described the total sample, the majority of participants reported an annual family income of over $20,000. Most of the study participants were employed; about one-half were Roman Catholic. None of the study participants reported use of oral contraceptives at the time of data collection except for one adolescent.

Menstrual cycle characteristics of subjects in all four groups were similar. Most study participants reported moderate to heavy menstrual flows of 3 to beyond 5 days duration every 28–35 days. Most were intermenstrual at the time of data collection.

### Experimental Hypothesis Testing

Hypothesis 1, predicting no significant differences between adolescents and their mothers on measures of menstrual attitudes, beliefs, self-care practices, communication patterns and symptom experiences, was only partially supported.

No significant differences were found between the overall scores of adolescents and their mothers, groups I and II (Table 1), or between the overall scores of the close girlfriend adolescents and their mothers, on the SMQ. There were, however, significant dif-

**Table 1. Paired *t*-Test Analysis of Stoltzman Menstrual Questionnaire Total Scores and Subscores by Group**

| Scale | Group I: Adolescents (N = 24) | | Group II: Mothers of adolescents (N = 24) | | Paired *t*-test | |
|---|---|---|---|---|---|---|
| | M | SD | M | SD | | |
| Overall (74 items) | 3.04 | 0.23 | 2.94 | 0.27 | t = 1.58 | (p = .129) |
| Subscale I: Attitudes and beliefs (29 items) | 3.01 | 0.24 | 2.70 | 0.34 | t = 3.77* | (p = .001) |
| Positive (6 items) | 2.70 | 0.57 | 2.98 | 0.39 | t = −2.11* | (p = .046) |
| Bothersome (6 items) | 3.75 | 0.62 | 3.20 | 0.54 | t = 3.12* | (p = .005) |
| Debilitating (7 items) | 3.05 | 0.40 | 2.60 | 0.64 | t = 2.93* | (p = .008) |
| Unsanitary (5 items) | 2.56 | 0.56 | 2.24 | 0.56 | t = 2.37* | (p = .026) |
| No sexual intercourse (5 items) | 2.86 | 0.70 | 2.45 | 0.76 | t = 2.21* | (p = .038) |
| Subscale II: Self-care practices (15 items) | 2.49 | 0.50 | 2.68 | 0.55 | t = −1.35 | (p = .190) |
| Activity (9 items) | 2.28 | 0.59 | 2.33 | 0.58 | t = −.34 | (p = .739) |
| Hygiene (6 items) | 2.82 | 0.61 | 3.16 | 0.67 | t = −2.22* | (p = .037) |
| Subscale III: Communication (30 items) | 3.37 | 0.40 | 3.28 | 0.34 | t = .93 | (p = .361) |
| Feelings about communication (17 items) | 3.40 | 0.42 | 3.46 | 0.39 | t = −.62 | (p = .539) |
| Practices of communication (13 items) | 3.33 | 0.45 | 3.05 | 0.39 | t = 2.38* | (p = .026) |

*Significant at $p < .05$.

ferences on several subscales. Data from SMQ suggests that menstruation was perceived as a slightly bothersome, debilitating and negative event by all four sample groups. Menstruation was not viewed as very unsanitary, and sexual intercourse during menstruation was considered acceptable. Additionally, the data suggest that study participants did not change their usual daily activities or routines when menstruating, and that all groups were slightly more concerned about personal hygiene during their menstrual periods. Although the total sample reported neutral to slightly positive feelings about discussing their menstrual periods with others, it appears that they engaged in more open communication about menstruation with members of the same sex of similar ages. Although there were no differences in overall SMQ scores, examination of Table 1 reveals significant differences between adolescents and their mothers on attitude and belief subscale scores, hygiene self-care subscale scores and communication patterns subscale scores. These differences suggest that adolescents were more likely to view menstruation as debilitating, bothersome, and unsanitary, and less likely to view it as a positive event than their mothers. They were less likely to be concerned about menstrual hygiene practices, but more likely to engage in open communication with others about menstruation than their mothers. These same trends were present between close girlfriend adolescents and their mothers, though not to a statistically significant degree.

The data from the modified Moos MDQ indicate that all four sample groups experienced subscale symptoms of pain, water retention, and negative affect during menstruation. Table 2 shows a significant difference ($p \leqslant .01$) between adolescents and their mothers on the overall scores and on three subscale scores suggesting that adolescents experienced menstrual symptoms of pain, water retention, and arousal more acutely than their mothers. This same trend was present, though not to a statistically significant degree, between the close girlfriend adolescents and their mothers.

Data from this study supported Hypothesis 2. No significant differences were found between adolescents and their close girlfriends on measures of menstrual attitudes, beliefs, self-care practices, communication patterns, or symptom experiences (Tables 3 and 4).

Hypothesis 3, that there will be significantly less difference between adolescents and their mothers than between adolescents and their close girlfriends on measures of menstrual attitudes, beliefs, self-care practices, communication patterns and symptom

**Table 2. Paired *t*-Test Analysis of Modified Moos Menstrual Distress Questionnaire Total Scores and Subscores by Group**

| Scale | Group I: Adolescents (N = 22) | | Group II: Mothers of adolescents (N = 22) | | Paired *t*-test | |
|---|---|---|---|---|---|---|
| | M | SD | M | SD | | |
| Overall (55 items) | 2.10 | 0.60 | 1.74 | 0.59 | t = 3.00* | (p = .007) |
| Subscale I: Positive affect (8 items) | 1.58 | 0.52 | 1.40 | 0.53 | t = 1.30 | (p = .209) |
| Subscale II: Concentration (8 items) | 1.45 | 0.62 | 1.34 | 0.60 | t = .92 | (p = .369) |
| Subscale III: Autonomic reactions (4 items) | 1.59 | 0.95 | 1.56 | 1.40 | t = .11 | (p = .917) |
| Subscale IV: Pain (6 items) | 3.27 | 0.87 | 2.34 | 0.81 | t = 4.46* | (p = .000) |
| Subscale V: Behavior changes (5 items) | 1.65 | 0.57 | 1.43 | 0.62 | t = 1.32 | (p = .202) |
| Subscale VI: Water retention (4 items) | 3.31 | 0.89 | 2.65 | 0.91 | t = 2.34* | (p = .029) |
| Subscale VII: Negative affect (8 items) | 2.74 | 1.17 | 2.32 | 0.93 | t = 1.75 | (p = .094) |
| Subscale VIII: Arousal (5 items) | 2.15 | 1.00 | 1.57 | 0.72 | t = 2.78* | (p = .011) |
| Subscale IX: Control (6 items) | 1.45 | 0.60 | 1.41 | 0.82 | t = .24 | (p = .816) |

*Significant at $p \leq .05$.

107

**Table 3. Paired *t*-Test Analysis of Stoltzman Menstrual Questionnaire Total Scores and Subscores by Group**

| Scale | Group I: Adolescents (N = 17) | | Group III: Close friend adolescents (N = 17) | | Paired *t*-Test | |
|---|---|---|---|---|---|---|
| | M | SD | M | SD | | |
| Overall (74 items) | 3.02 | 0.26 | 2.99 | 0.15 | $t = .44$ | $(p = .668)$ |
| Subscale I: Attitudes and beliefs (29 items) | 3.00 | 0.25 | 2.91 | 0.30 | $t = 1.01$ | $(p = .326)$ |
| Positive (6 items) | 2.68 | 0.54 | 2.62 | 0.65 | $t = .32$ | $(p = .753)$ |
| Bothersome (6 items) | 3.86 | 0.57 | 3.64 | 0.88 | $t = .72$ | $(p = .479)$ |
| Debilitating (7 items) | 3.06 | 0.42 | 2.75 | 0.61 | $t = 1.64$ | $(p = .120)$ |
| Unsanitary (5 items) | 2.36 | 0.55 | 2.56 | 0.72 | $t = -.87$ | $(p = .398)$ |
| No sexual intercourse (5 items) | 2.86 | 0.69 | 2.96 | 0.62 | $t = -.54$ | $(p = .600)$ |
| Subscale II: Self-care practices (15 items) | 2.40 | 0.50 | 2.66 | 0.38 | $t = -2.05$ | $(p = .06)$ |
| Activity (9 items) | 2.19 | 0.62 | 2.39 | 0.62 | $t = -.94$ | $(p = .359)$ |
| Hygiene (6 items) | 2.72 | 0.61 | 3.09 | 0.45 | $t = -2.39*$ | $(p = .029)$ |
| Subscale III: Communication (30 items) | 3.35 | 0.42 | 3.24 | 0.37 | $t = .89$ | $(p = .387)$ |
| Feelings about communication (17 items) | 3.40 | 0.44 | 3.26 | 0.49 | $t = .98$ | $(p = .343)$ |
| Practices of communication (13 items) | 3.28 | 0.48 | 3.18 | 0.35 | $t = .64$ | $(p = .530)$ |

*Significant at $p \leqslant .05$.

Table 4. Paired *t*-Test Analysis of Modified Moos Menstrual Distress Questionnaire Total Scores and Subscores by Group

| Scale | Group I: Adolescents (N = 17) | | Group III: Close friend adolescents (N = 17) | | Paired *t*-Test | |
|---|---|---|---|---|---|---|
| | M | SD | M | SD | | |
| Overall (55 items) | 2.08 | 0.63 | 1.99 | 0.49 | $t = .55$ | $(p = .591)$ |
| Subscale I: Positive affect (8 items) | 1.58 | 0.53 | 1.42 | 0.50 | $t = 1.14$ | $(p = .270)$ |
| Subscale II: Concentration (8 items) | 1.46 | 0.45 | 1.53 | 0.42 | $t = -.66$ | $(p = .519)$ |
| Subscale III: Autonomic reactions (4 items) | 1.74 | 1.31 | 1.73 | 1.25 | $t = .02$ | $(p = .987)$ |
| Subscale IV: Pain (6 items) | 3.26 | 0.93 | 2.99 | 1.043 | $t = 1.04$ | $(p = .313)$ |
| Subscale V: Behavior changes (5 items) | 1.68 | 0.68 | 1.92 | 0.82 | $t = -1.03$ | $(p = .313)$ |
| Subscale VI: Water retention (4 items) | 3.42 | 0.84 | 2.94 | 1.00 | $t = 1.44$ | $(p = .168)$ |
| Subscale VII: Negative affect (8 items) | 2.59 | 1.23 | 2.61 | 0.93 | $t = -.05$ | $(p = .958)$ |
| Subscale VIII: Arousal (5 items) | 2.02 | 1.07 | 1.66 | 0.85 | $t = 1.47$ | $(p = .162)$ |
| Subscale IX: Control (6 items) | 1.39 | 0.61 | 1.44 | 0.68 | $t = -.22$ | $(p = .832)$ |

*Significant at $p \leqslant .05$.

experiences, was not supported. An analysis of variance for a randomized complete block design tested this hypothesis, using only data from the 13 complete sets* of participants. A significant difference was found between the four groups on the SMQ subscale I—Attitudes and Beliefs—($p \leqslant .05$, F = 4.39) and on the overall score for the MDQ ($p \leqslant .05$, F = 3.17). Post hoc analysis of subscale I scores for the SMQ using Bonferonni's multiple comparison tests showed significant differences between the adolescents (group I) and their mothers (group II) and between the adolescents and the mothers of close girlfriend adolescents (group IV). A significant difference was also found between adolescents and their mothers on overall scores for the Modified Moos, MDQ. These findings seem to indicate that a generational difference exists between adolescents and their mothers on menstrual attitudes, beliefs, and symptom experiences. However, no significant differences were found between close girlfriend adolescents and their mothers (group III, IV) or between close girlfriend adolescents and the mothers of the adolescents in group I. Thus, the study data only partially supports this observation.

## DISCUSSION

Considering theories about the development of sex role identity among pubescent females and previous studies by Cain (1980) and Schick (1980), one would expect mothers and daughters to hold similar attitudes toward and beliefs about menstruation and to experience similar menstrual cycle symptoms. Results of this study, however, suggest that mothers and daughters may have different perceptions about menstruation. The unexpected findings of this study suggest that adolescents are more similar to their close girlfriends than to their mothers on measures of menstrual attitudes, beliefs, and menstrual cycle symptom experiences.

One explanation for the generational differences revealed in this study may be found by considering the influences of developmental stage and life experiences. Social learning theorists suggest that attitudes, beliefs, and behaviors are learned responses, reflecting one's actual life experiences (Bandura, Ross, & Ross, 1971). Initially, perceptions of new life events may be determined by expectations that have been learned through the observation and teachings of significant others; however, these perceptions may change with

---

*Set = an adolescent, her mother, her close girlfriend, and her close girlfriend's mother.

subsequent personal experiences (Peterson, 1980). It may be that the menstrual attitudes, beliefs, and cycle-related symptoms reported by the adolescent daughters of this study reflected their reactions to and perceptions of a relatively new life event—an event with which they had little experience. In contrast, the reports of the mothers participating in the study may in large part reflect long personal experience with menstruation. The adolescent participants may be more vulnerable to societal taboos and negative stereotypic beliefs about menstruation, due to their limited experience with menstrual cycles. In comparison with their mothers, adolescent deaughters have had fewer opportunities to experience and evaluate menstrual discomforts; their assessment of cycle-related symptoms may have been strongly influenced by what they expected to feel. In other words, the retrospective self-reports of menstrual symptoms for the adolescents in this study may more closely represent their expectations than their actual experiences. Adolescents may expect to feel acute menstrual discomforts because of their perceptions of societal taboos and media messages which imply that menstruation is often painful and debilitating. While mothers may receive the same negative messages about menstruation, they may perceive the implications of these messages differently; experiences with life events in general and with the menstrual cycle in particular may make menstrual taboos less influential during adulthood. It is also conceivable that mothers of adolescent females may sense the responsibility to model more realistic and positive views of the menstrual cycle for their daughters. Mothers' responses may reflect not only their more extensive experience with menstruation, but also a heightened consciousness of their importance as role models for their adolescent daughters. Thus, a female's perceptions about menstruation prior to menarche and during adolescence may not be the same ones she holds as an adult. Menstrual attitudes, beliefs, and symptom experiences may change throughout a woman's life, reflecting her recurring experiences of the menstrual cycle and, perhaps, other significant life events and experiences (e.g., childbirth, motherhood).

Considering the relatively complex and highly emotional impact of menarche and recurring menstrual cycles (Brooks-Gunn & Matthews, 1981; Whisnant & Zegans, 1975), both cognitive and psychoanalytic approaches to growth and development may provide additional insights into the study results. For example, the differences between mothers and daughters might be explained by considering the development of cognition; mothers' responses may reflect more formalized thought processes and a greater ability to conceptualize abstract ideas. Thus, the adult women in this study may have had different definitions and perceptions of relatively abstract terms (such as "pain") than their adolescent daughters. Mothers may view menstruation in a broad and relatively abstract sense, linking it to other aspects of sexuality and gender identity (e.g., potential motherhood), while adolescents, on the other hand, may view the menstrual experience from a concrete and somewhat limited level, focusing on the concerns of hygiene and on potential activity restrictions (Koff et al., 1981). The affective and emotional aspects of growth and development may also account for some of the differences observed in the study. Responses of the adolescents may reflect ambivalent feelings toward their developing sexuality and toward the inevitable physical and social changes that accompany the onset of menstruation. It is possible that the somewhat negative attitudes and beliefs of the adolescents in this study reflect feelings of resentment, confusion, fear, and uncertainty about the significance of menstruation. These feelings may diminish as a woman grows into adulthood and develops a sense of self identity that incorporates her menstrual cycle experience.

It is also possible that adolescents' reports of more acute menstrual distress may be explained by menstrual cycle physiology. Some investigators have asserted that the relatively unstable and unpredictable hormone shifts that occur during puberty may predispose adolescent females to more menstrual cycle symptoms than adult females (Dickey, 1976).

Factors such as parity and use of oral contraceptives may affect the amount and degree of cycle-related symptoms; after childbirth women have reported significantly less dysmenorrhea and other menstrual discomforts (Moos, 1978; Paige, 1976). If the retrospective self-reports of the females in this study are taken at face falue, the data partially support these observations. About two-thirds of the adolescent participants reported significantly more acute menstrual symptoms than their mothers. It is a reasonable speculation that painful or uncomfortable menstrual cycles are likely to generate somewhat negative attitudes toward menstruation; thus, acute cycle-related symptoms may, in part, account for the adolescent participants' attitudes toward and beliefs about menstruation.

In addition to the influences of socialization, developmental stage, and menstrual cycle physiology, the contradiction between this study and other studies reported in the literature may be explained by differences in data collection instruments, differences in methodology, and a nonrepresentative sample of mother-daughter dyads.

## SUMMARY

In summary, the females who participated in this study perceived menstruation as slightly bothersome, debilitating, and negative. They reported mild to moderate menstrual symptoms of pain, water retention, arousal, and negative affect. Partial support for generational differences was revealed through comparison of mother and daughter responses to both the SMQ and the Modified Moos MDQ. Adolescent daughters were more likely to view menstruation as debilitating, bothersome, and unsanitary, and less likely to view it as a positive event than their mothers. These adolescents reported significantly more acute pain, water retention, and arousal symptoms than their mothers. This investigation, limited by virtue of sample homogeneity and nonstandardized research instruments, nevertheless points to significant questions in the area of menstrual cycle research. Considering the differences between mothers and daughters revealed in this study, future investigators should continue to explore the influence of developmental stage on the menstrual experiences of women.

## REFERENCES

Bandura, A., Ross, D., & Ross, S. (1971). A comparative test of the status envy, social power and secondary reinforcement theories of identificatory learning. In A. G. Thompson (Ed.), *Social development and personality*. New York: Wiley.

Brooks-Gunn, J., & Matthews, S. W. (1979). *He and she: How children develop their sex-role identity*. New Jersey: Prentice-Hall.

Brooks-Gunn, J., & Ruble, D. (1980a). Menarche: The interaction of physiological, cultural, and social factors. In A. J. Dan, E. A. Graham, & C. P. Beecher (Eds.), *The menstrual cycle, Vol. I. A synthesis of interdisciplinary research*. New York: Springer.

Brooks-Gunn, J., & Ruble, D. (1980b). The menstrual attitude questionnaire. *Psychomatic Medicine, 42*(5), 503–512.

Cain, L. B. (1980). *A study of mother and daughter attitudes and beliefs regarding menstruation*. Unpublished thesis, Ohio State University.

Clarke, A. E., & Ruble, D. (1978). Young adolescents' beliefs concerning menstruation. *Child Development, 49*, 201–234.

Dalton, K. (1964). *The premenstrual syndrome*. Springfield, Illinois: Charles C Thomas.

Delaney, J., Lupton, M., & Toth, E. (1976). *The curse: A cultural history of menstruation*. New York: Dutton.

Deutsh, H. (1944). *The psychology of women: Volume I–Girlhood.* New York: Grune & Stratton.

Dickey, R. P. (1976). Menstrual problems of the adolescent. *Post Graduate Medicine, 60*(4), 183–187.

Friday, N. (1977). *My mother, my self.* New York: Delacorte Press.

Golub, S., & E. Harrington, D. M. (1981). Premenstrual and menstrual mood changes in adolescent women. *Journal of Perspective Social Psychology, 41*(5), 961–965.

Haft, M. H. (1973). *An explanatory study of early adolescent girls: Body image, self acceptance, acceptance of traditional female roles, and response to menstruation.* Unpublished manuscript, Columbia University, New York.

Hammer, S. (1975). *Daughters and mothers; Mothers and daughters.* New York: New York Times Books Co.

Koff, E., Rierdon, J., & Jacobson, S. (1978). Changes in representation of body image as a function of menarchial status. *Developmental Psychology 14,* 635–642.

Martin, L. L. (1978). *Health care of women.* Philadelphia: J. B. Lippincott.

Menke, E. (1979). *Mothers and daughters: Menstrual beliefs and attitudes.* Unpublished manuscript, Ohio State University, Ohio.

Moos, R. H. (1968). The development of a menstrual distress questionnaire. *Psychosomatic Medicine, 30,* 853–862.

Moos, R. H. (1977). *Menstrual distress questionnaire manual.* Palo Alto, California: Stanford University, March, 1977.

Moos, R. H., & Liedermann, D. B. (1978). Toward a menstrual cycle symptomatology. *Journal of Psychosomatic Research, 22,* 31–40.

Paige, K. E. (1976). Women learn to sing the menstrual blues. *Psychology Today, 7,* 41–46.

Peterson, A. C. (1980). Puberty and its psychological significance in girls. In A. J. Dan, E. A. Graham, & C. P. Beecher (Eds.), *The menstrual cycle, Vol. I. A synthesis of interdisciplinary research.* New York: Springer.

Schick, C. (1980). *A descriptive study of menstrual beliefs and experiences of mother-daughter dyads.* Unpublished thesis, Ohio State University.

Sommer, B. (1978). *Puberty and adolescence.* New York: Oxford University Press.

Weideger, P. (1976). *Menstruation and menopause: The physiology and psychology, the myth and the reality.* New York: Knopf.

Whisnant, L., & Zegans, L. (1975). A study of attitudes toward menarche in white middle-class American girls. *American Journal of Psychiatry, 132,* 809–814.

# SOCIALIZATION AND SOCIAL CONTEXT: INFLUENCE ON PERIMENSTRUAL SYMPTOMS, DISABILITY, AND MENSTRUAL ATTITUDES

Nancy Fugate Woods, RN, PhD, FAAN

Department of Parent-Child Nursing, University of Washington, Seattle, Washington

The purpose of this study was to examine the effects of socialization and exposure to a stressful milieu on women's experiences of perimenstrual symptoms, related disability, and menstrual attitudes. Women ($N = 179$) from 18 to 35 years of age were interviewed using the Index of Sex Role Orientation, Schedule of Recent Events, Moos Menstrual Distress Questionnaire, and Menstrual Attitudes Questionnaire. Path analysis was used to assess models based on Mechanic's concept of illness behavior for negative affect, pain and water retention symptoms during the perimenstruum. Exposure to a stressful milieu was useful in explaining cyclic, recurrent symptoms. Socialization and exposure to a stressful milieu were more useful in explaining negative affect than pain or water retention symptoms. Socialization and exposure to a stressful milieu are not as important in understanding disability as is the severity of symptoms, but socialization influences menstrual attitudes.

Many women experience symptoms immediately before and during menstruation including cramps, backache, headache, weight gain, painful or tender breasts, swelling, irritability, mood swings, depression, tension, anxiety, and fatigue. Thirty to fifty percent of menstruating women experience mild or moderate symptoms and 10-20 percent experience severe and disabling symptoms (Woods, Most, & Dery, 1982). Some investigators attribute school or work

This work was supported by grants from Sigma Theta Tau and BRSG S07 RR05758 awarded by the Biomedical Research Support Grant Program, Division of Research Resources, National Institutes of Health.

The assistance of Gretchen Dery and Ada Most in the earlier phases of this project is gratefully acknowledged.

absence to perimenstrual symptoms (PS) (Bergsjo, 1978), and some report that these symptoms frequently cause women to seek medical care (National Center for Health Statistics, 1981).

Variability of perimenstrual symptomatology occurs in both the variety of symptoms women experience and in the large variation in the prevalence of these symptoms across different populations (Ferguson & Vermillion, 1957; Pennington, 1957; Schucket, Daly, Herman, & Heinman, 1975; Moos, 1968; Tomonen & Procope, 1971; Sheldrake & Cormack, 1976; Bergsjo, 1975; Taylor, 1979; Van Keep, 1979; Woods, Most, & Dery, 1982; O'Rourke, 1983). Whether variability in the prevalence of PS can be attributed to variability in age, parity, or other demographic characteristics of the populations studied, to variation in research methods, or to variation in the processes that influence women's perceptions of and response to symptoms is unclear.

Biological explanations for PS include evidence linking prosta-glandins, particularly $PGF2\alpha$ to menstrual cramps, as well as to other systemic symptoms such as backache, nausea, vomiting, diarrhea, headache, tiredness, nervousness, and dizziness. How-ever, women with apparently normal $PGF2\alpha$ synthesis are not universally effective (Chan, Dawood, & Fuchs, 1981). Some in-vestigators are exploring the role of prolactin and vasopressin in producing symptoms (Carroll & Steiner, 1978; Backstrom & Aak-waag, 1981; Andersch & Hahn, 1981; Reed & Yen, 1981; Akerlund, Stromberg, & Forsling, 1979).

Other investigators believe that the autonomic nervous system may mediate perimenstrual symptoms. Some have found no menstrual cycle phase differences in catecholamine excretion (adrenaline and noradrenaline), skin conductance, heart rate, and respiratory rate (Slade & Jenner, 1979; Patkai, Johannsen, & Post, 1974) while others find higher or lower levels of ANS arousal in the premenstrual phase (Asso & Beach, 1975; Little & Zahn, 1974).

Psychoanalytic formulations suggest that PS are the result of inability to accept one's femininity (Shainess, 1961; Berry & McGuire, 1972), but contemporary theories relate the influence of individual expectations about menstruation (Brooks, Ruble, & Clarke, 1977), and feminine socialization (Paige, 1973) to PS. Others suggest that exposure to a stressful environment (Wilcoxon, Schrader, & Sherif, 1966; Siegel, Johnson, & Sarason, 1979; Woods, Dery, & Most, 1982) either exacerbates or causes PS. The prevalence of symptoms (Janiger, Reffenbergh, & Kersch, 1972; Most, Woods, & Dery, 1982) varies across ethnic groups, but little effort has been devoted to exploring how ethnicity influences PS. Most literature on PS addresses the pathophysiological origins of PS and personal and social factors that might exacerbate underlying physiologic changes during the perimenstruum.

The conceptual framework guiding this study focuses on PS as "symptoms" rather than disease, and emphasizes understanding women's responses to PS from the perspection of illness behavior. Illness behavior is the process of perceiving, evaluating, and responding to symptoms. The goal of this study is to extend understanding of the influence of two aspects of the social environment on individuals' adaptation to cyclic, recurring symptoms of varying types. Mechanic (1962, 1980) found that individuals' definitions of illness are shaped by bodily sensations which one labels as symptoms, hypotheses about what the individual is feeling, and environmental influences, particularly the stressful nature of the environment.

Each month some women perceive bodily sensations that occur concurrently with the menstrual cycle. Some women may find these bodily sensations evoke no distress whereas others may perceive them as unpleasant or disruptive and label them symptoms. A complex set of factors influences whether women label bodily sensations as symptoms, how they label them and the way in which they respond to them. The cognitive definitions women apply to their situations are influenced by the culture which conveys to women, through socialization processes, what to expect about menstruation and related symptoms. Common beliefs about menstruation and its effects on women's lives and what aspects of behavior to attribute to menstruation. A woman's exposure to cultural norms about women, health in general, and menstruation in particular, contributes to these cognitions (Ruble & Brooks-Gunn, 1979). Women with traditional attitudes about women and their roles report more symptoms of mental ill health and psychosomatic disorder than their counterparts with less traditional attitudes (Levy, 1976; Nathanson, 1975; Woods, 1985). Thus, it seems that women with traditional conceptions about the feminine role would be more inclined to perceive and report symptoms related to menstruation and to have more negative attitudes toward menstruation than their counterparts.

Exposure to a stressful social environment is also associated with the incidence of PS (Wilcoxon, Schrader, & Sherif, 1976; Woods, Most, & Dery, 1982; Siegel, Johnson, & Sarason, 1979). Moreover, exposure to a stressful milieu is also likely to predispose women to negative attitudes toward menstruation.

Response to symptoms is based on evaluation of the nature of the symptoms in terms of their presumed causality, treatability and likely prognosis against standards of the culture. Severity of the symptoms is evaluated on the basis of factors such as associated physical manifestations, the ability to conceal the symptom and familiarity of the condition. Responses to symptoms may include altering activity by going to bed or resting, engaging in self care such as use of over-the-counter drugs, seeking help or advice from a lay person, seeking help from a health professional or ignoring the symptoms. Socialization and the current social environment should also influence women's responses to symptoms, including the amount of disability they experience and their attitudes toward menstruation.

Mechanic's model of illness behavior has been tested with individuals who are experiencing acute, time-limited episodes of illness or chronic symptoms. To date, this model has not been tested with cyclic, recurring symptoms such as those occurring during the perimenstruum. Moreover, the utility of the model for explaining specific groups of symptoms has not been considered in previous studies.

The purpose of this study was to assess the extent to which the woman's environment and socialization influenced her experience of three types of PS, related disability and menstrual attitudes. We hypothesized that socialization to a traditional conception of the feminine role and exposure to a stressful life context would be positively associated with PS, particularly negative affect symptoms. We also hypothesized that traditional socialization would influence women's attitudes toward menstruation, but that these attitudes would also be affected by the symptoms themselves, and the amount of disability related to PS. We further hypothesized that perimenstrual disability would be a function of the PS, themselves.

## METHODS

We studied a population of women residing in five southeastern city neighborhoods which afforded variation in race and socioeconomic status. Each woman living in these neighborhoods who was 18 to 35 years of age, not pregnant at the time of interview, and who had not had a hysterectomy was identified. Of 650 households there were 241 potential participants and 179 (74%) agreed to participate in the study.

### Measures

We used the Moos Menstrual Distress Questionnaire (MDQ) which has been commonly used to document the presence and severity of symptoms associated with menstruation. The MDQ contains 47 symptoms attributed to the perimenstruum such as weight gain and insomnia. Women were asked to report their perceptions of each of the symptoms for 1) their most recent flow, 2) the week before their most recent flow, and 3) the remainder of the cycle. They were asked to use a rating scale in which responses range from 1 for "no experience of the symptom" to 6 for "acute or partially disabling."

We reasoned that for a symptom to be related to the perimenstruum it should differ in frequency and severity across cycle phases, being exacerbated during the perimenstruum. Of the symptoms on the Moos Menstrual Distress Questionnaire, only 16 differed significantly across cycle phase ($p < .01$) and had a mean difference of $<0.3$ (one-third of one unit on the MDQ scale). These 16 symptoms were grouped into four factors: pain, negative affect, water retention and impaired performance. The fourth factor contains items that reflect responses to symptoms such as, stayed home from work or school. In the following analyses the first three factors are considered for the entire perimenstruum, combining scores for both the premenstruum and the menstruum. Earlier analyses revealed few significant differences in premenstrual and menstrual symptom intensity and high correlation of symptom ratings across these cycle phases (Woods, Most, & Dery, 1982).

## Disability

We employed two MDQ items as indicators of disability: "lowered work or school performance" and "take naps or rest in bed." The premenstrual and menstrual scores on these items were summed and used as a single indicator of perimenstrual disability.

## Stressful Environment

We employed the 42-item Schedule of Recent Events as an indicator of a stressful environment. The Schedule of Recent Events (Holmes & Rahe, 1967) consists of items commonly judged to be stressful. The weighted score reflects the number and gravity of life events. We eliminated 2 items because of their inappropriateness in this population: wife beginning or ceasing work and retirement from work. Items related to personal illness and pregnancy were omitted due to their confounding effects on PS (Woods, Dery, & Most, 1982).

## Socialization

We employed the Index of Sex Role Orientation, a 16-item scale that differentiates women with a traditional role orientation from those with a more modern role orientation (Dreyer, Woods, & James, 1981). Items reflect female-male division of household labor, employment, family conflicts and women's work roles outside the home. The ISRO is internally consistent (alpha = .9) and reliable in a one-month retest trial.

## Menstrual Attitudes

We used one of the scales from the Menstrual Attitudes Questionnaire (Brooks, Gunn, & Ruble, 1980) as an indicator of women's attitudes toward menstruation. The Debilitation Scale consists of 12 items related to viewing menstruation as debilitating, such as, "Women are more tired than usual when they are menstruating." Internal consistency of the debilitation scale was high (alpha = .82).

## Analysis

We employed path analysis (SPSS Regression Procedure) to test the proposed relationships between stressful milieu, socialization, age, menstrual attitudes and disability for three groups of symptoms: negative affect, pain, and water retention.

## Participants

Most participants were in their late 20s and early 30s, married, white, employed and had an annual family income of $15,000–$20,000 (Table 1). Half of the women had been pregnant. Twenty-four percent used oral contraceptives and 12 percent used an IUD. The mean menstrual cycle length was 28.6 days (±4) with a mean of 4.7 (±1) days of flow.

## Stressful Environment, Socialization

The mean SRE score is 220 ± 147 with the highest score being 737 of a possible 1,374. The average ISRO score was 65 ± 8.7, on the modern end of the continuum and 3 points less than the cut point used to discriminate between traditional and modern norms.

Table 1. Characteristics of the Participants ($N = 179$)

| Characteristic | Frequency | Percentage |
|---|---|---|
| Age | | |
| 18–20 | 10 | 5 |
| 21–25 | 53 | 30 |
| 26–30 | 59 | 33 |
| 31+ | 57 | 32 |
| Marital status | | |
| Married | 105 | 59 |
| Single | 57 | 32 |
| Divorced | 9 | 5 |
| Separated | 6 | 3 |
| Living with a partner | 2 | 1 |
| Race | | |
| White | 120 | 67 |
| Black | 59 | 33 |
| Employed | | |
| Yes | 145 | 82 |
| No | 31 | 18 |
| Status of nonemployed | | |
| Students | 14 | 45 |
| Homemakers | 17 | 55 |
| Annual family income | | |
| to $2,000 | 1 | 1 |
| 2,000–3,999 | 7 | 4 |
| 4,000–6,999 | 5 | 3 |
| 7,000–9,999 | 21 | 12 |
| 10,000–14,999 | 26 | 15 |
| 15,000–19,999 | 22 | 13 |
| 20,000–24,999 | 27 | 16 |
| 25,000–29,999 | 32 | 19 |
| 30,000–39,999 | 21 | 12 |
| 40,000 or more | 9 | 5 |
| Educational level | | |
| Junior high or some high school | 4 | 2 |
| High school graduate | 17 | 10 |
| Some technical school or college | 50 | 28 |
| College graduate | 72 | 40 |
| Graduate degree | 35 | 20 |
| Religion | | |
| Protestant | 116 | 65 |
| Catholic | 19 | 11 |
| Jewish | 4 | 2 |
| Other | 13 | 7 |
| None | 27 | 15 |

Table 1. Characteristics of the Participants ($N = 179$) (*Continued*)

| Characteristic | Frequency | Percentage |
|---|---|---|
| Children | | |
| Yes | 78 | 44 |
| No | 101 | 56 |
| Pregnancy history | | |
| Positive | 88 | 49 |
| Negative | 91 | 51 |

## Perimenstrual Symptoms

Perimenstrual negative affect, water retention, and pain scores ranged from absent (1) to disabling (6). Means and standard deviations for each scale were negative affect, 2.2 ± .80; water retention, 2.2 ± .86; pain, 2.1 ± .85. These scores indicate that symptoms were, on the average, barely noticeable to mild.

## Disability and Menstrual Attitudes

Perimenstrual disability scores were rated from absent (1) to severe (6), with a mean of 3.2 ± 1.51. These scores reflect low average disability. The menstrual attitudes scale scores (Debilitation) reflected women's slight disagreement that menstruation was disabling ($X = 4.09 ± 10.0$).

## Models of Perimenstrual Symptoms, Disability, and Attitudes

Simple correlations for all variables are given in the matrix in Table 2. Stressful life events (STR) are positively related to negative affect (NA) whereas nontraditional socialization (SOC) is negatively related to menstrual attitudes as reflected in MAQ scores measuring debilitation (DE). Women who score high on one symptom scale tend to score high on the others (PP, NA, and WR are all significantly correlated). Perimenstrual pain and negative affect are positively related to disability (DI) and debilitation scores, whereas water retention is unrelated to either.

The influence of socialization, stressful milieu, and age on negative affect, disability and negative attitudes toward menstruation was examined first. As seen in Figure 1, women with a very stressful milieu (high SRE scores) reported the most severe negative affect

Table 2. Association between Stressful Life Events, Feminine Socialization, Perimenstrual Symptoms, Disability and Menstrual Attitudes; Pearson's R

| Variable | STR | SOC | PP | NA | WR | DI | DE |
|---|---|---|---|---|---|---|---|
| Stressful life events (STR) | (.78)* | | | | | | |
| Feminine socialization (SOC) | −.004 | (.90) | | | | | |
| Perimenstrual pain (PP) | .048 | −.005 | (.67) | | | | |
| Negative affect (NA) | .221** | .117 | .502** | (.86) | | | |
| Water retention (WR) | .134 | −.009 | .393** | .358** | (.66) | | |
| Disability (DI) | .100 | −.061 | .284** | .419** | .181 | — | |
| Menstrual attitudes (Debilitation) (DE) | .165 | −.265** | .333** | .461** | .202 | .489** | (.82) |

*Alphas are given in parentheses for scales.

**$p < .05$.

*Note.* $N = 153$; complete data were available from 153 participants.

123

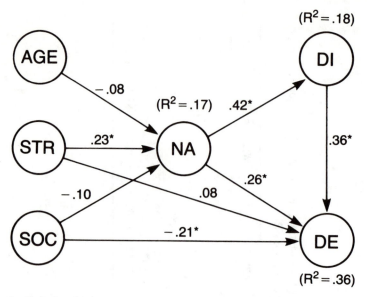

Fig. 1. Relationship between stressful milieu, socialization, age, perimenstrual negative affect, and viewing menstruation as debilitating. (All path coefficients are standardized beta weights.)

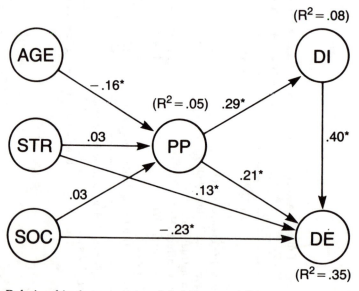

Fig. 2. Relationship between stressful milieu, socialization, age, perimenstrual pain, and viewing menstruation as debilitating. (All path coefficients are standardized beta weights.)

symptoms (NA). Women with more traditional socialization (SOC) were significantly more likely to see menstruation as debilitating (DE). Negative affect symptoms were related to greater disability (DI) and also to attitudes toward menstruation as debilitating (DE). Women with more severe negative affect (NA) and more disability (DI) had more negative attitudes toward menstruation (DE).

As seen in Figure 2, there was little influence of SOC or STR on perimenstrual pain (PP) but age was significantly associated with perimenstrual pain. Pain had a significant influence on disability and, along with disability and nontraditional socialization, had a negative influence on women's attitudes toward menstruation. A stressful environment was positively associated with viewing menstruation as debilitating.

As seen in Fig. 3, the influence of water retention symptoms on disability was significant, but modest. Instead, socialization and disability had a significant influence on attitudes.

## DISCUSSION

Although exposure to a stressful social milieu had a significant influence on perimenstrual negative affect symptoms, its influence

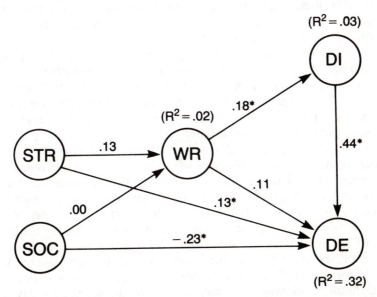

Fig. 3. Relationship between stressful milieu, socialization, age, water retention, and viewing menstruation as debilitating. (All path coefficients are standardized beta weights.)

on perimenstrual pain and water retention was not significant. Socialization did not influence the experience of any category of symptoms, but did influence women's attitudes toward menstruation as did the experience of pain or negative affect symptoms and the disability they experienced. Negative affect symptoms, pain, and water retention all significantly affected disability. Perimenstrual disability had a stronger effect on menstrual attitudes than did any of the symptoms, socialization, or stress.

The models examined here suggest that socialization plays a minor role in explaining severity of perimenstrual symptoms. On the other hand, women who have been socialized to traditional views about women's roles and place in society see menstruation as more debilitating than their nontraditional counterparts. Socialization does not have an important effect on disability. Instead, each group of symptoms has a significant effect on disability. These findings are in conflict with literature linking feminine socialization to symptom reporting (Gunn, 1972; Levy, 1976; Nathanson, 1975; Woods, in press); however, other investigators have examined the influence of socialization on symptoms in general, and this investigation was restricted to only those symptoms of which significant menstrual cycle phase variability was demonstrated. The influence of a stressful social milieu was an important predictor for negative affect symptoms, but had only a minor effect on water retention and little effect on pain symptoms.

Of all the symptom clusters, negative affect was most influential with respect to disability. It is interesting that negative affect was more disruptive than pain symptoms, despite the fact that dysmenorrhea is strongly linked to decreased productivity, absenteeism from work and school and use of medical care (Bergsjo, 1978; National Center for Health Statistics, 1981).

Both negative affect and pain symptoms had important effects on menstrual attitudes. Women who were more symptomatic had more negative attitudes. Thus it appears that menstrual attitudes are not merely a product of socialization but also a function of women's experiences with symptoms that disrupt their lives. Women who believe that menstruation is debilitating do so not only because of their attitudes about women's lot but also because of their lived experiences with painful, disruptive symptoms. Water retention symptoms, which seem to have little effect on disability, are not influential in women's menstrual attitudes. Apparently these symptoms are not sufficiently troublesome to affect women's usual activities or their attitudes.

Elements of Mechanic's model of illness behavior, primarily

exposure to a stressful milieu, have some utility in explaining cyclic, recurrent symptoms. The model seems more useful in understanding negative affect than pain or water retention symptoms. Socialization and exposure to a stressful milieu are not as important in understanding disability as is the severity of the symptom, but both variables may help explain menstrual attitudes.

## REFERENCES

Akerlund, M., P. Stromberg, & M. Forsling. (1979). Primary dysmenorrhea and vasopressin. *British Journal of Obstetrics and Gynecology, 86,* 484–487.

Andersch, R., & L. Hahn. (1982). Bromocriptine and premenstrual tension: A clinical and hormonal study. *Pharmatherapeutica, 3,* 107–113.

Asso, D., & H. Beach. (1975). Susceptibility to the acquisition of a conditioned response in relation to the menstrual cycle. *Journal of Psychosomatic Research, 19,* 337–344.

Backstrom, T., & A. Aakvaag. (1981). Plasma prolactin and testosterone during the luteal phase in women with premenstrual tension syndrome. *Psychoneuroendocrinology, 6,* 245–251.

Bergsjo, P., H. Jenssen, & O. Vellar. (1975). Dysmenorhea in industrial workers. *Acta Obstetrica Gynecologica Scandinavica, 64,* 355–359.

Bergsjo, P. (1978). Socioeconomic implications of dysmenorrhea. *Acta Obstetrica Gynecologica Scandinavica, 87,* 67–68.

Berry, C., & F. McGuire. (1972). Menstrual distress and acceptance of sex role. *American Journal of Obstetrics and Gynecology, 114,* 83–87.

Brooks, J., D. Ruble, & A. Clarke. (1977). College women's attitudes and expectations concerning menstrual related changes. *Psychosomatic Medicine, 39*(5), 288–298.

Brooks, J., D. Ruble, & A. Clarke. (1977). The menstrual attitude questionnaire. *Psychosomatic Medicine, 42,* 503–512.

Carroll, B., & M. Steiner. (1978). The psychobiology of premenstrual dysphoria: The role of prolactin. *Psychoneuroendocrinology, 3,* 171–189.

Chan, W., M. Dawood, & F. Fuchs. (1981). Prostaglandins in primary dysmenorrhea. *American Journal of Medicine, 70,* 535–541.

Chan, W., M. Dawood, & F. Fuchs. (1979). Relief of dysmenorrhea with the prostaglandin synthetase inhibitor ibuprofen: Effect of prostaglandin levels in menstrual fluid. *American Journal of Obstetrics and Gynecology, 13,* 102–108.

Dreyer, N., N. Woods, & S. James. (1981). ISRO: A scale to measure sex role orientation. *Sex Roles, 7,* 173–182.

Ferguson, J. H., & M. B. Vermillion. (1957). Premenstrual tension: Two survery of its prevalence and a description of the syndrome. *Obstetrics and Gynecology, 9,* 615–619.

Gump, J. (1972). Sex role attitudes and psychological well-being. *Journal of Social Issues, 28,* 79–92.

Halbreich, J., J. Endicott, S. Scach, & J. Nee. (1982). The diversity of premenstrual changes as reflected in the premenstrual assessment form. *Acta Psychiatrica Scandinavica, 62,* 177–190.

Holmes, T., & R. Rahe. (1967). The Social Readjustment Rating Scale. *Journal of Psychosomatic Research, 11,* 213–218.

Janiger, O., R. Reffenburgh, & R. Kersch. (1972). Gross cultural study of premenstrual symptoms. *Psychosomatics, 13,* 226–235.

Koeske, R. K., & O. F. Koeske. (1975). An attributional approach to moods and the menstrual cycle. *Journal of Personality and Social Psychology, 31,* 474–478.

Levy, R. (1976). Psychosomatic symptoms and women's protest: Two types of reaction to structural strain in the family. *Journal of Health & Social Behavior, 17,* 122–124.

Little, B., & T. Zahn. (1974). Changes in mood and autonomic functioning during the menstrual cycle. *Psychophysiology, 11,* 579–590.

Mechanic, D. (1962). The concept of illness behavior. *Journal of Chronic Disease, 15,* 189–194.

Mechanic, D. (1980). The experience and reporting of common physical complaints. *Journal of Health and Social Behavior, 21,* 146–155.

Moos, R. H. (1968). The development of menstrual distress questionnaire. *Psychosomatic Medicine, 30,* 853–867.

Most, A., N. Woods, G. Dery, & B. Most. (1981). Prevalance of perimenstrual in Israili women. *International Journal of Nursing Studies, 18,* 61–71.

Nathanson, C. (1975). Illness and the feminine role: A theoretical review. *Social Science & Medicine, 9,* 57–62.

National Center for Health Statistics. (December, 1981). *Patients' reasons for visiting physicians.* National Ambulatory Medical Care Survey. United States, 1977–78. U.S. Vital and Health Statistics Series 13, No. 6, DHHS Pub. No. (PHS) 82-1717. Hyattsville, MD: National Center for Health Statistics.

O'Rourke, M. (1983). Subjective appraisal of psychological well being and self reports of menstrual and non-menstrual symptomatology in employed women. *Nursing Research, 32,* 288–293.

Paige, K. (1973). Women learn to sing the menstrual blues. *Psychology Today, 7,* 41–46.

Patkai, P., G. Johannsen, & B. Post. (1974). Mood, alertness, and sympathetic-adrenal medullary activity during the menstrual cycle. *Psychosomatic Medicine, 36,* 503–512.

Pennington, V. (1957). Meprobamate (Miltown) in premenstrual tension. *Journal of the American Medical Association, 164,* 638–640.

Reed, R., & S. Yen. (1981). Premenstrual syndrome. *American Journal of Obstetrics and Gynecology, 138,* 85–104.

Ruble, D., & J. Brooks-Gunn. (1979). Menstrual symptoms: A social cognition analysis. *Journal of Behavioral Medicine, 2,* 171–193.

Schuckit, M., V. Daly, G. Herrman, & S. Hineman. (1975). Premenstrual symptoms and depression in a university population. *Diseases of the Nervous System, 36,* 516–517.

Shainess, N. (1961). A re-evaluation of some aspects of femininity through a study of menstruation. *Comprehensive Psychiatry, 2,* 10–26.

Sheldrake, P., & M. Cormack. (1976). Variations in menstrual cycle symptom reporting. *Journal of Psychosomatic Research, 20.* 169–177.

Siegel, J., J. Johnson, & I. Sarason. (1979). Life changes and menstrual discomfort. *Journal of Human Stress, 5,* 41–46.

Slade, P., & F. Jenner. (1979). Autonomic activity in subject reporting changes in affect in the menstrual cycle. *British Journal of Social and Clinical Psychology, 18,* 135–136.

Taylor, J. (1979). The timing of menstrual related symptoms assessed by a daily symptom rating scale. *Acta Psychiatrica Scandinavica, 60,* 87–105.

Timonen, S., & B. J. Procope. (1971). Premenstrual syndrome and physical exercise. *Acta Obstetrica Gynecologica Scandinavica, 50,* 331–336.

Van Keep, P. (1979). *The premenstrual syndrome.* Geneva: International Health Foundation.

Wilcoxon, L., S. Schrader, & C. Sherif. (1976). Daily self reports on activities, life events, moods, and somatic changes during the menstrual cycle. *Psychosomatic Medicine, 38,* 399–417.

Woods, N. (1985). Employment and family roles, and mental ill health among young married women. *Nursing Research, 34,* 4–10.

Woods, N., G. K. Dery, & A. Most. (1982). Stressful life events and perimenstrual symptoms. *Nursing Research.*

Woods, N., A. Most, & G. Dery. (1982). Prevalence of perimenstrual symptoms. *American Journal of Public Health, 72,* 1257–1264.

Woods, N., A. Most, & G. K. Dery. (1982). Toward a construct of perimenstrual distress. *Research in Nursing and Health, 5,* 123–126.

# TOWARD DELINEATING MENSTRUAL SYMPTOM GROUPINGS: EXAMINATION OF FACTOR ANALYTIC RESULTS OF MENSTRUAL SYMPTOM INSTRUMENTS

**L. A. Monagle, MS, and A. J. Dan, PhD**
University of Illinois, Health Sciences Center

**R. T. Chatterton, PhD**
Northwestern University Medical School

**F. A. DeLeon-Jones, MD**
West Side Veterans Administration Hospital, Chicago, Illinois

**G. A. Hudgens, PhD**
U.S. Army Human Engineering Laboratory, Aberdeen Proving Ground, Maryland

The present study objectives were three. First, the factor structure of Chesney and Tasto's Menstrual Symptom Questionnaire (MSQ) was reexamined to determine whether Chesney and Tasto's (1975a) two-factor or Webster's (1980) and Stephenson, Denney, and Aberger's (1983) multifactor result could be replicated. Second, the internal-consistency reliability of the MSQ in the present study was determined. Third, known and suspected menstrual symptom report confounders were deleted from the analysis to determine whether or not exclusion of menstrual symptom confounders results in a factor structure which differs significantly from samples which include known symptom confounders.

A "Heterogeneous" sample ($n = 330$), similar to samples used in previous studies, and a more "homogeneous" sample ($n = 230$), which deleted menstrual symptom confounders, were utilized in the MSQ factor analysis replication. Six factors resulted from both samples: premenstrual negative affect, menstrual pain, premenstrual pain, gastro-intestinal/prostaglandin, water retention, and asymptomatic. Cronbach's alpha internal-consistency reliability was determined to be .89 in the heterogeneous sample and .90 in the homogeneous sample. It was concluded that these results 1) supported the existence of multiple menstrual syndromes and 2) supported the high internal consistency reliability of the MSQ, and 3) indicated the robustness of the factor analytic structure of MSQ's menstrual symptoms to the inclusion of known menstrual symptom confounders.

## INTRODUCTION

A number of menstrual cycle researchers have attempted to clarify the existence of one, several or many groups of menstrual symptoms (Chesney & Tasto, 1975a, 1975b; Dalton, 1964; Moos, 1969; Nelson, Sigmon, Amodei, & Jarrett, 1984; Stephenson et al., 1983; Webster, 1980). In 1964, Katharina Dalton hypothesized that there were two clusters of menstrual symptoms, "spasmodic" and "congestive," based on her clinical observations. Moos, however, reported in 1969 eight symptom clusterings based on his factor analysis of data from 839 student wives who had completed the Menstrual Distress Questionnaire (MDQ). Six years later, Chesney and Tasto (1975a) developed the Menstrual Symptom Questionnaire (MSQ) building on Dalton's theory, and reported a two cluster result of menstrual symptoms from their factor analysis of the MSQ. The two cluster result was seen as support for Dalton's theory, and treatment approaches were developed for "spasmodic" and "congestive" types of dysmenorrhea (Chesney & Tasto, 1975b). Dalton's distinction between spasmodic and congestive dysmenorrhea, however, has since been subject to intense scientific scrutiny, and has been labeled "weak on psychometric grounds" and as not having "shown great utility . . . in the identification of different etiological factors or of differentially effective treatments" (Nelson et al., 1984, p. 614). The controversy over the validity of Dalton's theory and Chesney and Tasto's two cluster factor analytic result is due in part to Webster's (1980) and Stephenson et al.'s (1983) reports which replicated Chesney and Tasto's work with a larger sample size than had been utilized by Chesney and Tasto, and reported a seven factor result, findings which were more in agreement with Moos' hypothesis of multiple menstrual symptom groupings than Chesney and Tasto's two cluster theory. To date, the controversy over the number and types of menstrual symptom clusters, and therefore their treatment, remains unsettled. A first purpose of the present study, therefore, was the re-examination of the factor structure of Chesney and Tasto's Menstrual Symptom Questionnaire to determine whether the two factor or the multi-factor results could be replicated.

A second aspect of the debate over the validity of the two symptom clusters or multiple symptom clusters, the reliability of the MSQ, has received little research attention to date. Chesney and Tasto (1975a) in their original study reported a test-rest reliability of .87 when spasmodic symptoms were scored 1–5 (1 = never, 5 = always experienced) and congestive symptoms were scored in the opposite way (1 = always, 5 = never experienced). Cox (1977), however, criticized the reverse scoring method reporting that not only did the data not fall into two distinct clusters, they demonstrated a clear overlap between the two theoretically opposite dimensions, and that only when a consistent method of item scoring from one to five was used did the test-retest reliability reach an acceptable level (r = .80). Nunnally (1978) makes several points regarding an instrument's validity. First, he reiterates the principle that the establishment of an instrument's reliability is a necessary but not sufficient step in the establishment of the instrument's validity, and second, he advises that high correlations between tests and retests should not be taken as an indication of high reliability if the coefficient alpha internal consistency reliability measure is low for the test. A second purpose of the present report, then, was the determination of the coefficient alpha internal consistency reliability of the MSQ using a consistent method of item scoring since no such evaluation exists to date in the literature.

A third issue in the delineation of menstrual symptom groupings using factor analysis which has not yet been addressed in the literature is that of the inclusion/exclusion of known or suspected menstrual symptom confounders in the menstrual symptom grouping data analysis. Nunnally (1978) has cautioned that unless one is primarily interested in how factors relate to specific sample characteristics (e.g., structure of menstrual symptoms among oral contraceptive pill or IUD users), it is wise to delete these confounding factors. Otherwise, one may find general factors in heterogeneous groups that disappear when more homogeneous groups are studied. Chesney and Tasto, in their factor analysis of 48 college student's data, did not report how many of the women might have been oral contraceptive pill (OCP) or intrauterine device (IUD) users (Table 1). Forty-three percent of Webster's sample were OCP or IUD users and 18 percent of Stephenson's sample were OCP users. Use of OCP's and IUD's are known to confound menstrual symptom reports since OCP's are reported to decrease menstrual fluid prostaglandin content, uterine contractility (Chan, 1978) and to artificially provide relief of menstrual symptoms (Ylikorkala & Dawood, 1978). In addition, well documented side effects of the IUD include increased menstrual cramping, amount and duration of bleeding and intermenstrual pains (Ylikorkala & Dawood, 1978). The question arises, does the inclusion or exclusion of known or suspected menstrual symptom report confounders result in different factor structures? This third question was also addressed in the present study.

The present study, then, was designed to address three questions related to the delineation of the number and types of menstrual symptom groupings.

1. Is Chesney and Tasto's MSQ two factor result or Webster's and Stephenson et al.'s multifactor result replicable?
2. What is the internal-consistency reliability of the MSQ?
3. Does the factor analysis of a more "hetereogeneous" sample, similar to samples used in previous studies which includes known menstrual symptom report confounders, result in a different factor structure from that using a more "homogeneous" sample, which has deleted from it known or suspected menstrual symptom report confounders?

## SUBJECTS AND SAMPLE DETERMINATION

During a three-year period, questionnaires containing an extensive health history and demographic questions were distributed with the Menstrual Symptom Questionnaire to serve as a screening device for the selection of subjects to be followed longitudinally. Of the approximately 500 distributed questionnaires from a midwestern university student, secretary, and faculty member population, 330 were returned and usable. The mean age of the 330 subjects was 25.3 years (±5.5), and their average length of education was 15.7 years (±1.8). The majority of subjects were single (76%), and 85 percent were caucasion (Table 1).

The total sample of 330 subjects, a relatively heterogeneous sample which included known or suspected menstrual symptom report confounders, was labeled "Heterogeneous." The more "homogeneous" subsample was created by deleting all data from subjects with a history of diabetes, hypertension, current pregnancy, current oral contraceptive pill (OCP) or intrauterine device (IUD) use, hormone treatment, current breastfeeding, having irregular vaginal bleeding, irregular periods, or having had a hysterectomy or sterilization for contraceptive purposes. The resulting sample size was 230. The "homogeneous" sample, therefore, represented healthy, nonpregnant, nonlactating, regularly menstruating women who had not undergone surgical sterilization, and was designed to determine whether known or potential menstrual symptom confounders affected factor analytic structures.

**Table 1. Summary of Characteristics of Samples Used in Menstrual Symptom Factor Analyses**

| Author(s) | Sample size | Sample source by occupation | Age (x ± s.d.) (range) | Educ. (∝ of yrs.) | Cycle length (x ± s.d.) | Period length (x ± s.d) | % OCP % IUD | Confounding factors deleted |
|---|---|---|---|---|---|---|---|---|
| Chesney & Tasto, 1975 | n = 48 | 100% college students | NP[a] | NP | NP | NP | NP | None |
| Webster, 1980 | n = 275 | 79% college students, 21% students & working women | NP (18–30 yrs) | NP | NP | NP | 37 6 | None |
| Stephenson et al., 1983 | n = 423 n = 294 | 100% college psychology students | 19.4 (17–42 yrs) | NP | 29.2 | 5.1 | 18 NP | None |
| Monagle et al., 1985 | n = 330 | 74% students, 26% working women | 25.3 ±5.5 | 15.7 ±1.8 | 29.6 ±3.7 | 5.3 ±1.3 | 7 6 | None |
|  | n = 230[b] |  | 24.9 ±5.9 | 15.7 ±1.7 | 29.4 ±2.9 | 5.2 ±1.2 | 0 0 | b |

[a]Not published with the original report.
[b]Represents "Homogeneous" sample including deletion of data from women with histories of hypertension, diabetes, hysterectomy, tubal sterilization, currently pregnant, lactating, on hormone treatment, using OCP's, or having irregular vaginal bleeding or irregular periods.

135

## METHODS

Three methods were applied to the data obtained from the subject samples: 1) Principal components factor analysis (diagonals equal to 1) with varimax (orthogonal) rotation was performed on both the heterogeneous and homogeneous samples. 2) The heterogeneous and homogeneous samples were compared to Chesney and Tasto's and Webster's findings as well as to each other. 3) Cronbach's alpha internal-consistency reliability was determined for both the heterogenous and homogeneous samples.

## RESULTS

First, principal components factor analysis was performed on both the heterogeneous and homogeneous samples. A six-factor structure resulted in both cases, explaining 59 percent of the total variance. Table 2 outlines the factor structure of the heterogeneous sample. Table 3 reflects the factor structure of homogeneous sample. It is apparent that the multifactor structure and not Chesney and Tasto's two-factor structure is replicated.

Second, in the present study's analysis, Cronbach's alpha internal consistency reliability was equal to .89 in the heterogeneous sample and to .90 in the homogeneous sample (Table 3).

The third question addressed was whether or not menstrual symptom clustering was altered according to the inclusion/exclusion of known or suspected menstrual symptom report confounders. As noted, the factor structure of the homogeneous sample, representing healthy, nonpregnant, nonlactating currently menstruating women who were not using OCP's or the IUD, is presented in Table 3. Premenstrual negative affect explained the most variance (31.7%) followed by menstrual pain, explaining 8.5 percent. The factor structure, or symptom clustering, remained essentially the same in the two samples with the exception of the reversal of Factor 1 (premenstrual negative affect) and Factor 2 (menstrual pain) in the heterogeneous sample. It was concluded, therefore, that deletion of data from subjects with chronic debilitating diseases, with irregular or no current menses and those using IUD's and OCP's did not result in a major factor restructuring. That is, in general the factor structure appeared robust enough to withstand the inclusion of some confounding factors.

## DISCUSSION

The results from the present study indicate Chesney and Tasto's MSQ is a highly reliable instrument with a factor structure which

## Table 2. MSQ Factor Analysis: "Heterogeneous" Sample

| MSQ item no. | Factor loading | Description | Type of dysmenorrhea |
|---|---|---|---|
| | | **Factor 1: Premenstrual negative affect** | |
| 2 | .76 | Cramps 1st day | S |
| 19 | .70 | Pain, continuous dull ache (not intense) | C |
| 12 | .66 | Aspirin use | S |
| 15 | .65 | Hot water bottle, bath | S |
| 14 | .61 | Back, abdomen, thighs hurt 1st day | S |
| 18 | .55 | Pains disappear several minutes and reappear | S |
| 21 | .44 | Backache same day | S |
| | | **Factor 2: Menstrual pain** | |
| 3 | .83 | Depression several days before | C |
| 1 | .80 | Irritable few days before | C |
| 9 | .77 | Tense and nervous before | C |
| 5 | .61 | Exhaustion, lethargic, tired before | |
| 17 | .37 | Constipation during period | C |
| | | **Factor 3: Premenstrual pain** | |
| 20 | .76 | Abdominal discomfort $>$ 1 day before | C |
| 4 | .67 | Abdominal discomfort 1 day before | S |
| 24 | .58 | Headaches few days before | S |
| 8 | .54 | Weak and dizzy during period | S |
| 11 | .50 | Backaches several days before | C |
| | | **Factor 4: Gastrointestinal/Prostaglandin related** | |
| 7 | .81 | Pre. dr. for pain during | S |
| 10 | .54 | Diarrhea during period | S |
| 23 | .43 | Nauseous during 1st day | C |
| | | **Factor 5: Water retention** | |
| 13 | .64 | Breasts tender and sore | C |
| 16 | .61 | Gain weight before | C |
| 22 | .57 | Bloated abdomen before | C |
| 25 | .56 | Types of menstrual discomfort | C |
| | | **Factor 6: Asymptomatic** | |
| 6 | .81 | Only know period by calendar | S |
| 17 | .36 | Constipation during period | C |

## Table 3. MSQ Factor Analysis: "Homogeneous" Sample ($n = 230$)

| MSQ item no. | Factor loading | Description | Type of dysmenorrhea[a] |
|---|---|---|---|
| | | **Factor 1: Premenstrual negative affect** | **(31.7%)** |
| 3 | .82 | Depressed several days before | C |
| 1 | .82 | Irritable few days before | C |
| 9 | .78 | Tense and nervous before | C |
| 5 | .61 | Exhausted, lethargic, tired before | C |
| 17 | .44 | Constipated during period | C |
| | | **Factor 2: Menstrual pain** | **(40.2%)** |
| 14 | .71 | Back, abdomen, thighs hurt 1st day | S |
| 2 | .70 | Cramps first day | S |
| 15 | .68 | Hot water bottle, bath 1st day | S |
| 19 | .61 | Pain continuous dull ache | C |
| 21 | .60 | Backaches same day | S |
| 12 | .57 | Aspirin use | S |
| 18 | .57 | Pain disappear and reappear | S |
| | | **Factor 3: Premenstrual pain** | **(45.3%)** |
| 20 | .79 | Abdominal discomfort before | C |
| 4 | .74 | Abdominal discomfort one day before | S |
| 8 | .51 | Weak and dizzy during period | S |
| 24 | .48 | Headaches few days before | S |
| 11 | .47 | Backaches several days before | C |
| | | **Factor 4: Gastrointestinal/Prostaglandin related** | **(50.2%)** |
| 7 | .77 | Prescription drug for pain during | S |
| 10 | .68 | Diarrhea during period | S |
| 23 | .51 | Nauseous during 1st day | C |
| | | **Factor 5: Water retention** | **(54.9%)** |
| 25 | .77 | Types of menstrual discomfort (b) | |
| 13 | .58 | Breast tender and sore | C |
| 22 | .47 | Bloated abdomen before | C |
| 16 | .45 | Gain weight before | C |
| | | **Factor 6: Asymptomatic** | **(59.1%)** |
| 6 | −.75 | Only know period coming by calendar | S |

[a]C = congestive, S = spasmodic, Chesney & Tasto's menstrual symptom groups.

more closely replicates Webster's (1980) seven menstrual symptom grouping findings than Chesney and Tasto's (1975a) own two factor results. Both the heterogeneous and homogeneous sample factor analyses resulted in six factor solutions accounting for 59 percent of the variance. Beyond the similarity in the number of factors, four of the current report's factors closely duplicated four of Webster's seven factors (Table 4). However, whereas two of Webster's factors, 5 and 7, were unlabeled because of lack of conceptual item congruity, the factors in this analysis were each found to be relatively conceptually consistent (Table 2 and 3). For example, in the present study the only asymptomatic item, Factor 6 (I only know my period is coming by the calendar), behaved as expected by not correlating positively with any symptomatic items, whereas in Webster's study, it correlated with menstrual nausea and the factor was left unlabled (Factor 5).

The present study's factor analytic results of the MSQ symptom clustering is the third in a series (after Webster and Stephenson et al.) of attempts to replicate Chesney and Tasto's two symptom cluster results which was used to support Dalton's spasmodic and congestive theories. The adequacy of sample size when utilizing factor analysis techniques has been pointed to as an issue with Chesney and Tasto's factor analysis of the MSQ. According to Nunnally (1978), factor analysis is not a powerful data analytic tool when the number of subjects approximates the number of items. As Webster (1980) noted, in Chesney and Tasto's factor analysis report, data from 41 subjects were used to analyze a 25-item questionnaire. In this situation, the probability of results being due to chance is high (Nunnally, 1978). When a larger subject/item ratio was utilized in the present analysis (approximately 10 subjects/item), multiple factor results rather than Chesney and Tasto's two-factor results were supported.

It appears clear given the results of the series of studies that when the sample size is adequate for the statistical method use, Chesney and Tasto's results cannot be replicated. Furthermore, all three of the replication studies resulted in the delineation of six or seven factors, illustrating a stability and degree of reliability in the multifactor structure of the MSQ menstrual symptom groupings. While it is conceptually inappropriate to accept the structure of menstrual symptoms based on a menstrual symptom instrument, it is interesting to note the repetition of the number of factors across the three studies, which lends some support to the construct validity of these menstrual symptom groupings.

The internal-consistency reliability analysis resulted in r = .90 when unidimensional (Chesney & Tasto, 1975a, 1975b; Dalton,

Table 4. Summary of Factor Analytic Studies of Menstrual Symptom Questionnaire

| Item | Chesney & Tasto, 1975 | Webster, 1980 | Stephenson et al., 1983 | Monagle et al, 1985 |
|---|---|---|---|---|
| Reliability measure | test-retest r = .87 | —[a] | —[a] | Cronbach's alpha = .89 |
| No. of symptom clusters (factors) extracted | 2 | 7 | 6 ($n$ = 294)<br>7 ($n$ = 423) | 6 |
| Names of factors | 1. spasmodic<br>2. congestive | 1. PM negative affect<br>2. menstrual pain<br>3. PM pain<br>4. menstr. back pain<br>5. unlabeled<br>6. water retention<br>7. unlabeled | Factors not named; "substantial overlap" between Webster's factors and this study's factor results | 1. PM negative affect<br>2. menstrual pain<br>3. PM pain<br>4. gastroint./PG rel.<br>5. water retention<br>6. asymptomatic |
| Percentage of variance explained | 46.9% | 62% | 64% ($n$ = 423)<br>59% ($n$ = 294) | 59.1% |

[a]Not published with the original report.

1964; Moos, 1969, Nelson et al., 1984) scoring is used. This result, together with test-retest reliability information published previously, provide a solid examination of the MSQ's reliability according to Nunnally, a necessary but not sufficient step in the validation process.

The deletion of known or suspected menstrual symptom report confounders was not seen to affect the factor structure of the instrument in a significant way. Data from women who were OCP or IUD users as well as data from women with general systemic diseases such as hypertension and diabetes, and from women potentially experiencing endocrinological disturbances (as evidenced by their reported hormone treatments, irregular vaginal bleeding or irregular periods) were deleted owing to their possible confounding effect on reported menstrual symptomatology. The potential confounder of long-term memory recall on menstrual symptom reports was controlled for by deleting data from women having experienced a hysterectomy, and from women who were currently pregnant or lactating. Two changes did occur: 1) Factors 1 and 2 reversed themselves, suggesting a relationship whereby either one or the other might be used as the factor explaining the most variance within the MSQ instrument; and 2) Item 17, "constipated during period," loaded on Factor 2 and 6 in the heterogeneous sample, and on Factor 1 in the homogeneous sample, suggesting no strong contribution to any of the symptom clusters (Tables 2 and 3). Moreover, this lack of change in factor structure when menstrual symptom confounders were deleted was seen more clearly when factor structures across studies were examined. The Monagle et al. heterogeneous sample included only 13 percent of the known menstrual symptom confounders, OCP and IUD use, whereas the Webster sample contained 43 percent of subjects who were either OCP or IUD users, and as mentioned before, the structure, aside from the above mentioned increased conceptual clarity of the factors. Conceivable explanations for this consistent lack of predicted factor structure changes are several. The first is that the symptom reports of OCP and IUD users did in fact not differ in any significant way from the non-OCP and IUD users in the Webster sample and the Monagle et al. sample. This explanation is not consistent with a large body of literature which has focused on OCP and IUD users and the effects of these contraceptives. A second interpretation of the fact that deletion of physiological menstrual symptom confounders does not affect symptom clustering is that this finding supports the conclusions reached by Parlee (1974) and others (Paige, 1973; Ruble & Brooks-Gunn, 1979) that retrospective menstrual symptom questionnaires such as the MSQ and the MDQ more accurately represent social-cultural information than a physiological self-reporting of events. That is, analysis of the MSQ or MDQ appears to provide information regarding how women in varying cultures and environments view their experience of menstrual symptoms. The area of perception and reporting of menstrual symptoms needs further investigation, and could be well served by more cross-cultural studies than exist at present. More cross-cultural examinations of menstrual symptom reports would allow a closer analysis of the physiological versus social-cultural component of menstrual symptom reporting by determining consistent and universal patterns in symptoms reported versus systematic variation of symptom reports due to different cultural experiences. This route, in conjunction with others, is seen as useful in the determination of a more valid delineation of menstrual symptom groupings.

In conclusion, the present paper has addressed reported discrepancies in the number and types of menstrual symptom groupings. Previous work was replicated, and results were reported which, rather than supporting Dalton's two symptom group theory, were found to be consistent with a multiple menstrual syndrome approach to the characterization of menstrual symptoms. Further, instrument reliability and sample characteristics were evaluated as potential explanations for reported study discrepancies, and were found not to appear relevant as explanations. Results indicated that, on the contrary, the factor structure of menstrual symptoms remained stable even when known physiological menstrual symptom confounders were deleted, a finding which may contribute more understanding to what retrospective questionnaires such as the MSQ and the MDQ are measuring. More cross-cultural studies of menstrual symptom reports was seen as particularly needed and useful in the further delineation of valid menstrual symptom groupings.

## REFERENCES

Chan, W. Y., & Hill, J. C. (1978). Determination of menstrual prostaglandin levels in non-dysmenorrheic and dysmenorrheic subjects. *Prostaglandins, 15*(2), 365–375.

Chesney, M. A., & Tasto, D. L. (1975a). The development of the menstrual symptom questionnaire. *Behavior Research & Therapy, 13*, 237–244.

Chesney, M. A., & Tasto, D. L. (1975b). The effectiveness of behavioral modification with spasmodic and congestive dysmenorrhea. *Behavior Research & Therapy, 13*, 245–253.

Cox, D. (1977). Menstrual symptom questionnaire: Further psychometric evaluation. *Behavior Research & Therapy, 15*, 506–508.

Dalton, K. (1964). *The premenstrual syndrome.* Springfield, IL: Charles C Thomas.

Moos, R. H. (1969). Typology of menstrual cycle symptoms. *American Journal of Obstetrics and Gynecology, 103*(3), 390–402.

Nelson, R. O., Sigmon, S., Amodei, N., & Jarrett, R. B. (1984). The menstrual symptom questionnaire: The validity of the distinction between spasmodic and congestive dysmennorhea. *Behavior Research & Therapy, 6,* 611–614.

Nunnally, J. C. (1978). *Psychometric theory.* New York: McGraw-Hill.

Paige, K. E. (1973). Women learn to sing the menstrual blues. *Psychology Today, 7,* 41–46.

Parlee, M. B. (1974). Stereotypic beliefs about menstruation: A methodological note on the Moos Menstrual Distress Questionnaire and some new data. *Psychosomatic Medicine, 36,* 229–240.

Ruble, D. N., & Brooks-Gunn, J. (1979). Menstrual symptoms: A social cognition analysis. *Journal of Behavioral Medicine, 2,* 171–194.

Stephenson, L. A., Denney, D. R., & Aberger, E. W. (1983). Factor structure of the menstrual symptom questionnaire: Relationship to oral contraceptives, neuroticism and life stress. *Behavior Research & Therapy, 21*(2), 129–135.

Webster, S. K. (1980). Problems for diagnosis of spasmodic and congestive dysmenorrhea. In Dan, A. J., Graham, E. A., & Beecher, C. P., (Eds.), *The menstrual cycle: A synthesis of interdisciplinary research* (Vol. 1, pp. 292–304). New York: Springer.

Ylikorkala, O., & Dawood, M. Y. (1978). New concepts in dysmenorrhea. *American Journal of Obstetrics and Gynecology, 130*(7), 833–847.

# PREMENSTRUAL SYNDROME (PMS) EXAMINED THROUGH A FEMINIST LENS

**Esther Rome**
Boston Women's Health Book Collective

Though strong cycle changes affect some women it is anti-woman to classify these shifts as an illness. Labeling PMS as illness is political; it is a way to deny normalcy to cycle changes. There is a critique of Dalton's anti-feminist views of women and of the medical model used by one of the progesterone dispensing clinics. Alternative treatments are mentioned with a more detailed look at the possible role of self-help groups, based on the feminist consciousness-raising group model, to validate women's experiences and to increase their self-esteem.

The medicalization of premenstrual syndrome, or PMS, is one more step in the continuing medicalization of women's lives, that is, the labeling of increasing numbers of normal life events as appropriate for medical "expertise" and treatment. Katherina Dalton, the world's foremost proponent of progesterone therapy for PMS, who has run a PMS clinic in London for thirty years, claims that about half of all women become "ill" with PMS. She calls it "the world's commonest disease" (1979, p. 193). We need to recognize there *are* cycle changes which can be very uncomfortable and debilitating. Recognizing this as a fact of life for some women and not a defect in their characters is helpful and freeing. This does not mean the cycle changes are an illness. The illness label reflects a strong anti-woman bias. Treating women with strong cycle changes as ill is similar to treating pregnant and menopausal women as ill.

The analogy of PMS to menopause is particularly striking. First, both are called deficiency diseases, one of estrogen and the other of progesterone. They are treated with replacement hormones of mostly unproven value and unknown long-term risks.

Sophie Laws, a British sociologist, has called attention to the use of PMS as a political theory used to separate out a particular group of women and to divide women from each other (Laws, Hey, & Eagan, 1985). Some feminists have contributed to the problem by saying that most women are "normal" and only a few have problems. Rather than examining societal rules which classify a wider range of human experience as acceptable or unacceptable, this type of statement only serves to separate those who "pass" in our male regulated society from those who cannot or will not pass. Laws further suggests that the labeling of PMS as an illness is a way to ignore and invalidate women's rebelliousness. Some women who report deliberately using the premenstrual time to vent some of their rage and frustration understand this on an intuitive level. Calling these times of rage symptoms of disease is a handy way of not looking at what women are upset about and why. It is a way of "keeping us in our place." But trivializing and discounting anger is dangerous for women.

Golub and Harrington have found that women learn to attribute negative events in their lives to particular times of their cycles whether or not they actually correspond to cyclical changes in any measurable way (1981). Yet women today actively question the notion of the premenstrual time as *necessarily* negative. For some, it is a highly creative time, although Dalton never acknowledges this as a possibility. Emily Culpepper, who has run menstrual workshops for years, reports that after a workshop women will send her drawings, poems and other creative work that they have felt particularly inspired to do premenstrually. A letter to *Ms.* magazine suggests we change the name to Premenstrual Energy to help us think differently about it (1982). Dr. Barbara Parry suggests "premenstrual changes" as a more accurate name (Parry, 1985). We need to regard those times, even when we feel out of control, as teaching us something.

Now I wish to examine how social expectations and support that is or isn't available influence our perceptions to make the experience of PMS more negative than it needs to be. My phone conversations with women who call the Boston Women's Health Book Collective and who are looking for a progesterone dispensing clinic may be instructive. Though the numbers of women are small, their comments contain recurring patterns. First of all, they present their life situations as essentially positive. A typical example is, "I'm married, have a small child who was very much wanted, and a loving husband who has a good job." However, the woman has a premenstrual problem and is desperate. She may fell uncomfortable, depressed, edgy, or angry for days on end. The phrase I hear over and over is "out of control," the last thing a woman is brought up to be. She cannot live up to the image of herself as a good woman that she maintains through the rest of her cycle: that is, cheerful, compliant, easing everyone else's social relations. She often is embarrassed by her mood swings, sometimes humiliated. She feels she *should* be able to manage this on her own. Generally, she does not discuss this problem with friends or other family members and tends not to get help for it. This isolation makes PMS even harder. As the conversation goes on, it turns out that her partner is quite fed up with the whole business of her moods. What woman doesn't have trouble coping when she has an unsupportive and critical partner?

Even particular symptoms take on a value influenced by society. Bloating, for instance, can be painful in and of itself, but it would not carry a social stigma if we all wore loose clothing like robes and believed being fat to be beautiful.

Since Dalton's work has significantly influenced the dispensing of progesterone and overall medicalization of PMS, it is worthwhile to look at her view of women and the goals of her treatment, concentrating on her attitudes toward women and how that has shaped her work. Several scholars have already criticized Dalton's research methods (Parlee, 1973; Gonzalez, 1981), and there is additionally an unpublished literature calling her work into question. In view of Dalton's consistency in documenting her work, it does not appear necessary here to repeat those criticisms.

It becomes painfully clear that Dalton's goal is to help women function more smoothly in their traditional stereotypical role, subordinate to men. She wants to help women do what they "ought": function as housewives and mothers in an uncomplaining, cheerful way. In a typical book, *Once a Month* (Dalton, 1978), she tries to give women's "abnormal, unreliable" behavior a scientific basis. Noting that the volume was written to help males understand women's moods and varying temperaments, she argues that females can be interpreted exclusively in terms of her hormonal cycle. In several passages Dalton tells stories of women, normally calm, ever responsible for smooth family functioning, becoming moody, irrational, weepy or aggressive bitches, provoking male violence. Husbands are depicted as having their hands full in these unpleasant times as they strive to return calm to the domestic scene.

Dalton's opinion of women who might resist treatment is clear. It is women's "duty" and obligation to be treated. "Otherwise they will get what they deserve from men" (Coventry Evening Telegram, July 15, 1982, quoted in Laws et al., 1985). She really wishes to pacify women. Her solution, as the medical solution so often is, is to help women individually out of the context of their social setting, one by one, with drugs. In her defense, I will say that Dr. Dalton has acted within the context of her time and training. We must simply be aware of what it is and not necessarily continue to accept her treatment or her negative view of women.

Difficulties researchers have in agreeing on a definition of PMS have partly to do with their attitudes toward women. Some insist on a symptom-free time during the cycle; others include a premenstrual intensification of symptoms experienced to a lesser degree all though the cycle. Dalton is adamant in her definition of the syndrome as having at least a week symptom-free in the cycle, although this week does not have to include the time of menstruation. What is the significance of the symptom-free time? First, it means that a woman has a "normal" time when she is her "old self" even if it is the minority of the time when she is a good woman rather than a raging harpy or suicidally depressed. She still has a core which is self-confident as well as adjusted to male values, when she is loving and docile. *This* is her true self. The theory of a symptom-free time also provides a way to tell the hopeless (no cure yet) and the malingerers (just getting on the bandwagon) from the true PMS sufferers who deserve help. For Dalton, this serves an important function since no objective differences have been found so far in the hormone levels between PMS sufferers and others, although this difference is the rationale for her treatment. However, this definition invalidates the experiences of a whole set of women who report a worsening of symptoms premenstrually which otherwise come anytime during the cycle. Dalton classifies this as "menstrual distress" and claims only the "real" PMS sufferers respond to progesterone. We don't know if this is true, since no one has confirmed this with careful studies.

It is useful to present some impressions of how the progesterone treatment is being carried out. Clinics for dispensing progesterone are mushrooming in this country as if they were a new growth industry. Women learn about progesterone through the recent rash of newspaper and magazine articles, books, and TV programs on PMS. But many of the articles and shows do not make it clear how little we know about PMS, and often recommend progesterone as the treatment of choice. Progesterone advocates often talk or write in a way that suggests that the doctors are knights on white horses saving damsels in distress from the PMS dragon.

Reports of women using a PMS clinic in the Northeastern United States suggest a typical medical encounter. The woman sees only the medical staff on a one to one basis, although there is an initial group meeting before diagnosis and treatment begins. Women are not encouraged to get in touch with each other afterwards or during their treatment, nor are their complaints about the treatment always taken seriously. Supporters of progesterone treatment continue to claim that the only side effect of taking the drug is euphoria and excess energy at the beginning of treatment. Yet some women complain of chest pains, serious yeast infections while using the vaginal suppositories, severe diarrhea and cramping with the rectal suppositories, and an excessive drop in blood pressure with the sublingual form of the drug. There are reports of these complaints being brushed off or denied by the clinic. Numerous questions arise: What happens to women who go to a clinic like this one, which primarily dispenses progesterone, and fail to obtain the results they would like? What happens to their social and marital relationships? Do they become more isolated than before? We definitely need follow-up from the consumer's point of view.

The use of progesterone is alarming to all the feminist health workers with whom I have spoken. They fear that the progesterone treatments will prove to be another case of hormones being given to women in an untested and scientifically frivolous way. They point out that there are only a few studies investigating the safety of this drug, and these may indicate problems such as breast tumors, cervical cancer and arteriosclerosis. Progesterone is a sedative in large doses. Some of the women receiving treatment are also worried about being guinea pigs.

There *are* other treatments besides progesterone. These include rest, exercise, dietary changes, especially eliminating refined sugar and flours and caffeine, frequent meals, vitamin B-6, oil of evening primrose, reorganizing schedules, meditation, relaxation exercises, biofeedback, and acupuncture, some of which have been detailed by Dr. Michelle Harrison (1982). Harrison, who treats women with PMS as a large part of her medical practice, finds that women are about equally helped by any of the treatments. If, as is thought, any PMS treatment, including placebos, is about fifty to seventy percent effective in relieving symptoms, and in light of the little knowledge we have about the long term effects of progesterone, a powerful hormone, it appears that the ethical approach would be to try treatments first that pose no known harm.

Different women respond to different treatments, but each, after having found what seems to work for her, feels she has found her old self again. What then is happening with all these treatments? First, we should remember that the woman is finally being taken seriously and her cycle changes are being acknowledged; her reality is being validated. This in itself is enough help for some women.

Overwhelming response of women to articles or TV shows on the subject indicates how eager women are for confirmation of their experiences. (The Rhode Island Feminist Health Center had hundreds of inquiries to one short letter in the *Providence Journal.*)

Secondly, the woman may increase her self-esteem just by taking action on a perceived problem. In finding the "right" treatment, has the woman been learning how to assert herself?

Women-organized-and-run self-help groups can play an important role in enhancing both the validation of a woman's experiences and her self-esteem. The woman can gain encouragement and support just from talking with other women who have the same life problem. The support can function on many levels. On a practical level, the women could help lighten each other's loads during the premenstrual time by, for example, exchanging meals or finding baby sitters. Women do not need to see themselves as sick to benefit from doing this. (Dalton's quotes of women describing their difficulties in getting meals is one of the more compelling arguments for communal kitchens!) Women could share medical information, what they know about alternative treatments, and how well each has worked. This is one area in which an independent group is particularly useful—not one with a single point of view. Women could set up a phone-support system to help each other over the phone when feeling desperate. Women could discuss the conflicts, desperation, depression, or feelings of lack of control that surface during the premenstrual time. They could help each other figure out how they live with or avoid these feelings at other times of their cycles. They could identify what in their lives they *do* want to change. They could work together toward understanding PMS as something other than a disease.

This kind of discussion is equally valuable to women with less noticeable cycle changes and perhaps can help us see that our experiences with cycle change form a continuum. We cannot divide women into distinct and abrupt categories. We are all affected by how women with the most extreme experiences are classified.

## REFERENCES

Dalton, K. (1979). *Once a month.* Pomona, CA: Hunter House. (British edition first published 1978.)

Golub, S., & Harrington, D. M. (1981). Premenstrual and menstrual mood changes in adolescent women. *Journal of Personality and Social Psychology, 41*(5), 961–965.

Gonzalez, R. R. (1981). Premenstrual syndrome: An ancient woe deserving a modern scrutiny. *Journal of the American Medical Association, 245*(14), 1393–1396.

Harrison, M. (1982). *Self-Help for Pre-Menstrual Syndrome.* New York: Random House.

Laws, S., Hey, V., & Eagan, A. (1985). *Seeing red: The politics of pre-menstrual tension.* Dover, New Hampshire: Hutchinson and Co., Ltd.

Parlee, M. B. (1973). The premenstrual syndrome. *Psychological Bulletin, 83*(6), 454–465.

Parry, B. (1985). *Women and Health Roundtable Report.* IX(2), 1–2.

**Request reprints from Esther Rome, Boston Women's Health Book Collective, 465 Mt. Auburn St., Watertown, MA 02172.**

# PREMENSTRUAL SYNDROME: AN ASSESSMENT, EDUCATION, AND TREATMENT MODEL

Sharon A. Heinz, MSE
Eau Claire Clinic, Wisconsin

A description of a model for community programming in the area of Premenstrual Syndrome, as instituted in Eau Claire, Wisconsin. A team approach with medical and paramedical personnel who undertake to meet a growing demand for services to women suffering from hormonally related symptoms. This is an assessment, education, and treatment model that emphasizes self-responsibility for dietary, exercise, and life-style alterations shown to be helpful to women with the problem. In addition, there is a call for research based on the experience in Eau Claire, as well as suggestions as to how health professionals might respond in setting up such a program in their own areas.

## INTRODUCTION

Eau Claire, Wisconsin, is a small city with an area population of between 70 and 100,000 people. It is approximately 2 hours from the nearest cosmopolitan area which is Minneapolis/St. Paul, Minnesota. Eau Claire is the center of a largely rural area which provides goods and services to dairy farmers of the Western Wisconsin district.

The Eau Claire Clinic is a private psychiatric clinic with a psychiatrist, a psychologist, two clinical social workers, two Masters level professionals, incuding the author, who are trained in the fields of psychology and speech therapy. These latter two people have been additionally trained in the area of assessment, education, and management of Premenstrual Syndrome. The ensuing experience led to contact with a wide variety of area professionals and PMS sufferers, both primary and secondary, and expanded the knowledge of the entire staff.

The mass dissemination of material via television, newspapers, and magazines led to a growing awareness of premenstrual syndrome among area women, even in the most remote rural sections. Others learned through peer interaction. The initial publicity for the newly devised program for management of PMS at the Eau Claire Clinic elicited hundreds of phone calls. It became apparent that the interest in this problem among women, even in rural Wisconsin, was so high that professional response seemed warranted.

As we spoke with these women regarding their usually fruitless search for assistance with premenstrual symptoms, it became apparent that the health professionals in the area were not addressing a major need. In addition, attitudes communicated to the patients were rather negative so that women were becoming angry and disenchanted with physicians whom they had previously trusted. Interestingly, women told us that female doctors who themselves experience such symptoms were no more likely to take someone with disabling PMS seriously. Why, one might ask, this resistance among health professionals? Not only physicians, but nurses, therapists, and the legal system appeared to resist recognition of premenstrual syndrome, or at least, this was the impression given to women who approached them for help or information.

Our unique position in the community as two paramedical people working with a physician, who were talking to and attempting to advocate for women from all walks of life and educational levels, enabled us to observe several things. First, we found out that dealing with women who have concerns about premenstrual syndrome takes significant time. Each woman who contacted us had considerable anxiety about her experience and needed an opportunity to talk about it. Listening to the women and the extensive education necessary for management of the symptoms which ranges from specific strategies for dietary changes, through exercise, stress management techniques and possible medication management, can most productively be done by specially trained paramedical personnel.

## HOW THE PROGRAM WORKS

There are probably great numbers of women throughout the country who need at least counseling and reassurance, and probably a fair amount of education as well because of cyclicly recurring premenstrual symptoms. Direct medical treatment is necessary in only a small percentage of these cases. The Eau Claire Clinic program constitutes a model for community programming in the area of premenstrual syndrome.

Initially women are seen individually by a specially trained PMS counselor. Assessment is done which was developed by PMS Action

Incorporated of Madison, Wisconsin, under the leadership of Virginia Cassara. The assessment, which has been refined in our practice, is a detailed menstrual and reproductive history which provides a profile common to sufferers of PMS. The woman being assessed is compared to Dalton's diagnostic checklist. If she conforms to 60 percent of the diagnostic features found to discriminate PMS sufferers in Dalton's work in England, she is instructed in charting, which of course is the only known positive way to confirm the diagnosis. After the assessment is completed, the woman has the option of working either individually with the PMS counselor or in a professionally led small group educational program which deals with life-style changes and treatment options. The programming ranges from nutritional information helpful to women with premenstrual symptoms along with the effect of aerobic exercise on the body and stress management techniques.

One session is held with family members to provide them with a basic understanding of the problem. Treatment options are discussed which include vitamin therapies, tranquilizers and diuretics (these are not recommended) and progesterone replacement therapy. Throughout this period of time, the woman, who continues to chart her own symptoms, is assisted in evaluating her response to the nutritional changes and other life-style strategies she has elected to try. If a decision is made to request progesterone augmentation, the woman has the option of being referred back to her own physician with a synopsis of the assessment for his perusal along with any other advocacy from her PMS counselor which she may find necessary. In the event that she meets with a refusal from her physician or an inappropriately prescribed regimen, the medical supervisor of the Clinic consults at the woman's request to ensure that she receives effective treatment.

The final component of the Eau Claire Clinic's program is an ongoing monthly support group which is offered free of charge to women who have completed the program. Unlike other support groups which have no professional leadership and no common base of understanding, these women do not rehash "old war stories." They share efforts to manage the disorder and give one another support in the rather difficult job of making changes in their lives which will enable them to cope more productively whether they elect to use hormone therapy or not. Second, they maintain contact with the counselors who pass on new knowledge of the field as it becomes available.

Very little direct publicity has been necessary to keep the program busy and participants have proven to be a common source of referral.

The clinic has received positive feedback from participants about the success of the program in improving their lives.

In working with the problem over time, several issues have emerged which need further research. The first of these has to do with sleep disorders as related to the menstrual cycle. Secondly, a retrospective study on women who have had endometrial cancer to ascertain whether the premenstrual syndrome may have existed prior to menopause in their histories, and third, the relationship of the existence of breast cancer and prior undiagnosed premenstrual syndrome.

In summary, the experience in Eau Claire, Wisconsin, has shown that, although women are aware of PMS in large numbers, they do not seek treatment for the disorder as a panacea, or an excuse, as is assumed by some cynics. On the contrary, as they become more comfortable with the discussion of menstruation and come to understand the effect of this biological event on their functioning ability, they become willing to take more responsibility in their own care. They make difficult life-style changes, and only in the event of failure to obtain relief, do they request medication. Our program helps them to become informed consumers who recognize the seriousness of such a step. The medical profession has an obligation to serve these women in a responsible and thoughtful manner. It is likely that physicians will need inservice training in management of PMS. It will be necessary to train paramedical personnel to work along with them in the way that has been briefly described here.

## REFERENCES

### Articles

Backstrom, T. (1976). Epileptic seizures in women related to plasma estrogen and progesterone during the menstrual cycle. *Acta Neurologica Scandinavia, 54,* 321–347.

Beaumont, P. J. V., & D. H. Gelder (1975). A study of minor psychiatric and physical symptoms during the menstrual cycle. *British Journal of Psychiatry, 126,* 431–434.

Brush, M. G. (1977). The possible mechanisms causing the premenstrual tension syndrome. *Current Medical Research and Opinion, 4,* 9–15.

Dalton, D. (1961). Menstruation and crime. *British Medical Journal, 2,* 279.

d'Orban, P. T., & J. Dalton (1980). Violent crime and the menstrual syndrome. *Lancet, 2,* 1070–1071.

Gonzalez, E. R. (April 10, 1981). Premenstrual syndrome: An ancient woe deserving a modern scrutiny. *Journal of the American Medical Association, 245,* 1393–1396.

Hendler, N. H. (1980). Clinical drug trail: Spironolactone for premenstrual syndrome. *The Female Patient, 5,* 17–19.

Ivey, M. E., & Bardwick, J. M. (1968). Patterns of affective fluctuations in the menstrual cycle. *Psychosomatic Medicine, 30,* 336–345.

Moos, R. H. (1969). Typology of menstrual cycle symptoms. *American Journal of Obstetrics and Gynecology, 103,* 390–402.

Morton, J. H., H. Addition, R. G. Addison, L. Hunt, & J. J. Sullivan (1953). A clinical study of premenstrual tension. *American Journal of Obstetrics and Gynecology, 65,* 1182–1191.

Reid, R., & S. S. S. Yen (Jan. 1981). Premenstrual syndrome. *American Journal of Obstetrics and Gynecology.*

Sampson, G. (1979). Premenstrual syndrome: A double-blind controlled trail of Progesterone and placebo. *British Journal of Psychiatry, 135,* 209–215.

Steiner, M., & B. J. Caroll (1977). The psychobiology of premenstrual dysphoria: Review of theories and treatments. *Psychoneuroendocrinology, 2,* 221–235.

Taylor, J. W. (July, 1979). The timing of menstruation-related symptoms assessed by a daily symptom rating scale. *Acta Psychiatric Scandinavica, 60,* 87–105.

Warnes, H. (1978). Premenstrual disorders: Causative mechanisms and treatment. *Psychosomatics, 49,* 32–40.

## Books

Budoff, P. W. (1980). *No more menstrual cramps and other good news.* New York: G. P. Putnam's Sons. Distinguishes PMS from cramps; good diet suggestions for mild to moderate cases of PMS; dismisses Dalton's work by saying no one has been able to reproduce it but neglects to mention that only one person has tried. (Sampson)

Dalton, K. (1979). *Once a month.* Pamona, CA: Hunter House.

Dalton, K. (1977). *The premenstrual syndrome and progesterone therapy.* Chicago, IL: Yearbook Medical Press.

Seaman, B. (1977). *Women and the crisis in sex hormones.* New York: Rawson Wade. Good section on diet and nutritional needs of women. Don't let it frighten you about progesterone therapy as there's a crucial distinction between progestogens (synthetics) and progesterone.

Sherman, J. (1975). *On the psychology of women.* Springfield, IL: Charles C Thomas.

Shuttle, P., & Redgrove, P. (1978). *The wise wound.* New York: Richard Marek. A non-medical approach to dealing with premenstrual syndrome.

Unger, R., & Denmark, F. (Eds.). (1975). *Woman, dependent or independent variable?* New York: Psychological Dimension, Inc.

Weideger, P. (1976). *Menstruation and menopause, the physiology and psychology, the myth and reality.* New York: Knopf. An excellent book; well-researched and highly readable.

# PEER SUPPORT, PMS, AND STRESS:
## A PILOT STUDY

Diana Taylor, RN, MSN, and Laura Bledsoe, BS
Oregon Health Sciences University, Portland, Oregon

Premenstrual symptoms (PMS) may be aggravated by social or environmental stressors. An explanatory model incorporating the effects of stress, social support, and menstrual cyclicity is proposed. This paper discusses the effectiveness of social support as an adjunct to conventional treatment for PMS, and describes the results of a pilot study. The results indicate that peer social support, in combination with other treatments, may serve to educate; to provide support to adhere to difficult treatment regimens; and to indirectly reduce the severity of premenstrual symptoms.

## INTRODUCTION

The ever-increasing consumer demand for active participation in a wide range of services, including health care, has resulted in the advent of new therapeutic solutions. The use of self-management training for stress-related disorders (Kogan & Betrus, 1984) and the emergent role of mediating structures (Levin & Idler, 1981) in the form of self-help or mutual-support groups (Caplan & Killilea, 1976, Gottlieb, 1981) are examples of alternative health-related therapeutic modalities whose time has come.

However, more research is necessary to determine which therapeutic intervention is effective for specific health problems and in which context. As an attempt to clarify the therapeutic influence of social support, this paper will discuss the factors and health outcomes of a supportive peer network for women experiencing a particular menstrual dysfunction, premenstrual syndrome.

# A BIOPSYCHOSOCIAL PHENOMENON:
## PREMENSTRUAL SYNDROME

Premenstrual syndrome (PMS), a process first called "premenstrual tension" in 1931 (Frank) and later more generally labelled "perimenstrual symptom formation" (Woods, Most, & Dery, 1982) continues to remain an illusive problem 50 years later.

PMS may affect 30 percent of all women to a moderate or severe degree (Woods et al., 1982), and be so incapacitating that they require treatment. Although there is no clear definition of PMS, the definition accepted by contemporary researchers is a "disorder characterized by a complex of somatic, emotional, cognitive, and behavioral symptoms which regularly occur in the perimenstruum and affect work or lifestyle to a severe or incapacitating degree." (Backstrom, 1983, Taylor, 1984). Though the somatic symptoms such as headaches, fluid retention, and breast tenderness can be severe, it is often the psychosocial changes which are the most devastating and disruptive to the severe PMS sufferer. These symptoms (e.g., feeling "blue" crying, angry outbursts, avoidance of social contacts, and loss of self-control) may subsequently create strain in relationships at home and work as well as feelings of despair, worthlessness and loss of self-esteem.

What causes PMS is also unclear. Once thought to be psychological, then believed to be hormonal, it is now the subject of many neurohormonal and psychosocial theories. Just as a combination of theories might be responsible for the etiology of PMS, clinical research also suggests that a combination of treatments may be more satisfactory than a single treatment. Both pharmacologic and non-pharmacologic treatments have been used to treat PMS, but unfortunately, few controlled studies have been undertaken to test the efficacy of these treatments. Because the research on drug therapies is unclear, most clinicians prefer to try nonpharmacologic treatments for women experiencing mild to moderate symptoms. Even though non-drug therapies and self-help measures have been successful in reducing premenstrual symptoms, it is often difficult for women to adhere to a prescribed regimen because of the lifestyle changes they require. Social support in the form of peer-support groups may give women the knowledge and psychosocial support necessary to follow their treatment regimes.

In order to consider the effectiveness of social support as an adjunct to conventional treatment for PMS, a pilot study was undertaken at a Menstrual Disorder Clinic within a University Health

Science Center. The pilot study was conducted to determine whether or not 1) peer support had an effect on the severity of premenstrual symptoms, 2) peer support groups had an impact on patient compliance with a prescribed regimen of PMS treatment, and 3) peer support groups may actually be one component in a therapeutic model of PMS treatment.

## CONCEPTUAL LINKS: STRESS, PMS
## AND SOCIAL SUPPORT

Stress appears to play an important role in aggravating perimenstrual symptoms (Woods et al., 1982). Many of the neuroendocrine secretions associated with the human stress response can also be responsible for initiating or aggravating PMS. For example, during stressful events, secretion of aldosterone (Girdano & Everly, 1979); antidiuretic hormone (Ganong, 1983); ACTH, glucocorticoids and epinephrine (Selye, 1956) is increased. Aldosterone and antidiuretic hormone cause water retention and thus could play a part in symptoms such as breast swelling, abdominal bloating, headache, and edema of the extremities. An excess of glucocorticoids may lead to depression, and excess epinephrine, could lead to feelings of hostility, irritability, anxiety, and aggression. Stress may also disrupt the balance between estrogen produced by the adrenal glands as measured by urine analysis (Ganong, 1983). This stress-induced estrogen excess may be sufficient to increase perimenstrual symptoms. This evidence confirms what Selye (1956) first suggested and Cassel (1974, 1976) later hypothesized: that all disease processes are affected and enhanced by stress because the endocrine balance in the body is disrupted.

Women with PMS encounter many types of stress related to their disorder. Their relationships with husbands or partners, family, and friends are often strained by their unpredictable moods and angry outbursts. Women with moderate to severe symptoms may often isolate themselves from others, and isolation has shown to be stressful itself (Henry & Ely, 1980). The stress of trying to cope with a recurrent syndrome, in addition to the common stressors of everyday life, probably combine to increase the endocrine imbalance and aggravate PMS.

This same social environment which gives rise to the stressful stimuli may also provide a protective element against the interpersonal and social stressors. Individual personality characteristics allow the woman to use these social resources which have the potential to prevent illness and provide healthy outcomes. This protective social mechanism has been called "social support," and will be analyzed in terms of its therapeutic qualities.

There is evidence that social support can act as a buffer against the negative effects of life stresses and disease (Cassel, 1976; Cobb, 1976; Jordon & Meckler, 1982; Dean & Lin, 1977; Winnubst et al., 1982; Broadhead et al., 1984); and has a positive effect on health. Berkman and Syme (1979) led a long-term health study in which they discovered the single most important indicator of whether or not an individual would be alive nine years later was the degree to which the person's social network and contacts were developed. Nuckolls, Cassel, and Kaplan (1972) found that pregnant women with high life change and low social support were almost three times more likely to experience complications during delivery than women with high life change and high social support. Cobb (1976) stated that social support might serve to protect people from a variety of disorders such as arthritis, tuberculosis, depression, alcoholism, and low birth weight. He also held that social support would enable individuals to adhere to prescribed medical regimen and would reduce the amount of medication necessary for cure. Moreover, social support has been related to adjusting emotionally to abortion (Belsey et al., 1977) and to the adjustment to aging and retirement (Lowenthal & Haven, 1968). The concept of social support has been suggested as the basis for mutual-help organizations and self-help groups (Caplan & Killilea, 1976; Gottlieb, 1981).

Despite the diversity of definitions for social support, most definitions have focused on the helping elements, such as emotional or perceived support, and actual or material aid. The therapeutic effect of social support may be a combination of emotional and material aid, or it may modify the indivudal's stress response by altering the woman's perception of the stressor. Contact with a group of women who experience the same problem and situation may act to change the PMS sufferer's perception that she is alone or unique in her problem. A supportive network could also provide an outlet for women to discuss certain problems, anxieties, or thoughts which they may not freely express to friends or family members who have no direct experience with PMS (MacElveen-Hoehn & Eyres, 1982). An example is a woman who finds that her premenstrual irritability and aggressiveness are linked with negative or violent thoughts concerning her partner or child. Possibly only other women with PMS would understand these cyclical emotions and would not be so quick to condemn the woman for her strong negative emotions.

A supportive social network may actually change the woman's appraisal of her life-stressors. There is experimental evidence that social support can reduce the individual's susceptibility to physiological stress responses brought on by psychosocial stimuli (Kiritz & Moos, 1974). This research suggests that the social network influences the woman to alter her perception of the psychosocial stressor, or that the supportive network somehow aids the woman to withstand environmental stressors.

From this evidence, it is suggested that a peer support network with its complex of factors may be therapeutic in the clinical management of a chronic event like PMS. The factors have been previously described as emotional support, affirmation of self-worth, stress reduction, and instrumental aid (i.e., information, problem solving, and assistance). These components are hypothesized to act in combination to persuade individuals to adhere to their prescribed pharmacologic and nonpharmacologic regimens.

## PILOT STUDY

A peer support group was convened by a nonprofessional volunteer as part of the treatment program developed by a Menstrual Disorder Clinic within a University Health Science Center. Clinic personnel recruited subjects for the support group on a voluntary basis. The purpose of the group was explained to each subject as educational, supportive, and an ordinary component of the therapeutic regimen.

### Sample

The subjects were 22 women (23 to 43 years), diagnosed as having moderate to severe perimenstrual symptoms. The women were diagnosed in accordance with criteria established by the PMS and Menstrual Distress Clinic: symptoms must occur premenstrually and include both somatic and psychosocial components, symptoms must be severe enough to be disabling or disruptive of usual life patterns, and there must be a symptom-free period each cycle. The subjects were divided into an experimental and a control group. The experimental group was a convenience sample drawn from the files of the Menstrual Disorder Clinic and was invited to participate in a PMS support group. The control group was a matched sample selected from the same patient population. The groups were matched for age, marital status, pregnancy history, and occupation.

**Instruments**

Four questionnaires were administered: The Personal Resource Questionnaire (PRQ) (Brandt & Weinert, 1981); the Moos Menstrual Distress Questionnaire, form T (MDQ) (Moos, 1977); and two questionnaires (Questionnaire A and Q) developed by the investigator which consisted of questions about the subjects' experiences with PMS and the support group.

The Personal Resource Questionnaire (PRQ) was used to rate the subjects' social networks on five dimensions: intimacy, social integration, nurturance, worth, and assistance. Part I consists of nine problem situations, measuring both the number of people the women would turn to as well as the perceived satisfaction. Part II consists of 25 statements placed on a seven point Likert format, measuring each of the 5 dimensions of social support. Using Cronbach's alpha, Brandt and Weinert (1981) found an internal consistency reliability coefficient of alpha = .89 for Part II. Validity copfficients ranged from .21 to .23 ($p < .004$) for Part I and from .30 to .44 ($p < .001$) for Part II.

The number and severity of perimenstrual symptoms were measured by the Moos Menstrual Distress Quentionnaire (MDQ). The MDQ is made up of 41 common perimenstrual symptoms and six control symptoms. Respondents rated their experience of each symptom on a six-point scale ranging from "no reaction at all" to "acute or disabling." The items may be separated into eight subscales—pain, negative affect, autonomic reactions, water retention, behavior change, concentration, arousal, and control. Split-half correlations have been significantly high and women tend to have similar individual scores from cycle to cycle (Moos, 1977).

Questionnaire A consisted of questions about the subjects' experiences of PMS and the self-help measures they had taken in the prior four months. Questionnaire B contained open-ended questions about the support groups in which the experimental group was involved. Questionnaire B was adapted from work by Knight, Wollert, Levy, Frame, and Padgett (1980).

**Procedure**

At the beginning of the experimental period all subjects completed the PRQ and began a daily rating of premenstrual symptoms using the MDQ. After 8 weeks, the nubjects in both the experimental and control groups received second copies of the PRQ and Questionnaire A, which includes questions about their experience of PMS and the self help measures they had taken in the past four months. The experimental group received Questionnaire B, which asked about the peer support group in which they were involved.

The women in the experimental group participated in a PMS support group led by a nonprofessional. The groups met weekly for approximately 2.5 hours. Each week the members would discuss a topic that had been designated the week before. The meeting would loosely follow a format in which each member would take a turn speaking while the others were free to offer advice, additional comments, and anything else that seemed appropriate. After everyone had had a chance to talk, the discussion would open up to anyone who wanted to talk. Emphasis was placed upon encouraging each member to participate.

The control subjects received their materials by mail, and there was no collective meeting of the group. At the end of the experimental period, they were sent a second copy of the PRQ and Questionnaire A and were asked to complete them and return the packet by mail.

## Analysis

The PRQ was scored according to six subscores. First, the total number of people each respondent circled as sources of support were counted. Second, the number of times the respondent indicated that she had a problem over the past six months was tallied in order to obtain a general idea of the respondents' relative levels of stressful life events in the recent past. Third, the total satisfaction scores were divided by the number of problems reported. This provided the average satisfaction level the respondent experienced after asking people for help with a problem. Fourth, the number of times each respondent indicated she would seek help with a problem was counted. PRQ-Part II was scored by summing the total of the twenty-five statement ratings. Finally, the number of people or groups rated as "important" was tabulated.

The MDQs were divided into two phase categories, the luteal and follicular phases, and the two categories were scored separately. The luteal phases were assumed to be fourteen days long because time between ovulation and menses is approximately two weeks regardless of cycle length. The follicular phase was determined to be from the onset of menstrual flow to the day before ovulation. In the analysis of scores for the control and experimental groups, the luteal phase scores were the only ones used.

The MDQs were scored with respect to two factors: daily number of symptoms and severity of daily symptoms. The number of symptoms were counted on each questionnaire for a daily total score. For each subject, the total number of symptoms reported in each phase was summed and then divided by the number of days in that phase. In this way a mean daily symptom number was calculated for the luteal and follicular phases. A mean daily severity score was calculated by adding up the daily ratings, "no reaction at all" (0) to "acute or disabling" (5), and dividing by the number of symptoms that day to get a daily average severity score. The daily severity averages were then added together (separately for the two phases), and divided by the number of days in that phase. This resulted in two mean daily severity scores for each woman, one for the luteal and one for the follicular phase. The mean daily luteal symptom number and symptom severity scores were calculated for the control and experimental groups by summing each subject's mean daily score and dividing by the number of subjects in that condition.

Questionnaires A and B were scored with a modified content analysis strategy. For open-ended questions, the number of times a particular response was given was counted. The responses that subjects gave most frequently were considered. For example, Questionnaire A includes a question asking the respondent to list and rate the life style changes she has made which have a beneficial effect on her PMS. If the subject gave "education" as her first response, education would be recorded as being mentioned and assigned a ranking of "1." If another respondent listed education as her third response, this second mention of education would be recorded and its ranking of "3" would be recorded. If no one else mentioned education, the final scoring would show that education was mentioned by two subjects and that was given a mean ranking of "2" $[(1 + 3)/2 = 2]$. As a rule, responses were recorded only when reported by more than 30 percent of the subjects in either group. This method enabled measurement of the outstanding elements and common beliefs with respect to the effectiveness of the peer groups and the other treatment strategies for reducing premenstrual symptoms.

Frequency tables were established for each multiple choice question (such as "yes," "no," or "unsure"). There were two within group analyses of Questionnaire A, (one for each condition), to test whether responses were due to chance or due to an agreement among the members of each group. A between group analysis of Questionnaire A was performed to test whether or not the support group members' responses differed from those of the control group.

Questionnaire B was analyzed to test for favored responses that were not due to chance.

## RESULTS AND DISCUSSION

The subjects in support groups did not statistically differ from the control subjects in terms of symptom severity or number, or in social network size or satisfaction. However, with a larger sample size, group differences may be statistically significant. The results of this pilot study suggest that peer support might be a therapeutic adjunct in the treatment of menstrual distress.

The importance of a peer support group as a therapeutic method does deserve discussion in spite of the lack of statistically significant differences. The group members' comments, attitudes, and involvement in the group indicate that it was helpful to them.

Questionnaire B showed that 8 of the 10 women in the peer support group believed their meetings were 'somewhat to very' effective in satisfying the goals they expected the group to satisfy (see Table 1). The women stated that the support group provided the following types of benefits: education, emotional support, information that they were not alone with their problem, and people with whom to share problem situations and advice. When these functions were provided by the group, the women found that making the necessary life-style changes was facilitated. As evidenced by the responses to Questionnaire A, the women attributed the improvement of their symptoms to the pre-existing treatments such as diet change, natural progesterone therapy, vitamin and mineral supplements, and to education and awareness. It may be that the support group is not the key element in treatment, but rather works indirectly by informing the women about the life-style changes and their importance and by facilitating the life-style changes.

Table 1. Questionnaire B Responses: Support Group Only (before and after support group)

| Multiple-choice question | Chi-square | $p$ |
| --- | --- | --- |
| 5. Support group changed outlook on PMS? | 2.600 | ns |
| 6. PMS outlook changed at all? | 4.667 | .10 |
| 8. Support group effective in helping you with what you expected it to? | 10.410 | .01 |

*Note.* $N = 32$.

The positive attitudes of the women toward the support group and their beliefs that it helped them with their disorder warrangs further investigation of the hypothesis that social support may be an important factor in the treatment of premenstrual syndrome. In addition, further investigation of the relationship of social support and its mediating effect on stressors which may influence menstrual distress is warranted. Questionnaire responses from the subjects in the support group indicate that what they had learned from other group members had helped them to cope with their own cyclic symptoms and stressful life events. This seems to suggest that symptom severity was reduced (by subjective report) even though, statistically, the severity of symptoms did not decrease.

This pilot study will be repeated with a larger sample and a longer interval between the completion of the first and second sets of questionnaires. Ideally, the second set would not be administered until the support group members felt that the group had fulfilled its purpose and the group meetings were terminated. A strong test of the hypothesis would also requie some refinement of the social support measure. It would be desirable to have "support group" and "support group member" as choices for the respondent to turn to with a problem. This would facilitate measuring the importance of the support group to each member. The PRQ is not particularly sensitive to the benefits or costs of individual members within the subject's social network. The instrument assumes that important people in one's network are also supportive. Clinical observations contradict this premise and suggest that while part of a woman's social network is supportive, others are nonsupportive.

In summary, peer social support in combination with the other treatments, may be a very effective method of reducing the experience of premenstrual syndrome. It may serve to educate, to provide the necessary strength and support to adhere to the difficult treatment regimen, and to provide an outlet for the anxieties and frustrations felt by PMS sufferers. As one support group member put it, "I never feel quite sure that nay of the treatments or coping mechanisms are all that successful. One thing I feel sure about is that support groups, such as the one I'm involved with, are the best way to remain hopeful and sane."

## REFERENCES

Abraham, G. E. (1980). The premenstrual tension syndromes. In L. K. McNall (Ed.), *Contemporary obstetric and gynecologic nursing,* (Vol. III). St. Louis, MO: Mosby.

Abplanalp, J. M. et al. (1977). Cortisol and growth hormone responses to psychological stress during the menstrual cycle. *Psychosom. Med., 39,* 158.

Backstrom, T., & Mattsson, B. (1975). Correlation of symptoms in premenstrual tension to estrogen and progesterone in blood plasma. *Neuropsychobiology, 1,* 80.

Backstrom, T., & Aakvaag, A. (1981). Plasma prolactin and testosterone during the luteal phase in women with premenstrual tension syndrome. *Psychoneuroendocrinology, 6,* 245–251.

Backstrom, T., Sanders, D., et al. (1983). Mood, sexuality, hormones and the menstrual cycle. *Psychosomatic Med., 45,* 487.

Belsey, E. M., Greer, H. S., Lal, S., Lewis, S. C., & Beard, R. W. (1977). Predictive factors in emotional response to abortion. *Social Science and Medicine, 11,* 71–82.

Berkman, L. F., & Syme, S. L. (1979). Social networks, host resistance, and mortality: A nine-year follow-up study of Alameda County Residents. *American Journal of Epidemiology, 109,* 186–204.

Brandt, P. A., & Weinert, C. (1981). The PRQ—a social support measure. *Nursing Research, 30*(5), 277–280.

Broadhead, W. E., Kaplan, B. H., James, S. A., Wagner, E. H., Schoenbach, V. J., Grinson, R., Heyden, S., Tibblin, G., & Gehlbach, S. H. (1983). The epidemiologic evidence for a relationship between social support and health. *American Journal of Epidemiology, 117*(5), 521–537.

Caplan, G., & Killilea, M. (1976). *Support systems and mutual help: Multidisciplinary explorations.* New York: Grune & Stratton.

Cassel, J. (1974). Psychosocial processes and stress: Theoretical formulations. *Int. J. Health Services, 4,* 471–482.

Cassel, J. (1976). The contribution of the social environment to host resistance. *American Journal of Epidemiology, 104*(2), 107–111.

Cobb, S. (1976). Social support as a moderator of life stress. *Psychosomatic Medicine, 38*(5), 300–314.

Coyne, C., Woods, N., & Mitchell, E. (1985). Premenstrual tension syndrome— a review. *J. Ob-Gyn Nursing, 14*(6), 446–458.

Dean, A., & Lin, N. (1977). The stress buffering role of social support: Problems and prospects for systematic investigation. *Journal of Nervous and Mental Disease, 165,* 403–417.

Frank, R. T. (1931). The hormonal causes of premenstrual tension. *Arch. Neurol. Psychiatry, 26,* 1031.

Ganong, W. F. (1983). *Review of medical psysiology* (11th ed.). Los Altos: Lange Medical Publishers.

Girdano, D., & Everly, G. (1979). *Controlling stress and tension: A holistic approach.* Englewood Cliffs, NJ: Prentice-Hall.

Gottlieb, B. H. (1981). Social networks and social support in community mental health. In B. H. Gottlieb (Ed.) *Social networks and social support.* Beverly Hills, CA: Sage.

Henry, J. P., & Ely, D. L. (1980). Ethological and physiological theories. In I. L. Kutash & L. B. Schlesinger (Eds.). *Handbook on stress and anxiety.* San Francisco: Jossey-Bass.

Jordan, J., & Meckler, J. R. (1982). The relationship between life change events, social supports, and dysmenorrhea. *Research in Nursing and Health, 5,* 73–79.

Kahn, R. L., & Antonucci, T. D. (1980). Convoys over the life course: Attachment, roles and social support. In P. B. Baltes & O. G. Brim, Jr. (Eds.), *Life span development and behavior, 3.* New York: Academic Press.

Kaplan, B. H., Cassel, J. C., & Gore, S. (1977). Social support and health. *Medical Care, 15*(5, suppl.), 47–58.

Kiritz, S., & Moos, R. H. (1974). In F. M. Insel & R. H. Moos (Eds.), *Health and the social environment.* Lexington, MA: D. C. Heath & Co.

Knight, B., Wollert, R., Levy, L., Frame, C., & Padgett, V. (1980). Self help groups: The members' perspectives. *Am. J. of Community Psychology, 8,* 53–65.

Kogan, H. N., & Betrus, P. (1984). Self-management: A nursing mode of therapeutic influence. *Advances in Nursing Science, 7,* 55–73.

Krieger, D. T. (1980). The hypothalamus and neuroendocrinology. In D. T. Krieger & J. C. Hughes (Eds.). *Neuroendocrinology.* New York: HP Publishing Co., Inc.

Levin, L., & Idler, E. (1981). *The hidden health care system: Mediating structures and medicine.* Cambridge, MA: Ballinger.

Lowenthal, M. F., & Haven, C. (1968). Interaction and adaptation: Intimacy as a critical variable. *American Sociological Review, 33,* 20–30.

MacElveen-Hoehn, P., & Eyres, S. J. (1982). Social support and vulnerability: State of the art in relation to families and children. Paper presented at March of Dimes Conference, "Social Support and Families of Vulnerable Infants," October 24, 1982.

Mason, J. W. (1975). A historical view of the stress field. *J. Human Stress, 1,* 22.

Moos, R. H. (1977). *Menstrual distress questionnaire.* Palo Alto, CA: Stanford University Press.

Norbeck, J. S. (1982). The use of social support in clinical practice. *Journal of Psychiatric Nursing, 20*(12), 22–29.

Nuckolls, K. B., Cassel, J., & Kaplan, B. M. (1972). Psychosocial assets, life crises, and the prognosis of pregnancy. *American Journal of Epidemiology, 95,* 431–441.

O'Rourke, M. W. (1983). Self-reports of menstrual and nonmenstrual symptomatology in university-employed women. *J. Ob-Gyn Nursing, 5,* 317.

Selye, Hans. (1956). *The stress of life.* New York: McGraw-Hill.

Sommer, B. (1978). Stress and menstrual distress. *J. Human Stress, 4,* 5.

Taylor, D. L. (1984). Unpublished manuscript submitted to Sigma Theta Tau. School of Nursing, Oregon Health Sciences University.

Thoits, F. A. (1982). Conceptual, methodological, and theoretical problems in studying social support as a buffer against life stress. *Journal of Health and Social Behavior, 23*(2), 145–159.

Turner, R. J. (1983). Direct, indirect, and moderating effects of social support on phychological distress and associated conditions. In B. H. Kaplan (Ed.). *Psychosocial stress.* London, UK: Academic Press.

Walker, K., MacBride, A., & Vachon, M. (1977). Social support networks and the crisis of bereavement. *Social Science and Medicine, 11,* 35–41.

Weiss, R. S. (1974). The provisions of social relationships. In Z. R. Rubin (Ed.). *Doing unto others.* Englewood Cliffs, NJ: Prentice-Hall.

Winnubst, J., Marcelissen, F., & Kleber, R. (1982). Effects of social support in the stressor-strain relationship: A dutch sample. *Social Science and Medicine, 16,* 475–482.

Woods, N. F., Most, A., & Dery, G. (1982). Estimating perimenstrual distress: A comparison of two methods. *Res. Nursing and Health, 5,* 81.

# HELP–SEEKING FOR PREMENSTRUAL SYMPTOMATOLOGY: A DESCRIPTION OF WOMEN'S EXPERIENCES

**Marie Annette Brown, RN, PhD, and Phyllis Arn Zimmer, RN, MN, FNP**
Family Nurse Practitioner Program, University of Washington, Seattle, Washington

The new consumer-oriented literature on PMS both directly and indirectly suggests that the health care system, and in particular physicians, offer little acknowledgement, understanding or assistance to women seeking care for perimenstrual distress. In fact clinical reports point to disrespectful, dismissing and antagonistic attitudes on the part of health care providers as an important stress for women seeking help. Although some writers claim that physician bias and female stereotypes pervade all aspects of women's health care, others charge that gynecological and reproductive health care is even more prone to these abuses because of the nature of the problems. This pilot study was conducted to explore the experiences of women seeking help for premenstrual symptomatology. The sample consisted of 83 women who attended an evening lecture on premenstrual symptoms sponsored by a local civic group. Single, brief overview questions were used to obtain general information about symptoms, experiences with the health care system and motivations for attending the seminar. All of the participants had previously sought help for their symptoms and the majority had tried several different types of providers. Nurse practitioners were most frequently positively rated, while physicians were evaluated most negatively. The majority of the sample felt they were treated disrespectfully and were not taken seriously. Only one third of women currently in treatment were satisfied with the assistance they were receiving. These data support the informal descriptions of widespread dissatisfaction with current health care provider responses to women seeking assistance with premenstrual symptoms.

This project was supported in part by BRSG S07 RR05758 awarded by the Biomedical Research Support Grant Program, Division of Research Resources, National Institutes of Health.

## INTRODUCTION

Specific and supportive health care for women can be considered "an idea whose time has come." The proliferation of lay and professional books about women's health has been striking over the past decade. Particularly notable has been recent media attention directed toward a previously ignored and denied phenomenon—severe premenstrual symptomatology. *Science* (1984) summarized this phenomenon:

> Thus, it happened in the summer of 1982 that premenstrual symptomatology or PMS arrived. A disease that thousands of women had been told didn't exist suddenly became a media event. Newsweeklies, talk shows, style pages, bookstores, all had something to offer on PMS. There was no news, no cure, not even a better idea of its cause. What happened was less tangible: PMS acquired medical legitimacy. After years of telling women their problems were all in their head, the proportion of doctors who accepted PMS as a real disease reached critical mass.

The new consumer-oriented literature on PMS both directly and indirectly suggests that the health care system, and in particular physicians, has offered little acknowledgement, understanding, or assistance to women seeking care and upon occasion have been disrespectful, dismissing and antagonistic (Dalton, 1984; Lark, 1984; Lauersen, 1983; Norris & Sullivan, 1983). Consequently, there has been a demand for more comprehensive and supportive health care for women. As a result, special clinics and treatment programs have emerged which deal specifically with premenstrual syndrome or PMS.

The literature to date, however, does not document or evaluate provider responses to premenstrual cycle problems. This pilot study was conducted to explore the experiences of women seeking help for premenstrual symptomatology.

Women in the reproductive age group utilize considerably more physician services (exclusive of utilization due to pregnancy) than men (Nathanson, 1977). They also experience greater morbidity, days of illness, and disability (Verbrugge, 1979). A wide range of explanations have been posited for why women are more frequent users of health care than men. There is some indication that they have more interest in health-related issues and information (Feldman, 1966) and may utilize more preventive health services (Woods, 1981; Langlie, 1977). Other researchers have offered the following hypotheses: women's socialization as the primary caretakers of health in families (Albino & Tedesco, 1984), their increased responsiveness to discomfort and pain (Mechanic, 1976; Verbrugge, 1979), their more stressful roles and responsibilities, and their lower prestige and satisfaction in work, both inside and outside the home (Nathanson, 1975). Recently Hebbard and Page (1985) found a correlation between women's roles and concern with health and their reported symptoms.

In the past two decades reproductive health care services have been scrutinized from a political as well as a public health perspective (Dunbar, Paterson, Burton, & Stuckert, 1981; Boston Women's Health Collective, 1985; Harrison, 1982). There has been criticism of the fact that normal female life cycle events, such as menstruation, childbirth and menopause are treated in the context of pathology, disease and illness (Woods, 1981b). Attention has focused on "negative attitudes toward women patients" and medical textbooks depicting women in traditional and demeaning images (Dunbar et al., 1981; Stevenson, 1979; Scully & Bart, 1973; Woods, 1981b). "Physicians are thought to be less thorough in their diagnostic procedures for women patients, to give more superficial information about treatment regimens, and to recommend more unnecessary drugs, surgery, and follow-up care" (Verbrugge & Steiner, 1981, p. 610).

Although some writers claim that physician bias and female stereotypes pervade all aspects of women's health care (Scully & Bart, 1973; Frankfort, 1972; Howell, 1974), others charge that gynecological/reproductive health care is more prone to these abuses because of the nature of the problems (Lannane & Lannane, 1973; Woods, 1981b; Boston Women's Health Collective, 1985). Further investigation is necessary. Although a number of interesting insights have been elucidated, blatant and pervasive sex bias in health care has not been confirmed, to date.

Armitage, Schneiderman, and Bass (1979) analyzed the differential physician responses to males and females (52 married couples) seeking care for one of five primary complaints—back pain, headache, dizziness, chest pain, or fatigue. They observed that for all the complaints, workups were less extensive for women and concluded that stereotypical views of the hypochondriacal female contributed to biased care.

Wallen, Waitzken, and Stoekle (1979) studied tape recordings of male physician interactions with 184 male and 130 female patients. They found that men received fuller explanations without asking as many questions as women. Furthermore, the women's questions were often more technically sophisticated than the responses they received, indicating physicians may be "talking down" to their female patients. The physicians also attributed more psychological causes to women's illnesses and tended to be more pessimistic in their prognoses.

Verbrugge and Steiner (1981) examined data from the National Ambulatory Medical Care Survey and found a number of significant sex differences in medical care for men and women. These differences, however, suggested an opposite trend from the previously reported work. Women received more total and extensive services: laboratory tests, blood pressure charts, drug prescriptions, and return appointments. They suggest that sex bias can sometimes lead to more services for women than men:

> Physicians may offer more care to women because they believe women are more willing to spend time and money on health care, that women want more overt attention. . . . There is an extra incentive for having stereotypic views about women—income. It is highly remunerative to provide services and follow-up care for chronic, ambiguous problems. Together, this incentive and stereotypic views can lead some physicians to offer unnecessary and biased care. (Verbrugge and Steiner, 1981, p. 631)

In Berstein and Kane's study (1981) physicians tended to give women a psychosomatic diagnosis and to consider emotional factors important in their health problems. When female patients were less expressive and provided the physician with less cues, the physicians tended to employ stereotypic approaches.

Other authors have not found evidence of physicians' bias in care delivery. McCranie, Horowitz, and Martin (1978) used simulated patient profiles. No differences were noted in diagnoses, ratings of severity and prognosis, and treatment decisions. Verbrugge (1980) noted no difference in how often men and women reporting symptoms were declared "not sick" and the number of diagnoses received.

These studies raise questions about women's treatment as they seek health care, particularly in the area of reproductive health. The purpose of this study was to describe women's experiences with health care providers when seeking assistance with premenstrual symptoms. The current work was a pilot study designed to determine specific areas appropriate for more in-depth exploration of the interface between women's perimenstrual needs and the response of the health care delivery system.

## SAMPLE

The sample consisted of 83 women who attended an evening lecture on premenstrual symptoms sponsored by a local civic group. The age of the women ranged from 18 to 43 with a mean age of 33. Ninety-five percent of the women were caucasian. The educational level of the women included high school graduates (26%), additional trade/business school (26%), college degree (34%), and graduate school degree (14%). Thirty-nine percent of the women described themselves as homemakers and 61 percent reported that they were employed outside the home.

The mean occupational status of the employed women was 5.3 using a 10-point scale adapted from Hollingshead (Hollingshead, 1975). Higher scores indicated a greater status given to the occupational category. Thirty-one percent of the women stated they attended the meeting with their partner, 10 percent were accompanied by other family members, 30 percent came with a friend, and the remainder (29%) attended the seminar alone.

## QUESTIONNAIRE

The current study used an exploratory design. The subjects completed a short questionnaire prior to the lecture. Single, brief overview questions were used to obtain general information about symptomatology, experiences with the health care delivery system, and motivations for attending the seminar.

Women were asked to "briefly list their premenstrual symptoms." It was expected that this open-ended approach would minimize overreporting of premenstrual symptoms noted by other investigators (Woods, 1982) who used symptom checklists. Because premenstrual symptomatology can vary from month to month (Moos, 1968; Taylor, 1979; Shildrake & Cormack, 1976), women were asked to give a summary of their symptoms. This method yielded a retrospective reporting of symptoms, with all the accompanying questions of validity. This method did not provide an opportunity for careful assessment of the frequency or severity of each particular premenstrual symptom or the establishment of a diagnosis of premenstrual syndrome. Women were asked, however, to rate the degree of the disruption that they perceived from their premenstrual symptoms, as well as the overall frequency with which they experienced premenstrual symptomatology. The number of symptoms reported were summed for a total symptom score.

Women were questioned about their experiences when consulting others for assistance with their premenstrual symptoms. They were asked to describe the role (i.e., nurse, psychologist, friend) of those individuals they had asked for help, and to evaluate whether these consultations were positive or negative. Subjects were also questioned about the content and outcome of these consultations and their feelings about these interactions. The multiple choice responses to these questions were generated by the investigators based on their clinical experience working with women in gynecologic clinics and premenstrual syndrome support groups.

## RESULTS

A total of 74 unique regularly recurring premenstrual symptoms were reported spontaneously, of which the most frequently reported category was the "tension states," such as irritability and agitation. The maximum number of symptoms reported by any one subject was 22. Although the mean number of symptoms reported by women was six, half of the subjects reported five or more symptoms and one-fourth of the sample stated that they regularly experienced 10 or more premenstrual symptoms. Almost all of the subjects reported that symptoms "always or usually" occurred every menstrual cycle.

All of the study participants had sought previous consultation regarding their premenstrual symptoms. The majority of women in this sample had sought consultation from several different categories of individuals, with the range of one to eight categories of helpers. Furthermore, while the questionnaire did not delineate the number of different individuals consulted in each category, a number of the subjects spontaneously offered that they had sought out several different individuals in some categories, particularly physicians. Twenty-four percent reported consulting only one category of helpers, 25 percent of the subjects consulted two categories, 14 percent sought three categories, 17 percent consulted four categories, and 20 percent of the women sought the advice of between five and eight different categories of helpers.

The greater the total number of consultations a woman reported, the more frequent ($p = .20$; $r = .04$) and disruptive ($r = .39$; $p = .001$) her premenstrual symptoms. The most frequently consulted categories of health care providers were physician (87%), nurse practitioner (42%), counselor/psychologist (31%), nurse (24%), psychiatrist (21%), chiropractor (12%), nutritionist (9%), doctor of osteopathy (6%), and clergy (6%). In addition, 62 percent of the subjects sought help from their friends and 69 percent from the "other" category. The greater the total number of premenstrual symptoms, the more likely women were to seek assistance from psychologists/counselors (r = .26; p = .009), clergy (r = .20; p = .03), and friends (r = .33; p = .002). Table 1 presents the quality of experience (positive or negative) reported by women who sought consultation from each of the categories of individuals. In particular, of those who saw a physician or psychiatrist, 77 percent and 66 percent, respectively, reported this to be a negative encounter. On the other hand, encounters with nurse practitioners were more frequently positive than with other health professionals.

The women were then asked about their feelings and experiences surrounding these consultations. Fifty-four percent of the women reported that they were treated disrespectfully and 46 percent were treated respectfully by health care providers; 34 percent were told their symptoms were "all in their head," 47 percent reported that they were informed that their premenstrual symptoms were "part of being a woman," 72 percent felt they were not taken seriously and 24 percent were told to "go home and pull themselves together." Only 20 percent of the women felt they were given useful information. Of these, 16 percent thought their symptoms improved as a result of the help they received.

The management plan most frequently included psychiatric

Table 1. Quality of Experience with Consultants

| Consultant | Positive[a] (%) | Negative[a] (%) |
|---|---|---|
| Other | 69 | 31 |
| Nurse Practitioner | 67 | 33 |
| Friend | 61 | 39 |
| Nurse | 60 | 40 |
| Nutritionist | 60 | 40 |
| Clergy | 60 | 40 |
| Psychologist/Counselor | 50 | 50 |
| Doctor of Osteopathy | 50 | 50 |
| Chiropractor | 40 | 60 |
| Psychiatrist | 37 | 63 |
| Physician | 33 | 67 |

[a]Percent of those women who consulted the category of individuals.

referral (38%) or medications (47%), often tranquilizers (35%). Women who received tranquilizers were more likely to report a higher degree of life disruption from their premenstrual symptoms (r = .22; p = .03). Seventeen percent of the subjects were told nothing could be done to help them. The women with a greater total number of symptoms were more likely to be referred to a psychiatrist (r = .25; p = .01) or given tranquilizers (r = .19; p = .05). They were also more likely to report that they felt that they were not taken seriously (r = .20; p = .04).

Several of the women's motivations for attending the seminar can be viewed in light of the responses they received from health care providers. Subjects who stated that they attended the seminar to find out what they could do to alleviate their own symptoms were more likely to have received tranquilizers (r = .20; p = .04) or other medications (r = .26, p = .01), to have felt that they were not treated seriously (r = .26; p = .01), and to have been referred to a psychiatrist (r = .22; p = .03). Women who stated that their attendance motivation related to the desire to talk with other women who have similar symptoms were more likely to report they had been told by helath care providers that their symptoms were "all in their heads" (r = .19; p = .05) and to feel that they were not taken seriously by their provider (r = .21; p = .04).

And finally, 27 percent of the women reported that they were presently involved in a treatment program for their premenstrual symptoms. The greater the perceived life disruption from her premenstrual symptoms the more likely the subject was to be currently involved in treatment for her symptomatology (r = .34, p = .001). Of those currently receiving help, only 30 percent reported that they were satisfied with their assistance.

## DISCUSSION

The idea that women are expressing dissatisfaction with their health care is not new or surprising. "The literature is replete with accounts of sexism—in personal health services, in education of professionals and in research on women's health" (Woods, 1981b, p. 40).

This brief pilot study does not allow conclusions of physician bias but does reflect women's perceptions of providers as unsupportive, rejecting, disrespectful, or, at the least, unhelpful. Only one-third of the women currently in treatment were satisfied with the assistance they received.

It is striking to note that all of the participants had sought health care for their perimenstrual distress, with 20 percent having seen at least five different categories of helpers. It is likely that the actual number of different helpers, especially physicians, is under-represented.

Although this sample of women who have actively sought help for PMS is not necessarily representative, the pattern of help-seeking demonstrated here raises a number of questions. Why did these women persist in seeking help despite the large number of negative experiences they had? Did their high frequency of recurring premenstrual symptoms increase their motivation? Does their persistence in seeking help correlate with the amount of life disruption caused by their symptoms?

Almost half the participants in this study received some type of medication for the problem though the pathophysiologic base of premenstrual syndrome has not yet been clearly delineated (Reid & Yen, 1981, 1983). There are a number of explanations for this: Waldron (1977) discussed the idea that medication is often the easiest way of "doing something;" Woods (1981b) points out that there is often a sexist bias in the prescription of medications; and Cooperstock (1971) suggests that women are often given mood-altering drugs because of their propensity to bring their emotional problems to the attention of physicians.

One-fifth of the participants reported that they were told nothing could be done to help them. It is not clear whether they were also directed towards self-help in the areas of nutrition and lifestyle, or they were simply told "It's all in your head" or "It's just part of being a woman." In both situations they felt they were not being taken seriously, either because the tone and manner of the clinicians was pejorative or the women were reluctant to hear the message of self-responsibility for health.

Several clinicians have noted that it is critical for women to understand the contributions of stress and lifestyle to premenstrual symptomatology (Dalton, 1984; Harrison, 1982; Lark, 1984; Lauerson & Stukane, 1983; Norris & Sullivan, 1983). However, the necessity for self-responsibility must not be used to discourage women, but to inspire them.

The most popular interventions are currently in the areas of nutrition and lifestyle modifications, specifically exercise and stress management. The attitude with which this information is presented to the patient will determine whether it is received positively or negatively. In fact, the participant's more positive perceptions of nurse practitioners may be due to the nurse practitioners' empathic and practical emphasis on self-help preventive measures. McBride

(1984), commenting on the relationship between the Women's Movement and Nursing, writes, "Nurses are particularly well prepared to meet the health needs of women. . . . They are schooled to build their assessments on client's perception of their experience and to promote self-help, and that is exactly what women are demanding. . . . The emphasis is on valuing ordinary thoughts and feelings, and analyzing them for patterns that can guide action" (p. 66).

Dissatisfaction with traditional approaches and providers' negative attitudes may be responsible for these women's frequent use of alternative healers, who comprised the "other" category, second in choice only to physicians. A variety of provider options was available to these women. Woods (1981b) observes that "the most striking change occurring in women's health over the last decade has been movement from a nearly universal, traditional authoritarian approach in delivery of personal health services to the pluralistic array of the late 1970s" (Woods, 1981b, p. 46).

This study, unfortunately, did not differentiate women's levels of satisfaction according to the degree of traditional authoritarianism exhibited by the providers. It would be intersting to note whether, for example, those nurse practitioners and physicians who received a more positive rating by the women were associated with a setting that emphasized a less traditional approach such as a feminist clinic or community clinic.

These data were collected in 1983 at the very beginning of the national media surge of information on PMS and this seminar was the first on this topic held in the community. It would be interesting to conduct a follow-up study now, after several years of public education about PMS, to determine whether women's perceptions about their treatment for premenstrual symptomatology have changed.

## REFERENCES

Armitage, K. J., Schneiderman, L. J., & Bass, R. A. (1979). Response of physicians to medical complaints of men and women. *Journal of the American Medical Association, 241,* 2186–2187.

Bernstein, B., & Kane, R. (1981). Physicians' attitudes toward female patients. *Medical Care, 18,* 600–610.

Boston Women's Health Collective (1985). *Our bodies, ourselves.* New York: Simon and Schuster.

Cooperstock, R. (1971). Sex differences in the use of mood-modifying drugs: An explanatory model. *Journal of Health and Social Behavior, 12,* 238–244.

Dalton, K. (1984). *The premenstrual syndrome and progesterone therapy.* Chicago, IL: Yearbook Medical Publishers.

Dunbar, S. B., Patterson, E., Burton, C., & Strikert, G. (1981). Women's health and nursing research. *Advances in Nursing Science, 3,* 1–10.

Feldman, J. (1966). *The dissemination of health information.* Chicago, IL: Aldine.

Frankfort, E. (1972). *Vaginal Politics.* New York: Quadrangle Press.

Harrison, M. (1982). *Self-help for premenstrual syndromes.* New York: Random House.

Hibbard, J. H., & Pope, C. R. (1985). Gender roles, illness orientation and use of medical services. *Social Science and Medicine, 17*(3), 129–137.

Hollingshead, A. (1975). *Four factor index of social status.* New Haven: Yale University Press.

Howell, M. C. (1974). What medical schools teach about women. *New England Journal of Medicine, 291*(6), 304–307.

Langlie, J. K. (1977). Social networks, health beliefs and preventative health behaviors. *Journal of Social and Health Behavior, 18,* 244–260.

Lark, S. M. (1984). *Premenstrual syndrome self help book.* Los Angeles: Forman.

Lauersen, N. H., & Stukane, E. (1983). *Premenstrual syndrome and you.* New York: Simon and Schuster.

Lennane, K. J., & Lennane, R. J. (1973). Alleged psychogenic disorders in women: A possible manifestation of sexual prejudice. *New England Journal of Medicine, 288*(1), 288–292.

Mechanic, D. (1976). Sex, illness, illness behavior and the use of health services. *Journal of Human Stress, 2,* 29–40.

McBride, A. B. (1984). Editorial: Nursing and the Women's Movement. *Image: The Journal of Nursing Scholarship, 16*(3), 66.

McCranie, E. W., Horowitz, A. J., & Martin, R. M. (1978). Alleged sex role stereotyping in the assessment of women's physical complaints: A study of general practitioners. *Social Science and Medicine, 12,* 111–119.

Moos, R. H. (1968). The development of a menstrual distress questionnaire. *Psychosomatic Medicine, 30,* 853–867.

Nathanson, C. A. (1977). Sex, illness, and medical care: A review of data, theory, and method. *Social Science and Medicine, 11,* 13.

Nathanson, C. A. (1975). Illness and the feminine role: A theoretical review. *Social Science and Medicine, 9,* 57–62.

Norris, R. V., & Sullivan, C. (1983). *PMS: Premenstrual Syndrome.* New York: Rawson Associates.

Reid, R. L., & Yen, S. S. C. (1981). Premenstrual syndrome. *Clinical Obstetrics and Gynecology, 139*(1), 85–104.

Reid, R., & Yen, S. S. C. (1983). The premenstrual syndrome. *Clinical Obstetrics and Gynecology, 26*(3), 710–718.

Scully, D., & Burt, P. (1973). A funny thing happened on the way to the orifice: Women in gynecology textbooks. *American Journal of Sociology, 78,* 1045.

Sheldrake, P., & Cormack, M. (1976). Variations in menstrual cycle symptom reporting. *Journal of Psychosomatic Research, 20,* 169–177.

Stevenson, J. S. (1979). Women's health research: Why, what, and so what? *CNR Voice* (Ohio State University School of Nursing), Fall, 2-3.

Taylor, J. (1979). The timing of menstrual related symptoms assessed by a daily symptom rating scale. *Acta Psychiatrica Scandinavica, 60,* 87-105.

Verbrugge, L. M. (1979). Female illness rates and illness behavior: Testing hypotheses about sex differences in health. *Women and Health, 4,* 61-79.

Verbrugge, L. M. (1980). Sex differences in complaints and diagnoses. *Journal of Behavioral Medicine, 3,* 327-337.

Verbrugge, L. M., & Steiner, R. P. (1981). Physician treatment of men and women patients: Sex bias or appropriate care? *Medical Care, 19*(6), 609-632.

Waldron, I. (1977). Increased prescribing of Valium, Librium, and other drugs: An example of the influence of economic and social factors on the practice of medicine. *International Journal of Health Services, 7*(1), 91-94.

Wallen, J., Waitzkin, H., & Stoeckle, J. D. (1979). Physician stereotypes about female health and illness: A study of patient's sex and the informative process during medical interviews. *Women and Health, 4,* 135-146.

Woods, N. F. (1981a). Women and their health. In C. I. Fogel & N. F. Woods (Eds.), *Health care of women: A nursing perspective.* St. Louis: C. V. Mosby.

Woods, N. F. (1981b). Women and health care. In C. I. Fogel & N. F. Woods (Eds.), *Health care of women: A nursing perspective.* St. Louis: C. V. Mosby.

Woods, N. F., Most, A., & Gery, G. (1982). Estimating perimenstrual distress: A comparison of two methods. *Research in Nursing and Health, 5,* 81-91.

# INDEX